El Salvador in Transition

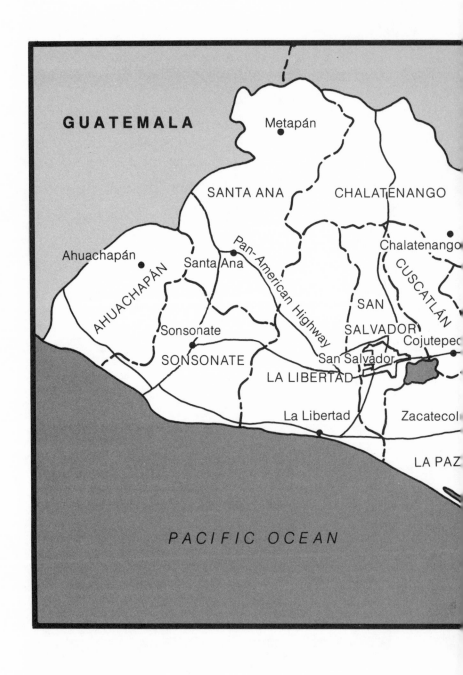

GUATEMALA

Metapán

SANTA ANA

CHALATENANGO

Chalatenango

Ahuachapán

AHUACHAPÁN

Santa Ana

Pan-American Highway

CUSCATLÁN

Sonsonate

SAN

SALVADOR

Cojutepe

SONSONATE

San Salvador

LA LIBERTAD

La Libertad

Zacatecol

LA PAZ

PACIFIC OCEAN

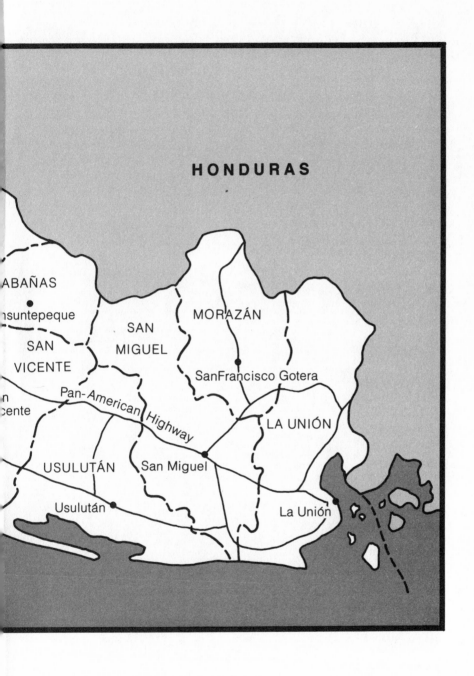

HONDURAS

ABAÑAS

nsuntepeque

SAN
VICENTE

SAN
MIGUEL

MORAZÁN

SanFrancisco Gotera

n
cente

Pan-American Highway

LA UNIÓN

USULUTÁN

San Miguel

Usulután

La Unión

Enrique A. Baloyra

El Salvador
in Transition

The University of North Carolina Press
Chapel Hill & London

© 1982 The University of North Carolina Press

All rights reserved.

Manufactured in the United States of America
First printing, December 1982
Second printing, April 1983

Library of Congress Cataloging in Publication Data

Baloyra, Enrique A., 1942–
El Salvador in transition.

Bibliography: p.
Includes index.

1. El Salvador—Politics and government—1944–1979.
2. El Salvador—Politics and government—1979–
3. El Salvador—Foreign relations—United States.
4. United States—Foreign relations—El Salvador.
5. United States—Foreign relations—1981–
I. Title.
F1488.B34   972.84'05   82-4815
ISBN 0-8078-1532-2   AACR2
ISBN 0-8078-4093-9 (pbk.)

To Pepe and Márgara and their ideals,
and the *cipotes* and their future

And to Tom, Steve, and Barry,
in praise of the courage and professionalism
they displayed during a firefight
on election morning at Apopa

Contents

Map, Figures, and Tables

Acknowledgments

I owe a very large debt to many persons whose support and collaboration were essential to the writing of this book. Part I relies in part on materials prepared originally as part of the project "Democracy in Latin America: Prospects and Implications." My coinvestigators, professors Federico G. Gil and Lars Schoultz, provided insightful commentary and much needed encouragement. Professor Schoultz, in particular, assumed additional responsibilities in the second stage of the project so that I could complete what was originally conceived as a very concise report on the Salvadoran situation. Professor Gil's leadership and oversight of our work proved to be indispensable.

Matthew Hodgson, director of the University of North Carolina Press, and Iris Tillman Hill, its editor-in-chief, made a very generous commitment to produce the book in a very short time. I thank the staff of the Press for having stood behind that commitment. My editor, David Perry, deserves much praise for the superb job he did improving the manuscript. I also want to acknowledge the professionalism and dedication of the two referees who read the expanded version during the Christmas vacation of 1981. Two Salvadoran friends, José Simán and Dr. Rómulo Colindres, made a major contribution by giving me access to their personal libraries. Most of the Salvadoran sources that I was able to consult would not have been available to me otherwise. I thank them for this indispensable contribution. In addition, Pepe Simán spent long hours poring over the manuscript, raising very important questions and educating the author on some of the subtleties and intricacies of Salvadoran society.

My colleague Professor Thomas Anderson, the foremost North American scholar on El Salvador, did much to make me rethink and distill many of the issues involving the background and contradictions of the Salvadoran crisis. Knut Walter also made a valuable contribution in this regard.

Last, but not least, I would like to thank Elizabeth Taylor, who typed the first draft on a very tight schedule, and Emily Anderson, who served the many requests for copies of that draft.

The opinions expressed in this book are the sole responsibility of the author, and do not, in any way, represent the views of the Department of State or of the government of the United States. The shortcomings and inconsistencies that may still be found in the argument are the result of my own limitations in dealing with a very difficult and complex subject. I hope to make a contribution by trying to clarify this complexity and by identifying the real issues confronting El Salvador.

List of Acronyms

ABECAFE Asociación Salvadoreña de Beneficiadores y Exportadores de Café
(Salvadoran association of processors and exporters of coffee)

AD Acción Democrática (Democratic action)

AFL-CIO American Federation of Labor-Congress of Industrial Organizations

AGEUS Asociación General de Estudiantes Universitarios Salvadoreños
(General association of Salvadoran university students)

AID Agency for International Development

AIFLD American Institute for Free Labor Development

ANEP Asociación Nacional de la Empresa Privada (National association of
private enterprise)

ANSESAL Agencia Nacional de Servicios Especiales de El Salvador (National agency of special services of El Salvador)

AP Alianza Productiva (Productive Alliance)

ARENA Alianza Republicana Nacionalista (Nationalist republican alliance)

ASI Asociación Salvadoreña de Industriales (Salvadoran industrialists'
association)

ATACES Asociación de Trabajadores Agropecuarios y Campesinos de El
Salvador (Association of agricultural workers and peasants of El
Salvador)

BPR Bloque Popular Revolucionario (Popular revolutionary bloc)

CCE Consejo Central de Elecciones (Central electoral council)

CCEA Consejo Coordinador de Empresas Agropecuarias (Coordinating
council for agricultural and livestock enterprises)

CCS Central Campesina Salvadoreña (Salvadoran peasants' central)

CEDEN Comité Evangélico de Emergencia Nacional (Evangelical committee
of national emergency)

CEL Comisión Ejecutiva Hidroeléctrica del Río Lempa (Lempa River
hydroelectric authority)

CELAM Conferencia Episcopal Latinoamericana (Latin American conference
of bishops)

CEPA Comisión Ejecutiva del Puerto de Acajutla (Acajutla port
authority)

CGS Confederación General de Sindicatos (General confederation of unions)

CGTS Confederación General de Trabajadores Salvadoreños (General confederation of Salvadoran workers)

CONAPLAN Consejo Nacional de Planificación (National planning council)

COPEFA Consejo Permanente de la Fuerza Armada (Permanent council of the armed force)

COSCAFE Compañía Salvadoreña de Café (Salvadoran coffee company)

CRM Coordinadora Revolucionaria de Masas (Revolutionary coordinative of the masses)

CUTS Confederación Unitaria de Trabajadores Salvadoreños (Unitary confederation of Salvadoran workers)

DRU Dirección Revolucionaria Unificada (Unified revolutionary directorate)

ERP Ejército Revolucionario del Pueblo (People's revolutionary army)

FAL Fuerzas Armadas de Liberación (Armed forces of liberation)

FALANGE Fuerzas Armadas de Liberación Anticomunista de Guerras de Eliminación (anti-Communist armed forces of Liberation by wars of elimination)

FAN Frente Amplio Nacional (Broad National Front)

FAPU Frente de Acción Popular Unificada (Front of Unified Popular Action)

FARN Fuerzas Armadas de Resistencia Nacional (Armed forces of national resistance)

FARO Frente de Agricultores de la Región Oriental (Front of agriculturalists of the eastern region)

FBI Federal Bureau of Investigation

FDN Frente Democrático Nacionalista (Nationalist democratic front)

FDR Frente Democrático Revolucionario (Democratic revolutionary front)

FECCAS Federación Cristiana de Campesinos Salvadoreños (Christian federation of Salvadoran peasants)

FENASTRAS Federación Nacional Sindical de Trabajadores Salvadoreños (National federation of unions of Salvadoran workers)

FESINCONSTRANS Federación de Sindicatos de la Industria de la Construcción, Similares, Transporte y de Otras Actividades (Federation of unions of the construction industry and kindred activities, transportation, and other activities)

FESTIAVTSCES Federación de Trabajadores de la Industria del Alimento, Vestido, Textil, Similares y Conexos de El Salvador (Federation of food, garment, textile, kindred and related activities of El Salvador)

FENAPES Federación Nacional de la Pequeña Empresa de El Salvador (National federation of small enterprises of El Salvador)

FEPRO Federación de Profesionales (Federation of professional associations)

FMLN (Frente) Farabundo Martí de Liberación Nacional (Farabundo Martí national liberation [front])

FPL Fuerzas Populares de Liberación (Popular liberation forces)

FRTS Federación Regional de Trabajadores Salvadoreños (Regional federation of Salvadoran workers)

FSR Federación Sindical Revolucionaria (Federation of revolutionary unions)

FUDI Frente Unido Democrático Independiente (United independent
democratic front)

FUSS Federación Unitaria Sindical Salvadoreña (Unitary federation of Salvadoran workers)

ICR Instituto de Colonización Rural (Rural settlement institute)

IDB Inter-American Development Bank

IMF International Monetary Fund

INAZUCAR Instituto Nacional del Azúcar (National institute of sugar)

INCAFE Instituto Nacional del Café (National institute of coffee)

INS Immigration and Naturalization Service

IRCA International Railroad of Central America

ISSS Instituto Salvadoreño del Seguro Social (Salvadoran institute of social
security)

ISTA Instituto Salvadoreño de Transformación Agraria (Salvadoran institute
of agrarian transformation)

IVU Instituto de la Vivienda Urbana (Urban housing institute)

LP-28 Ligas Populares 28 de Febrero (Popular leagues 28
February)

MIPTES Movimiento Independiente de Profesionales y Técnicos de El
Salvador (Independent movement of Salvadoran professionals and
technicians)

MLP Movimiento de Liberación Popular (Movement of popular liberation)

MNR Movimiento Nacional Revolucionario (National Revolutionary
movement)

MPSC Movimiento Popular Social Cristiano (Popular social Christian
movement)

NPR National Public Radio

ORDEN Organización Democrática Nacionalista (Nationalist democratic
organization)

PAC Partido Auténtico Constitucionalista (Authentic constitutionalist party)

PAD Partido Acción Democrática (Democratic action party)

PAN Partido Acción Nacional (National action party)

PAN Partido Auténtico Nacional (National authentic party)

PAR Partido Acción Renovadora (Renewal action party)

PCN Partido de Conciliación Nacional (National conciliation party)

PCS Partido Comunista de El Salvador (Communist party of El Salvador)

PDC Partido Demócrata Cristiano (Christian democratic party)

PDN Partido Demócrata Nacionalista (Nationalist democratic party)

PID Partido Institucional Democrático (Democratic institutional party)

POP Partido de Orientación Popular (Popular orientation party)
PPS Partido Popular Salvadoreño (Popular Salvadoran party)
PRAM Partido Revolucionario Abril y Mayo (April and May revolutionary
    party)
PREN Partido Republicano de Evolución Nacional (Republican party of
    national evolution)
PRI Partido Revolucionario Institucional (Institutional revolutionary party)
PRTC Partido Revolucionario de los Trabajadores Centroamericanos
    (Revolutionary party of Central American workers)
PRUD Partido Revolucionario de Unificación Democrática (Revolutionary
    party of democratic unification)
PRUD(a) PRUD auténtico (Authentic PRUD)
PDS Partido Social Demócrata (Social democratic party)
PUCA Partido de Unificación Centroamericana (Party of Central American
    unification)
PUD Partido Unión Democrática (Democratic union party)
SI Socialist International
STISSS Sindicato de Trabajadores del Instituto Salvadoreño del Seguro Social
    (Union of workers of the Salvadoran institute of social security)
STIUSA Sindicato Textil de Industrias Unidas, S.A. (Industrias Unidas, S.A.,
    textile union)
UCA Universidad Centro Americana (Simeón Cañas) ([Simeón Cañas]
    Central American university)
UCS Unión Comunal Salvadoreña (Salvadoran communal union)
UDES Unión de Directores de Empresa de El Salvador (Union of directors of
    enterprises of El Salvador)
UDN Unión Democrática Nacionalista (Nationalist democratic union)
UGB Unión Guerrera Blanca (White warriors' union)
UNO Unión Nacional Opositora (National opposition union)
UNT Unión Nacional de Trabajadores (National workers union)
UPD Unión de Partidos Democráticos (Union of democratic parties)
UTC Unión de Trabajadores Campestres (Rural workers union)

Part One

Salvadoran Reality

On 15 October 1979 a progressive faction of the military overthrew the government of General Carlos Humberto Romero, ending an experiment in institutionalized military rule that had lasted over thirty years and plunging the country into a political crisis from which it has yet to emerge. To locate the origins of this crisis, however, one must go much further back in Salvadoran history. In the late nineteenth and early twentieth centuries El Salvador was an oligarchic republic, sustained by a system of export agriculture. The prime beneficiaries of this system were a group of wealthy coffee planters, who dominated Salvadoran politics and monopolized key sectors of the economy. This coffee oligarchy was unable to spare its republic from the ravages of the Depression. A peasant uprising in 1932, which was bloodily put down by the armed forces in the *matanza*, made it evident that the oligarchy was no longer able to manage the system by itself.

There followed a period of personalistic rule (1932–44). General Maximiliano Hernández Martínez introduced some changes during this period to make the operation of the economy somewhat more orderly and to extend the power of the state to some areas that had been the domain of the oligarchy, but the crises of 1944 and 1948 finally led to institutional military rule. Under this arrangement, formalized in the Constitution of 1950, the military tried to evolve a political formula patterned after the Mexican model of one-party domination. There were important differences between Mexico and El Salvador, however, and in addition the military made some crucial mistakes which enabled the oligarchy to continue to play a very influential role in Salvadoran affairs. The oligarchy's opposition and the military's indecision doomed all attempts to change the basic features of the system of export agriculture and authoritarian politics.

Between 1932 and the late 1960s the military and its allies in the oligarchy were able to defuse the more serious political crises and defeat their adversaries with relative ease. Each time a military ruler was overthrown and there was even a distant possibility of democratization, the oligarchy and the more conservative military officers were able to revive their formula of political domination and restore the system to its usual mode of operation.

The taproot of the present Salvadoran crisis must be sought in what was required to maintain this system of military rule and oligarchic economic control. In order to remain competitive, maximize its profits, and survive periods of low export prices, the Salvadoran oligarchy relied on low agricultural wages. In addition, it remained adamantly opposed to any attempt to change a very unequal system of land tenure, which enabled it to monopolize the profits of the export trade and to use these to control the financial sector as well. Therefore, military reformism could not include agrarian reform or the unionization of agricultural workers.

Military rule was legitimized through elections that, as long as the opposition remained disorganized and divided, were relatively honest. Yet there can be very little doubt that this system was exclusionary, not pluralist, and that it could not really accommodate effective political opposition. Beginning in the late 1960s, the opposition, now much better organized, made some inroads into the legislature, and gained control of the government of some municipalities. Opposition coalitions won the general elections of 1972 and 1977, and the military perpetrated massive frauds to remain in power and used repressive measures to quell the protests that followed.

The suppression of moderate parties advocating incremental reforms through electoral means brought about a radicalization of the opposition and an increased polarization of the political process. To counter this, President Arturo Molina tried to implement a modest program of agrarian reform during 1975–76, which he hoped would ease tensions and increase the legitimacy of his government. The oligarchy resisted this so ferociously and effectively that Molina was not only defeated in the initiative but rendered unable to select his successor. Following the fraud of 1977, President Carlos Humberto Romero took the opposite tack, unleashing the security forces and paramilitary assassination squads on his increasingly mobilized opposition. Romero's public order law and the excesses of his government attracted a lot of international attention. Guerrilla groups and popular organizations emerged as the principal opposition to Romero. Relations with the United States deteriorated considerably.

This was the scene when the more progressive element of the military moved to overthrow Romero in October 1979. While short-term factors played an important role in the deterioration and breakdown of Romero's government, historical antecedents, serious structural imbalances, and substantial unresolved questions loomed large in Romero's inability to restore order. The consequence of all this was a crisis which, one has to conclude, the Salvadorans brought upon themselves. The oligarchy, for its obstructionism, and the military, for its unwillingness or inability to challenge the oligarchy, must share major responsibility for bringing about that crisis.

The Salvadoran Crisis in Historical Perspective

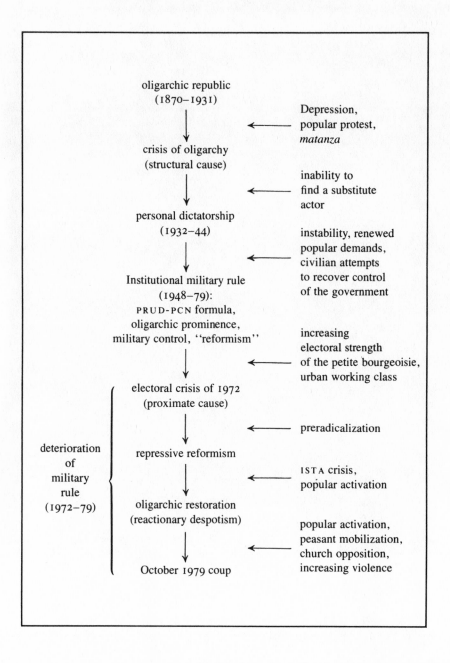

oligarchic republic
(1870–1931)

Depression,
popular protest,
matanza

crisis of oligarchy
(structural cause)

inability to
find a substitute
actor

personal dictatorship
(1932–44)

instability, renewed
popular demands,
civilian attempts
to recover control
of the government

Institutional military rule
(1948–79):
PRUD-PCN formula,
oligarchic prominence,
military control, "reformism"

increasing
electoral strength
of the petite bourgeoisie,
urban working class

electoral crisis of 1972
(proximate cause)

preradicalization

deterioration
of
military
rule
(1972–79)

repressive reformism

ISTA crisis,
popular activation

oligarchic restoration
(reactionary despotism)

popular activation,
peasant mobilization,
church opposition,
increasing violence

October 1979 coup

Chapter 1

Historical Roots

Consolidating the National Government

The beginnings of export agriculture and oligarchical domination in El Salvador can be traced back to the 1850s. At that time, the government was becoming increasingly concerned about the consequences of the country's reliance upon a single cash crop, indigo. The efforts to diversify, however, resulted instead in the monocultivation of coffee and the concentration of capital in only one sector of the economy. Rather than diversify the country's agriculture, the government succeeded only in substituting one agricultural product for another, and this substitution had far-reaching consequences.

The expansion of coffee growing radically altered patterns of land utilization and the political economy of El Salvador. The exploitation of indigo had been accomplished with relatively archaic methods and had not created a dominant social group; nor had government policy reflected the interests of a dominant group whose strength was based on agricultural exploitation. The "coffee boom" created tremendous pressure for the commercial utilization of land. As a result communal and ejidal lands were abolished, and they quickly passed into private hands.[1] The emergence of coffee as the dominant crop and of the oligarchic group that the boom supported helped consolidate the national government in El Salvador despite the lack of a unifying "national dictator" in the style of Mexico's Porfirio Díaz, Guatemala's Manuel Estrada Cabrera, or Venezuela's Antonio Guzmán Blanco.

The crisis of the traditional system in El Salvador culminated in the "bourgeois revolution" of 1870. After that time "liberals" controlled the Salvadoran government. The cultivation of coffee entailed a modernization of the economy, and a preindustrial capitalist state emerged. The government was oligarchic because the principal leaders were recruited from a narrow social stratum which, in some cases, can be identified with two or three families: Araujo, Meléndez, and Quiñónez Molina. More important, they ruled in a manner that served the interests of the dominant group whether or not these coincided with the national interest. During these years the government was stable, since the economic base produced by the system of export agriculture afforded increased revenue. The average tenure of presidential incumbents increased during 1898–1930, and they left office peacefully (see Table 1-1). Finally, the ideology or value system that supported this form of political domination was "liberal." The liberal Constitution of 1886—in force until 1944—provided legal justification and political legitimacy for a system that was relatively stable and successful until 1930.

Therefore, one can say that a preindustrial capitalist state has existed in El Salvador since the late nineteenth century. The powers of that state crystallized in a liberal-oligarchic government which evolved a political regime of markedly authoritarian character. Elements of this system included limited participation, decision making by elites, repression of discontent and of any attempt to organize by the popular classes, and a subordinate role for emerging urban middle-income groups. This system had only limited success, however, for, unlike in Colombia, where the typical unit of coffee production was of a small or intermediate size, in El Salvador the *finca*—a large estate—became the characteristic unit. These relatively few large estates also embraced satellite systems of subsistence agriculture that allowed for different forms of tenancy (small proprietors, *arrendatarios* [renters], and so forth) based on dependent relationships and, very frequently, coerced labor. In the Salvadoran case, the emergence of the *finca* as the basic unit of coffee production was not inevitable; it was simply a result of the manner in which capital and land became concentrated in a few hands. Control of the government and control of the process of land appropriation were the province of the same group.

The extent of oligarchic domination by the large cultivators of coffee becomes obvious in a closer observation of their role in the economy and government. The value of coffee exports increased from slightly over 2 million pesos in 1880 to 22.5 million in 1914. Between 1910 and 1914, coffee exports represented 86.9 percent of the average value of all exports, excluding gold and silver.[2] Other export products, primarily gold and silver ores, were under foreign control and exploited through an "enclave" system. Therefore, they had very little impact on the socioeconomic system.

The connection between the coffee industry and government revenue was indirect. The government did not tax production or export but taxed instead the imports brought into the country and paid for with the foreign currencies earned by coffee. For the period 1870–1914 import duties contributed an average of 58.7 percent of government revenue, in contrast to an average of 40.5 percent during 1849–71.[3]

The political dominance of the coffee cultivators is reflected in the tariff policies of the governments. These were not intended to protect nascent industries that could grow to challenge the economic preeminence and political domination of the coffee oligarchy. In general, the symbiotic relationship between the government and the coffee industry operated in favor of the latter. During the period 1870–1914 government expenditures for infrastructure catered to the needs of the coffee establishment; military expenditures were reoriented from the defense of previously insecure borders against invasions by Honduras and Guatemala to the maintenance of order in the Salvadoran countryside. The government was able to pay back the public debt—the second largest category of public expenditures during 1870–1914—acquiring additional independence from social groups outside the oligarchy. Thus these groups had an even harder time making themselves felt on public policymaking, for not only was their access to policy decisions limited but their importance as fiscal contributors was reduced to relative insignificance.

Looking at organized interests, there is nothing comparable to the Asociación Cafetalera, the coffee growers' association, which was under the control of the largest planters and represented their interests. Some have argued that this functioned as a second state or invisible government of El Salvador.[4] This is a matter for conjecture, but there can be little doubt that government policy did serve the interests of the planters and that government leaders viewed this as one—if not the most important—objective of the government. Yet it would be inaccurate to limit this oligarchy to fourteen or some other such number of families, as many have done. To be sure, the economic resources of El Salvador have been managed by relatively few actors who, for the most part, have provided most of the investment capital.[5] But one should not assume that this oligarchical group was perfectly homogenous and native. From the first, the coffee oligarchy incorporated some of the old *latifundistas* and merchant middlemen into its ranks, but a host of foreign immigrants also participated in the coffee boom and, later on, monopolized retail and wholesale trade.[6] These immigrants ended up marrying into the "old money," and therefore it may be better to speak of fourteen or quite a few more surnames that appear mixed in an endless stream of permutations.

Family connections are a crucial element in any attempt to understand the complexity and evolution of an oligarchical group. Whether by marriage to outsiders or as a consequence of family growth and the maturation of new generations, an oligarchical group is forced to diversify and, in so doing, to become more heterogeneous. In spite of their preference for labor-intensive methods and of their extravagant patterns of consumption, the coffee planters of El Salvador were a group of capitalists who understood their business. One finds them setting up their own banks to finance the operations of their *fincas* and *beneficios* (processing plants), trying to raise money for railway construction, or backing a government bond issue destined to subsidize one aspect of the business. They understood the requirements of their activities and the kinds of political mechanisms necessary to keep them going.

In comparison with Guatemala and Costa Rica, the conflict between merchant and planter appears muted in El Salvador, but there was some cleavage between the two, especially over such issues as the gold standard versus the silver standard, convertibility, devaluation, and the issuance of currency. In El Salvador, commercial banks—including the Banco Internacional (est. 1880), the Banco Particular (est. 1885), the Banco Occidental (est. 1889), and the Banco Agrícola Comercial (est. 1885)—were allowed to issue currency. It is difficult to tell which of these were controlled by the planters and which by the merchants, and which group benefited more. But in any case, the chaotic currency situation was not straightened out until the 1930s and the 1940s, when the Salvadoran monetary system was finally brought under public control. This division between the agricultural and business cliques seems to have existed from relatively soon after the consolidation of the liberal victory in 1870.

The appearance of some light industry in the early twentieth century did not alter the basic composition of the oligarchy or of the lower economic classes. The country remained a two-class society in which the peasants were effectively controlled, the urban working class was yet to appear, and middle-income groups were closely tied to the upper class. Any change in this structure would either have to originate outside it or be the result of an accumulation of pressures that the existing system of domination could no longer control.

The crisis of the oligarchical coffee republic of El Salvador came in 1931 as a result of demographic pressures on land tenure patterns, combined with a severe economic crisis and the activation of popular groups. Even though the state managed to survive, the nature of the government and of the regime was altered and a different system of political domination emerged. In a crisis of oligarchy it is no longer possible to form a *legitimate* government made up of members of the oligarchy and oriented to serve its interests exclusively. In the Salvadoran case, this did not mean that the coffee oligarchy disappeared as a social actor or that it lost most of its political power. If the oligarchy could no longer govern by itself, it remained the most influential among the few actors who were represented in the government. The crisis of the oligarchy in El Salvador marked the end of the period in which the control of the government by the coffee oligarchy was regarded as natural.

From Oligarchic Republic to Personal Dictatorship

Custom prevailing under the Constitution of 1886 allowed Alfonso Quiñónez Molina to select Pío Romero Bosque to be his successor as president of El Salvador during 1927–31. A social conservative, Romero broke with the Meléndez-Quiñónez clan, forced his predecessor into exile, and held what was perhaps the only open and truly competitive election in Salvadoran history. During his term, Romero was forced to use repressive measures to quell increasing popular and labor discontent over economic conditions, and he wanted to make amends for this at the end of his term by allowing a free election. However, the high level of popular mobilization, the lack of effective party organizations, the obstructionism of the oligarchy, and the difficult problems confronting the nation made the chances for democratic transition through an electoral solution extremely poor in El Salvador at that time.

A field of five candidates contested the election, which was won by Arturo Araujo with a plurality of 101,069 of the 217,405 valid votes. In order to prevent a maneuver by the oligarchy in the unicameral legislature that would have given the election to runner-up Alberto Gómez Zárate, who had obtained 62,931 votes and was the personal candidate of the Meléndez-Quiñónez clan, Enrique Córdova, the second runner-up with 32,778 votes, threw his support behind Araujo.[7] Córdova's Republican Party of National Evolution (PREN) was the outlet of landowners severely affected by the Depression, while Araujo's Labor Party was really an ad hoc coalition, supported by student and labor activists looking for a replacement for radical leader Agustín Farabundo Martí, who was incarcerated at the time.

The fact that the oligarchy considered Araujo a renegade was not as significant as the fact that Araujo could not accommodate the demands of his popular and lower-class supporters without comprehensive changes in the society. To make matters worse the members of his Labor Party cadre were very much out for themselves and had no interest in creating a viable national organization. While thousands of peasants and workers staged demonstrations to press their demands for reform, Labor Party operatives enjoyed themselves. Student unrest aggravated matters. There was little hope that any member of the oligarchy would collaborate with the government. When coffee prices slumped even further, bankers refused to lend and the coffee crop was threatened. Army salaries were also in arrears. Finally, on 2 December 1931, Araujo was overthrown by a coup.[8]

The coming to power of Araujo and his subsequent overthrow seem to parallel events elsewhere in Latin America, where several leaders coming to power for the first time suffered from problems very similar to those confronting Araujo. In many cases the first time that populist and social democratic parties reached power in Latin countries, they were beset by similar problems and met the same fate. A direct and relevant comparison would probably be the government of Juan Arévalo in Guatemala, although Arévalo was a very different person and a more astute politician than Araujo.

The immediate outcome of the Araujo overthrow was the *matanza* (massacre) of 1932, which put down the popular insurrection led by Communist leader Farabundo Martí. Taking advantage of the crisis brought on by the

Depression, of the desperation of the lower classes, and of the general confusion reigning in the country, Martí tried to organize and mobilize the popular
classes. There had been a significant increase in labor militancy since the
summer of 1930, when close to eighty thousand rural workers had joined the
Regional Federation of Salvadoran Workers (FRTS). The level of political
involvement was also high among the peasants. These developments convinced the Salvadoran Right that extreme measures were necessary.

General Maximiliano Hernández Martínez proved capable of performing
such a task. The vice-president and minister of defense in the Araujo government, Hernández Martínez had managed not only to survive the coup but to
become the president of a "provisional" government and, in the words of
Abel Cuenca, a rebel participant, "to crush in blood and fire the mass campe-
sino movement."[9] Martínez—as Salvadorans call General Hernández Martínez—had a simple solution for the revolt instigated by Farabundo Martí and
his coconspirators. According to Cuenca, "The government exacted reprisals
in the rate of about one hundred to one. . . . It appears that the rebels killed
about one hundred persons altogether during the uprising; [but] about ten
thousand rebels may have lost their lives afterwards in the *matanza*."[10]

Thomas Anderson's meticulous historical study of the *matanza* is comple-
mented by a broader picture of the crisis of the Depression provided by
Alejandro Marroquín. The latter attributes the severity with which the crisis
hit El Salvador to (1) the leadership's lack of sophistication, which left it
unable to understand and react to the crisis; (2) an economic system which
was too dependent on external sources for machinery, capital goods, con-
sumer goods, monetary stability, and services; (3) the paucity of institutions
that could plan and implement an orderly adjustment to the Depression and
distribute its impact among different economic sectors and social strata; and
(4) a social structure that passed the weight of the crisis on to the weaker and
less influential members of the society.[11]

Marroquín's essay provides some useful information concerning the class
structure that existed in El Salvador during this time and also of some subtle
yet real changes that took place in the state and in the government that made
the regimes that followed the *matanza* different from their predecessors. Using occupation as an indicator of class, Marroquín utilized data from the 1930
census of El Salvador to estimate that less than 1 percent (640 or 0.2 percent)
of persons with a known occupation at that time (854,127) could be classified
"upper class"—primarily bankers, some industrialists, and the more successful planters. By contrast, 4.4 percent were "middle class" (38,247) and 95.4
percent, or the remaining 815,359, were "lower class." Among those engaged in agriculture, only 8.2 percent were proprietors, that is, 117,680 of
1,316,681.[12] Although these are only estimates, since objective measures of

class *status* require education and income in addition to occupation and since one cannot assume that class identification patterns follow objective criteria, they indicate a very uneven and unequal social structure. The *matanza* put down the unrest brought about by the Depression, but this did not end the Depression crisis in El Salvador.

As a response to the Depression the governments of many capitalist countries sought a more active role for the state in the economy or enacted some redistributive policies. For example, in Mexico, where a commitment to reform existed but resources were not plentiful, an "active state" emerged to minimize similar crises in the future.[13] In the United States, the New Deal put forth a new public philosophy of "positive government," in which the state and the leaders of the different economic sectors came closer together.[14] In short, the Depression brought about changes in the economic model in many capitalist countries. No "active state" emerged in El Salvador, however; nor does one find a philosophy of "positive government" coming to dominate the thinking of policymakers in the post-Depression era in the country. In essence, the Salvadoran capitalist state remained basically *unreformed*, although there were attempts to make the operation of the system of export agriculture more orderly and to make the formulation of economic policy truly public. In addition, measures adopted by the Araujo and the Martínez administrations opened the door slightly to some middle-class elements, who derived some concrete benefits from these measures, plus an increased capacity to survive future crises.

In 1931, in order to prevent a total economic collapse, the government had begun to increase its participation in the economy. Beginning with the decree of 7 October 1931 the Araujo government had attempted to impose some order on the chaotic monetary system. Convertibility was suspended and the government took over custody of gold in a special fund. Banks were required to extend credit to businessmen and to issue currency only in amounts authorized by law. Furthermore, they were prevented from raising interest on reissues and from foreclosing on nationals. Since the Araujo government was relatively weak and incompetent, the bankers flaunted their disregard for the decree and continued to demand convertibility, to withdraw currency from circulation, and to try to renegotiate credit on usurious terms.[15] In 1929 three major banks held about 84.1 percent of the mortgages, and since the value of the properties had decreased by 50 percent—reflecting an identical decline in the export price of coffee—the crisis threatened to result in a tremendous concentration of the country's wealth in a few hands, and at a bargain price.[16]

With Martínez in power the picture changed somewhat. Attempts to stop the wild and scandalous speculations by a few big planters and bankers had to be taken more seriously. Assisted by Miguel Tomás Molina and Napoleón

Viera Altamirano, Martínez tried to put the house in order. He first addressed the problem of loans from the United States. Tom Anderson has given us a good description of this process.

> El Salvador defaulted on her loan from the United States for $21 million, which had been contracted in 1922, [and] payments of foreign debts were temporarily suspended [by a decree of 29 February 1932]. The government further ordered that customs duties which had previously been given over to a representative of the American bankers, under terms of the 1922 loan, were to be paid directly into the treasury of El Salvador. The bankers, of course, protested; but although the United States had not recognized Martínez, the State Department refused to come to their aid, perhaps because it did not want to embarrass the dictator who seemed the only bulwark against communism.[17]

On 12 March 1932 the Moratorium Law ratified and reformed the decree, making the moratorium general, suspending convertibility, and cutting interest by 40 percent. There was resistance to this new attempt by government to deal with the economic crisis, but the flurry of decrees continued—with those of 28 May and 14 November 1932. The oligarchy was still strong enough to force a repeal of the Legislative Bill of 25 August 1933, establishing exchange controls—which were finally imposed in mid-1935.

The government was more successful in its attempt to create two new banking institutions. The Moratorium Law of March 1932 had been aimed directly at the three large banks that controlled most of the mortgages—the Banco Agrícola Comercial, the Banco Salvadoreño, and the Banco Occidental. On 19 June 1934 the government bought out the stock of the Agrícola Comercial and established the Banco Central in its stead. The Banco Central was to control credit and the money supply, supervise a newly created central reserve bank fund, assume responsibility for printing money, monopolize the gold trade, control the rates of discount and interest, and supervise the operation of private banks.[18] These measures were "statist" in nature, for the Banco Central was chartered as a private company and modeled after the Bank of England.[19] While this was not a blueprint for "state capitalism," the creation of the Banco Central may have produced a realignment within the oligarchic power structure, making the groups interested in diversification somewhat less dependent on the more traditional elements.

Marroquín believes that the creation of the other major new financial institution aimed to compensate these ruling elements for the creation of the Banco Central—which had deprived them of the opportunity to engage in reckless monetary speculation. On 18 December 1934 the Banco Hipotecario de El Salvador was created by a legislative decree.[20] The Banco Hipotecario was created as a *sociedad anónima* to take over the lending functions monopolized by the Agrícola Comercial, the Salvadoreño, and the Occidental. The aim was to make credit cheaper and more available to growers of other crops as well.[21] The stock of the Banco Hipotecario was subscribed by the coffee growers' association, the Asociación de Cafetaleros de El Salvador, which had 40 percent of the shares, and by the livestock association, the Asociación de Ganaderos de El Salvador, which had 20 percent.[22] The Martínez government also organized a federation of savings and loans associations (Federación de Cajas de Crédito), and after reorganizing the coffee growers' association he formed the Compañía Salvadoreña de Café, which became the chief marketer of Salvadoran coffee, buying from the *beneficios*, grading the beans, and servicing export orders.[23]

The consequences of these reforms have been summarized by Webre:

> All [these changes] helped bring order to an anachronistic system and served to protect the interests of *property owners at all levels*. The fact that all these institutions, although organized on state initiative to serve public functions, *were in fact private corporations* subscribed by private capital indicates that the advance in El Salvador from the sacred principles of laissez-faire liberalism to the concept of the economically *active state* was still quite tentative. *Although these reforms were prejudicial to the interests of individual oligarchic families* heavily engaged in banking and finance who might have hoped to profit from a credit squeeze upon less dynamic landholders, they were beneficial to the industry as a whole. During the Martínez period and for years thereafter, oligarchs dominated these new organizations and operated them to their benefit. Future governments, however, would take advantage of their existence to increase state participation in the economy and augment the capacity of *the state to function as a defender and promoter of capitalism as a system* rather than the not infrequently contradictory interests of a few individual capitalists [emphasis added].[24]

In a class sense, the reorganization protected Salvadoran capitalists from future crises, prevented the financial sector from becoming predatory, and allowed for the orderly operation of the sensitive sectors of the economy, such as agriculture, banking, and finance, as well as the emerging industrial sector. It was less a reform of the capitalist state than an attempt to put everyone in his place. The policy measures were not reformist but *corporatist*.

Yet these were not simply policies imposed on the oligarchy by a relatively strong government. To be sure, Martínez was able to make the banking and currency reforms stick, but he was acting on behalf of a wide array of capitalists who were hard hit by the Depression and vulnerable to the maneuvers of oligarchic speculators playing with the currency. Efforts that dated back to the previous century finally resulted in a stable national currency—the colón was pegged at 2.50 to the dollar and stayed there for a long time—and instruments for the pursuit of monetary and fiscal policies were put in place. The oligarchy's controlling interest in the new banking institutions, however, suggests that Martínez's measures did not lay the foundations for state capitalism or state corporatism. The dominant group retained its ability to participate in decision making in economic policy.

The fact that the reorganization carried out by Martínez fell considerably short of social reform is witnessed by the fraudulent attempts made by his administration to improve the lot of the popular classes. Once the *matanza* had been completed, Martínez realized that it would be necessary to redress some grievances. But the thoroughness of the repression enabled him to make only token moves. Bogus redistributions of (non–coffee producing) lands were enacted through the Mejoramiento Social, with less than 2 percent of the *campesinos* benefiting from them. The real benefits from these went to the friends of the dictator.

In summary, the experience of the Depression did not shake the commitment of the Salvadoran ruling class to laissez-faire liberalism; nor did it question the logic of the system of export agriculture on which the coffee republic had rested. The republic was gone, but the oligarchy remained a ruling class in a social and economic sense. The personal dictatorship of Maximiliano Hernández was made possible by the crisis of oligarchic power culminating in the *matanza*, which created a new division of political labor. The regime had become explicitly authoritarian, and grounded in a personal dictatorship.

The "ruling elite" and a personalistic dictator found it convenient to collaborate because their objectives coincided. The oligarchy did not want reform and redistribution, since these would come at its expense; Martínez did not want them because he did not believe them possible or necessary, and he insisted that El Salvador had to live within its means. This suited the oligarchy fine.

But Martínez was not merely a trustee of the oligarchy. He showed his ability to implement some measures that were not exactly welcomed by the financial speculators and the big planters. His ability to enforce their acceptance of these shows that Martínez could play a very strong hand in certain areas. While this does not imply that the oligarchy had lost all its power, it does indicate that it had to accommodate a new reality. The system of oligarchic domination was in crisis. The oligarchy retained the ability to prevent others from usurping its role and the power to resist attempts by any administration to enact reformist policies that could erode its economic base. This crisis of the oligarchy created a political vacuum. The lack of legitimate rule in El Salvador—with the possible exception of the Osorio (1950–56) and Rivera (1962–67) administrations—added a crisis of hegemony to that vacuum.

Chapter 2

The Salvadoran Model of 1948–1972

A Paradigmatic Failure

On 2 April 1944, while the dictator was out of the capital, a coup d'etat was staged against Martínez. The movement was suppressed with considerable violence, but a general strike and strong pressures from the United States persuaded Martínez to resign on 8 May. Martínez named a sixty-two-year-old general, Andrés I. Menéndez, to serve as interim president. With the support of progressive elements clustered around Arturo Romero, Menéndez appointed a fairly representative cabinet and issued a call for elections. He also allowed labor to organize, and the National Workers Union (UNT) quickly grew to about fifty thousand affiliates by October. Assisted by Agustín Alfaro Morán, Romero organized the Partido Unión Democrática (PUD), and after a brief absence to undergo surgery in the United States, Romero began to campaign vigorously for the presidency. The other main contender was General Salvador Castaneda Castro, a former minister of the interior during the Martínez era, who counted on the support of most of the military who opposed a return to civilian rule and of the landowners who were adamantly opposed to Romero's reformist platform.

As the government of Arturo Araujo had done earlier, the junta of General Menéndez was embarked on an attempt to bring about a peaceful process of transition to a democratic regime in El Salvador, and under very difficult circumstances. Economic conditions were more favorable in 1944, but that was not the problem. The basic obstacle that this attempt could not overcome was the obstructionism of the military and the oligarchy, who for different reasons would not tolerate the inauguration of a democratic regime. The military was reluctant to allow a return to civilian supremacy, while the oligarchy perceived a democratic regime, which would allow the rise of other institutions and interests, including true political parties and labor unions, as a direct threat to its economic predominance.

Lacking the unequivocal support of the military the Menéndez junta could do little to prevent the violence directed against the campaign of Romero and his PUD. On 30 June 1944 the military high command forced Menéndez to postpone the August election and to name Colonel Osmín Aguirre, an architect of the massacre of 1932, as his chief of police. This diluted the already feeble control that the government had over the security forces. Moreover, *aperturista* elements could not count on the PUD, which was only an embryonic political organization. Lacking an experienced cadre to maintain discipline and perform the indispensable work of building up a viable organization at the grass-roots level, the party was incapable of well-coordinated action.

On 20 October 1944 the attacks against Romero culminated in a violent incident. About ten thousand *romeristas* were marching to their party headquarters after holding a rally at the Parque de la Libertad in San Salvador. Marching past the headquarters of Castaneda, they were fired upon. As though acting on cue, Aguirre reacted by incarcerating hundreds of *romeristas*, as well as the entire cabinet. Menéndez was forced to resign, and the members of the legislature were assembled at the Zapote barracks to witness the swearing in of Aguirre as provisional president. He immediately cracked down on the opposition, driving most of the *romerista* leadership out of the country and conducting a very thorough repression against the UNT. In December he crushed a revolt in San Miguelito and beat back an invasion launched by the opposition from Guatemala. Aguirre went through with the election, but he made sure that Castaneda Castro's victory was all but certain. The new president was inaugurated on 5 March 1945.[1]

During the 1940s three factions were clearly discernible in the Salvadoran armed forces. One consisted of senior officers of the Martínez generation, including Aguirre and Castaneda. They were able to neutralize a faction which had been involved in the April 1944 attempt to overthrow Martínez. This second group was no longer influential by the time that Castaneda took office. A third faction, composed of junior officers, waited in the wings.

Such patterns of cleavage were relatively common in contemporary Latin American military institutions. Factors of training, generation, career orientation, and social class were probably more important contributors to these cleavages than any real or imagined ideological differences that could be derived from readings of the documents put forth by military groups when they assumed power. In El Salvador the cleavages were important, since the armed forces were on the point of embarking on a civil-military experiment in "controlled democracy" and "military reformism" that was to last almost three decades. It must not be forgotten, however, that in their relations with civil society different military factions will overlook their disagreements when the integrity of their institution is threatened. This drive for unity and consensus becomes as important as any specific policy or project that the military *in the government* may pursue.

The "majors coup" of 14 December 1948 sought to inaugurate a new model in Salvadoran politics. The coup was precipitated by moves by Castaneda Castro that were apparently aimed at extending his mandate to a second term, but it is probable that a new and more institutionalized system of military rule would have come about sooner or later. The political roots of the present crisis in El Salvador may be found in the failure of this experiment and of the deterioration of the form of domination that it entailed. The more profound reasons for the crisis stem from the inability of the new model to solve some basic problems of political organization.

Military Reformism

The experiment inaugurated in 1948 accepted the conventional wisdom that coffee was of predominant importance and that the operation of that sector should be spared any dangerous reforms that might upset the delicate balance of a country with a small territory, a protean economy, and a rapidly growing population. What the military failed to understand was that the operation of the coffee sector was not inextricably bound to the oligarchy in some kind of historical spell that could not be broken.

The country needed structural reform to correct inequities; this was not a matter of ideological preference but a basic question of economic necessity and political viability. For such change a political "opening" was necessary, and this was impossible without the support of the military. Furthermore, despite the unresolved crisis of hegemony, the oligarchy retained enough political influence and economic power to veto any reforms. Any changes had to be produced from the outside by a new coalition. The military could have played a crucial role in this, as it did in other Latin American countries, but it failed to do so.

Instead, during the next three decades in El Salvador, the military controlled but did not dominate the society. It failed to become the hegemonic actor that could replace the oligarchy; it missed a number of opportunities to form a dominant coalition, and it prevented others from doing so. Unable to evolve a lasting social pact that could legitimize its rule, unwilling to turn the control of the government over to civilians, and incapable of articulating a developmental strategy that would modernize the country and erode the socio-economic foundations of oligarchic power, the military in its political experiment of 1948–72 must be considered a failure. Unable or at least unwilling to make some crucial decisions, it allowed events to take their own course. Moreover, it stood in the way of the emergence and consolidation of participatory institutions that could have rivaled the social influence of the dominant group and introduced a more balanced picture. Although the military lionized some of the more dynamic and progressive forces in El Salvador, it implemented only half-hearted substitute policies, and these seldom got far beyond the blueprint stage.

Essentially, military reformism left Salvadoran society intact. Whatever changes did occur were not planned and were, in most cases, unforeseen. Military government was not oligarchic, but it benefited the oligarchy. Worse still, these governments were all military dictatorships. Republican institutions were never allowed to prosper or even to operate for any length of time. The regime remained authoritarian, torn between the contradictory tendencies of "populism," "Nasserism,"[2] and "reactionary despotism."[3]

The Comparison with Mexico

The basic dynamics of this Salvadoran model may be clarified through a contrast with the Mexican model of single-party domination and development through industrialization. This is a frequently made comparison. According to Monteforte Toledo, El Salvador was the only Central American country in which the Mexican formula could have been replicated successfully. Monteforte believed that the following factors made this possible:

1. The *matanza* of 1932 neutralized the possibility of "revolution from below," or, more specifically, of a peasant uprising, at least for some time (in Mexico the *agraristas* were defeated and the peasant faction proved incapable of organizing a government; thus, the chance for a peasant revolt was lost).

2. The military *institution* emerged as the dominant political actor, filling the power vacuum created by the crisis of oligarchy that began in 1932; this rule was not personal but institutional (in Mexico, the charismatic authority was institutionalized in the office of the presidency itself, and not in its incumbent).

3. The system found equilibrium in a formula of "triple veto," which defined the power relations between the dominant actors and guaranteed their integrity. The *oligarchy* retained the veto against developmentalism and against structural changes in agriculture; the industrial bourgeoisie accepted the domination of the army and the oligarchy, but it preserved a veto which excluded the petite bourgeoisie from power and thwarted any attempt to implement a populist formula; and the military monopolized the powers of the government through its control of the presidency and of the political ministries (Interior, Defense, Labor) in order to maintain order and veto any civilian attempt to regain hegemony.

4. The single-term presidency and the renewal of the top governmental positions every five years reduced tensions and allowed different factions to share in the running of the incumbent administration, diminishing instances of violence and conspiracy (removal of top governmental and party elites every six years gives a fluidity to the Mexican system that facilitates the circulation of elites).

5. The middle sectors of the petite bourgeoisie were incorporated into the system through their recruitment into a bloated public bureaucracy.

6. The official party of El Salvador utilized the military command structure as a political machine, particularly during electoral campaigns when local commanders of the national guard acted as agents of the party, mobilizing support, neutralizing opponents, and, when necessary, stuffing ballots or keeping people away from the polls.

7. Urban labor was allowed to organize within certain limits, co-opting the leadership and making it difficult for dissident unions to compete with the tame unions tolerated by the government. The very limited organizational rights of urban workers, primarily industrial workers and commercial employees, were not extended to the peasantry.

8. The peasant sector remained outside the system, since the existing system of coffee exploitation could not be changed. Wages had to remain low, production had to remain labor intensive, and any changes in land tenure patterns had to be made without "serious disruptions," which would bring about "dire consequences."[4]

Even though these elements show a strong resemblance between the system that evolved under the control of the Partido Revolucionario Institucional (PRI) in Mexico and the Salvadoran system from 1948 to 1972, they mask a number of fundamental differences. An examination of these will help us understand some of the basic flaws and contradictions of the Salvadoran copy.

In Mexico the revolution of 1910 destroyed the liberal oligarchy that grew out of the Reforma and the Porfiriato, laying the foundations for a *reformed* capitalist state which finally crystallized during the administration of General Lázaro Cárdenas (1934–40). The "active state" that emerged under Cárdenas was based upon a social pact between a new industrial bourgeoisie, government officials, and urban labor, with the exclusion of the military from the dominant party, the compulsory inclusion of the peasantry, and the optional participation of the middle class. The manner in which the Salvadoran state operated and the basic coalition that was accommodated within the official party could not have been more different. Moreover, the Mexican formula altered the nature of the capitalist state that had evolved under the Porfiriato, and it destroyed or neutralized the power of precisely the two actors who not only had managed to survive in El Salvador but, more importantly, had organized a very different party with a very different coalition. These two, the military and the oligarchy, were not interested in promoting a model in which the inclusion of other groups in the official coalition would result in a diminution of their influence.

Party-government relations were also different in El Salvador. The selection of the president was primarily a military and not a party decision. The president ruled as a military man, and not as a civilian or, much less, as a party leader. I say "primarily" and not "exclusively" a military decision because this depended upon the incumbent's power base, the popularity of his administration, and the oligarchy's ability to influence the decision. For example, Colonel Oscar Osorio chose his minister of the interior, Lt. Colonel José María Lemus, to succeed him in the presidency for 1956–62. Lemus had not bothered to join the official party until 1955. By contrast, President Molina did not get his first choice to succeed him in 1977. Probably, this was the result of the very bitter confrontation between Molina and the oligarchy over the creation of the Instituto Salvadoreño de Transformación Agraria (ISTA) and Molina's attempt to introduce some mild reforms into the agrarian sector.[5] Thus, Molina's inability to choose his successor was not the product of an intraparty squabble but was instead a consequence of conflict in the always delicate relation between the oligarchy and the military. Defeated by the oligarchy on a substantive issue, Molina found his ability to sell his candidate to his military peers impaired. In short, the influence of the oligarchy on the selection was indirect, and the president's inability to choose his successor did not result from a *party* decision.

At no time were the civilian elites of the party in a position to impose a decision on their military colleagues on the basis of party discipline. The military elites, on the other hand, were more concerned with the integrity of their institution than with the institutionalization of *any* party. In the process of presidential selection, as well as in decisions on important issues, the military had to reconcile the ambitions and designs of individual officers and officer factions with the need to maintain the principles of hierarchy and discipline and, furthermore, to reconcile these with the exigencies of public policy and the demands of political influentials. Since all of these considerations had priority over party development, it is difficult to see how the normal operation of the Salvadoran model could have contributed to the institutionalization of an official party.

This contrast between Mexico and El Salvador underlines a basic distinction and deeper contradiction which the *salvadoreños* were not able to solve: in order to build the party the leadership had to become "politicians." They could do this only at the risk of losing their grip on the armed forces. But the Salvadoran military had a conception of politics which viewed parties, elections, and opposition as a minor annoyance during times of prosperity, and as a threat during times of crisis. According to Juan Felipe Leal, in the Mexican case the differentiation between military elites who became politicians and created the bureaucracies of the government and of the party and those who remained military officers brought about a demilitarization of the party.[6] Eventually, civilian supremacy became a fact of political life there. The Salvadoran military was reluctant to abandon the uniform and equally reluctant to accept civilian supremacy.

The other major actor in the Salvadoran coalition, the oligarchy, was able to exercise its influence very effectively through the manipulation of the ideological symbols that it monopolized. Military deference to the laissez-faire liberalism advocated by the oligarchy put all the marbles on the side of the latter. For example, in spite of its relative success in deriving legitimacy from the revolution of 1948, the Salvadoran military could not find a language or set of ideological symbols to challenge those utilized by the oligarchy. Military rhetoric remained a mixture of populism, McCarthyism, and progressivism, which clouded the basic objectives and normative underpinnings of government policy. Declarations of reform were toned down with guarantees of private property; promises of agrarian reform were a double entendre. Since the oligarchy viewed all reforms with suspicion anyway, and since it had sufficient economic muscle and social prestige to command the attention of the media, it was always able to put the military on the defensive.

In Mexico, by contrast, the PRI has the ability to utilize a revolutionary heritage to defend itself and its policy initiatives from conservative attacks. This is not to imply that the Mexican party is truly revolutionary, for anyone familiar with Mexico knows of the ability of the "liberal Machiavellians" of the PRI to clothe everything in lofty rhetoric. However, the Mexican government can justify some of its policies by labeling them revolutionary. In El Salvador this was not possible. The military sought to defend incremental reformism with anti-Communist rhetoric. This only made it and its reformism more vulnerable to attack by the oligarchy, which continued to monopolize the proper vocabulary. Thus military reformism could always be castigated as hasteful, demagogic, and dangerous and injurious, not to the interests of a small and narrow group, but to some basic pillars of Salvadoran society, such as the right of property and the free enterprise system.

The Salvadoran military was also at a serious disadvantage in maintaining the legitimacy of its regime. Its "controlled democracy" remained militaristic, and was resented by civilians. Its rule was tolerated by the oligarchy, but not supported enthusiastically, except when used to curb any stirrings from the lower classes. The military's inability to transform the state and to produce a new social pact distanced it from other political actors who could have taken the place of the oligarchy in a new coalition. In turn, those actors lacked

the ability to match the economic power and political influence of the oligarchy, which they could challenge in only two ways: through a system of
genuinely competitive elections or by a new alliance. Neither scheme could
succeed without the decided support of the military. A scheme based on
competitive elections was out of the question since it would bring to power a
coalition unacceptable to the oligarchy and would imply civilian supremacy,
which was anathema to the military. A new alliance could have been formed
in 1944, 1948, 1960, or, later on, in 1979, but the military lacked the nerve,
the desire, and the consensus to do so. This problem remained unsolved in
1980–82.

The military experiment, or the series of military experiments between
1948 and 1972 in El Salvador, failed to resolve the crisis of oligarchy of 1931,
which became a crisis of hegemony after the overthrow of Maximiliano
Hernández Martínez in 1944. The military failed to supplant the oligarchy as
hegemonic actor, it fell considerably short in taking the measures necessary to
produce a better balance of political forces, and it stood in the way of others
who tried. If, as the Purcells suggest, the Mexican state is characterized by a
constant bargaining among elites with different political interests, the Salvadoran state did not provide that option in 1972 and 1979, as we shall see.[7]

Oligarchic Domination

Before we proceed any further, it may be prudent to clarify what is meant by
"oligarchy" in the Salvadoran context. In the language of the classics, oligarchy was simply the selfish rule of a few governing for themselves. In more
contemporary terms, the word usually implies a situation in which a relatively
small and closed group of economic actors manipulates the market, derives
social prominence from that manipulation, and acquires an unchecked amount
of political influence as a result. In El Salvador the members of that oligarchy
are certainly more numerous than the notorious "fourteen families," a meta-
phor that has acquired a reality of its own. Of course this is not an inquiry into
the social register but an attempt to determine the composition of that oligarchy, the degree to which it overlapped with the bourgeoisie, and the types of
resources which enabled it to continue to play a prominent role in Salvadoran
politics and, more specifically, to check the reformism of the military.

A study by Robert Aubey offers some evidence about the nature of the
Salvadoran oligarchy. In his analysis of economic family groupings in El
Salvador, which admittedly did not include all the relevant families yet never-
theless produced a representative and valid sample of this social stratum,
Aubey detected the existence of three major groups in the oligarchy: planters,
merchants, and a "mixed" group of entrepreneurs.[8] Rearranged in tabular

form, Figure 2-1 presents evidence to show the diversification of this nucleus of the Salvadoran oligarchy.

The Aubey scheme could be expanded as follows: the Dueñas family is also involved in real estate (massively in San Salvador), banking, investment, and manufacturing (the Palomo group is really Dueñas); the Alvarez family (oldest branch) is also involved in cattle and the dairy industry; the Escalón family also deals in real estate; the Meza Ayau and Quiñónez families also have ties to banking (through intermediary junior partners) and real estate. These modifications were suggested by someone who is a well-qualified observer, but since it is difficult to determine how much change has taken place in the overall configuration of relations between the top entrepreneurial groups, these changes have not been included in the Aubey scheme.[9] But even considering these new data, the fact that some of the information is incomplete, and the relative obsolescence of the study, his survey remains fairly accurate.

Using Aubey's data, we can make the following conclusions. First, "diversification" in El Salvador did not increase the social heterogeneity of the dominant group. The older families, represented in the first group (planters), simply moved outside the coffee sector into other areas of the agricultural sector and into other areas of production. It is difficult to assert their dominance over these other areas, but given the concentration of ownership and the small number of large enterprises, it is probable that their presence in those other sectors was, to say the least, influential. Eduardo Colindres suggests that this presence was indeed very strong.[10]

Second, the economic diversification of the planter group did not extend into retail trade, which remained very much under the control of the merchant group. The families in this group are of more recent vintage in Salvadoran society and of varying national background—notice the probable differences in ethnic origin among the surnames of this group. Conversely, very few merchant families seem to have gone into agriculture. This could suggest, on the one hand, that the classic cleavage between planters and *comerciantes*, so characteristic of the nineteenth century in some of the countries of the Isthmus, was still present in El Salvador scarcely a decade ago. On the other hand, Aubey's awareness of such a notorious division may have influenced his perception of the contemporary configuration. In either case there is little doubt that the data presented in Figure 2-1 show one group of families with a relatively tight control over coffee and some spillover into the service sector, and a different group of families concentrating its activities in commerce and manufacturing.

These tentative inferences lead to two questions: first, which of these was really dominant and, second, what was the difference between the oligarchy and the bourgeoisie?

Lacking interview data on the normative perspectives of members of these

FIGURE 2-1

Patterns of Ownership and Sectoral Specialization of Some Salvadoran Families

	Planters: Alvarez	Battle	Dueñas	Escalón	Guirola	Magaña	Mathies	Meza Ayau	Quiñonez	Regalado	Mixed Group: Deininger	De Sola	Hill	Wright	Merchants: Batarse	Bernheim	Borgonovo	Frenkel	Freund	Gadala María	Goldtree-Liebes	Hasbun	Nasser	Poma	Safie	Schwartz	Simán	Sol-Millet	Vairo	Zablah
Agriculture:																														
coffee cultivation	x	x	x	x	x	x	x	x	x	x	x	x	x				x													
coffee processing			x	x		x	x			x	x	x	x				x				x									
coffee export	x		x	x				x			x	x	x				x				x									
dairy											x																			
cattle		x	x								x																			
sugar cultivation									x	x	x	x																		
sugar refining									x	x	x	x																		
other											x	x		x			x													
Banking	x				x							x	x						x											
Insurance			x									x																		
Investment, finance					x			x	x			x	x	x										x				x		
Real estate												x							x	x										
Utilities																					x									
Construction												x															x	x		
Dealership, distributorship	x	x										x			x								x	x	x				x	
Manufacturing	x						x	x	x	x	x	x	x	x	x	x	x	x	x	x	x	x	x	x	x	x	x	x	x	x
Retail																		x	x	x	x	x	x	x	x		x	x	x	x
Other	x			x		x																x								x

Source: Adapted from Robert T. Aubey "Entrepreneurial Formation." pp. 272–76.

groups, it is impossible to state definitively who was really who. According to the results of important research, moreover, social background is a poor predictor of elite attitudes, which, in turn, are poor predictors of elite behavior. In short, membership in one economic group is a relatively unreliable indicator of oligarchy status unless this is validated by members of the group in question. In this case, at least a partial validation of the composition of the core element of the oligarchy is at hand.

It is a bit harder to determine who was really dominant, for some of the relevant data are difficult to get or even unobtainable: for example, data on rates of profit by sector for the Salvadoran economy or the balance sheets of individual enterprises.[11] Colindres's "La Tenencia de la Tierra," a condensed version of his *Fundamentos Económicos de la Burguesía Salvardoreña*, however, as well as a series of articles and sources, shed some light on this question and allow additional inferences on how much control existed in the agricultural sector, who benefited from it, and what the consequences of this concentration were.[12]

Using the Third Agricultural Census as a point of departure, Colindres estimated that in 1970–71 approximately 250,539 *explotaciones* (farms), or 92.5 percent of all the farms, accounted for only 27.1 percent of the land under cultivation.[13] By contrast, the 1,941 farms larger than 100 hectares,[14] representing 0.7 percent of all farms, accounted for 38.7 percent of the land under cultivation at that time.[15] This situation had not changed in 1978–79, since only 4 percent of the estimated 40,800 growers controlled 67 percent of all the coffee produced in that harvest year.[16]

A lopsided distribution of agricultural property, however, is only one aspect of the economic domination by the oligarchy in El Salvador. According to Luis de Sebastián, as one moves from tenure to cultivation to processing and to export, the number of enterprises declines—as one may expect—and therefore, the chances for excessive concentration increase. In Sebastián's view, El Salvador witnessed even more concentration, as most of the processors were also exporters.[17]

Data compiled by the Seminario Permanente de Investigación of the Universidad Centroamericana Simeón Cañas (UCA) show that twenty-three of the twenty-six family groups producing ten thousand quintals or more were also *beneficiadores*, that is, engaged in processing.[18] In addition, these twenty-six included twelve of the fourteen largest producers of cotton and nine of the top ten sugar growers—although the tenth happened to be the largest sugar grower.[19] If these twenty-six family groups are compared to the top twenty-four identified through the standard used by Colindres—exporting at least 1 percent of the total export of Salvadoran coffee—one gets a fairly precise idea not only of the extent of the concentration but also of the overlap in ownership in different aspects of the exploitation of coffee and of the main agricultural exports (see Figure 2-2).

The determination of who were the core families of the oligarchy will be left to others, since this is not, after all, the main purpose here. What the evidence presented thus far suggests is that Sebastián did not exaggerate. To put it in his own words: "In summary, the power pyramid of agricultural exports rests on the large landed estate and it culminates in the [control] of exports. . . . In the Salvadoran economy oligarchic power does not consist of concentration but omnipresence, that is, that this [concentration] extends to all the key productive sectors."[20] The names of the groups and individuals included in Figures 2-1 and 2-2 belie the conclusion that there was a perfectly identifiable set of fourteen key families who dominated the Salvadoran economy. But the data here presented should at least establish a plausible and valid case for the argument that too many crucial aspects of the economy were in the same hands.

A number of Salvadoran social scientists have offered more precise descriptions of the makeup and internal dynamics of the oligarchy power block. Rafael Guidos Véjar talks about two main factions:

> A *frente agrario* [an agrarian front] and *grupos industrializantes* [industrializing groups]—[the former are] political forces who . . . identify with the interests of agrarian capital [while the latter are] those political forces who, although they share in and reenforce the interests of agrarian capital, strive to make their own industrial capital faction dominant economically and hegemonic politically. [The relationship between the two factions resembles a] permanent process of integration and disintegration of these *frentes* and *grupos* [in which] their internal dynamics, the circumstances in which they redefine themselves vis-à-vis the popular groups . . . produce "equilibrating compromises."[21]

Italo López Vallecillos perceives a similar configuration consisting of

> a faction denominated *agrario-financiera* [agro-financial] opposed to any attempts to transform the rigid framework of land concentration [and] low salaries, [cornerstones of] a plantation economy that serves as the basis of its profits . . . and the *agrario-industrial-financiera* [agro-industro-financial] faction which seeks to impose new patterns of agricultural diversification. [During crises] both factions are forced to joust with respect to the type of domination that ought to prevail in the country. This hegemonic dispute . . . allows that other class factions mobilize themselves . . . seeking to increase their own influence. . . . For example, whenever the price of export products is relatively stable, the agro-industro-financial faction seeks to introduce changes in the

FIGURE 2-2

Top Economic Actors in Agricultural Exports and Coffee Exports

Top 26 Groups in Agricultural Export Products	Coffee[a]	Cotton[a]	Cane[b]	Top 24 in Coffee Exports (percent of total)	
1. Regalado Dueñas, Mathies Regalado	85	—	105	1. De Sola (sons and successors)	14.37
2. Guirola	72	67	9	2. Salvadoreña de Café	8.16
3. Llach-Schonenberg	50	27	—	3. Liebes	7.03
4. Hill-Llach Hill	49	77	—	4. Daglio	6.66
5. Dueñas	46	124	44	5. Prieto	5.92
6. Alvarez Lemus	42	—	—	6. Borgonovo	5.76
7. Meza Ayau	41	—	—	7. Cafeco, S.A.	4.15
8. Sol Millet-Luis Escalante	37	—	—	8. Battle	3.93
9. Daglio	39	18	—	9. Dueñas (Miguel)	2.88
10. Alvarez, other	33	—	—	10. Llach	2.87
11. Salaverría	32	31	10	11. Salaverría-Durán	2.80
12. Deininger	22	—	—	12. Cristiani-Burkard	1.80
13. Alfaro (Castillo-Liévano-Vilanova)	22	—	48	13. Homberger	1.79
14. Dalton	22	35	—	14. Salaverría (José Antonio)	1.64
15. Lima	20	—	—	15. Salmar	1.59
16. García Prieto-Miguel A. Salaverría	20	92	—	16. Herrera Cornejo	1.55
17. Avila Meardi-Meardi Palomo	19	18	—	17. Castro Liebes	1.46
18. Liebes	18	—	—	18. Industrias de Café, S.A.	1.41
19. Battle	18	—	—	19. Bonilla (Sons)	1.32
20. Alvarez Drews	16	—	22	20. Rengifo Núñez	1.15
21. Quiñónez	15	—	45	21. Regalado (bros.)	1.10
22. H. de Sola	14	—	22	22. Monedero	1.09
23. Kriete	13	100	—	23. J. Hill	1.07
24. Cristiani Burkard	13	79	51	24. Sol Millet	1.02
25. Salaverría (Eduardo)	12	10	—		
26. Bonilla	10	—	—		

Source: Colindres, "La Tenencia de la Tierra," p. 471.
a. Thousands of quintales
b. Thousands of metric tons

economic system, redistributing more social benefits to labor and
favoring less authoritarian political structures.[22]

The duocentric models of the Salvadoran power block presented by
Guidos Véjar and López Vallecillos are naturally not without fault, but they
do have much empirical validity and conceptual sophistication. In addition,
these models parallel others that may be found in the Salvadoran literature on
this question, suggesting a consensus of scholarly opinion. They depict a
scheme of "shared economic power," in which the more traditional (agro-
financial) faction adjusted to the limited industrialization afforded under the
model of export agriculture without having to accept the social and political
consequences of that transformation. Under the existing circumstances it was
unlikely that industrialization would be the key to a new system of political
domination in El Salvador.[23]

The continued dominance of the traditional faction was inextricably bound
to a process of concentration described as a "magic square" of oligarchic
domination, which included control of production, export, finance, and land
tenure.[24] The description of how this concentration came about deserves a
major historical essay, a task undertaken in part by David Browning and by
Knut Walter.[25] For our purposes here it is more important to understand how
this mechanism has operated in contemporary times, reproducing and rein-
forcing itself.

The profits realized by the major planters were exceedingly high through
most of the period from 1948 to 1979. In the late 1940s El Salvador was, in
the opinion of an expert source, the most efficient producer of "mild arabica"
coffee in the world. Production costs were estimated by the Compañía Salvadoreña de Café at 12 cents per pound for 1948, and in the 18 to 20 cents per
pound range for 1949. A different computation by a more impartial source,
however, suggested that the real costs may have been closer to 7.3 cents per
pound during those years.[26] In addition, a careful study by Daniel and Ester
Slutzky calculated the profits of the large planters at 30 percent during the late
forties, 45 percent in 1950–57, and 34 percent in 1962–64.[27]

All of these estimates are subject to criticism and revision. Yet there is little
question that the Salvadoran economy produced the levels of investment
needed to keep export agriculture going, as well as a surplus to apply to other
sectors.[28] According to careful calculations by Joseph Mooney, gross fixed
domestic investment jumped from 4.5 to 14.6 percent of GDP between 1945
and 1965—in real terms, fixed at 1962 prices.[29] In his conclusions, Mooney
stated that investment had not only strengthened but acquired a cyclical insensitivity. In other words, investment capital was available regardless of the
level of export prices. Mooney seemed correct in saying that manufacturing
and commerce had become important sources of growth at the time; however,

his appraisal that this picture signified a "break from the pattern of development which prevailed in the past" seems to have been optimistic and
premature.[30]

One reason why a new pattern of development failed to take root was
precisely because the control of the profits and the surplus remained in few
hands. According to Luis de Sebastián, Salvadoran finance had originated in
the circulation of the surplus generated by agricultural exports. In recent
times, the link between agriculture and finance has remained strong. For
example, the ownership "of the four oldest banks—Salvadoreño, Comercio,
Agrícola Comercial, and Capitalizador—is linked to [that sector, while] the
nexus between the four other largest banks—Crédito Popular, Cuscatlán,
Financiero, and Internacional—and the agro-exporting sector is not so notorious. . . . [Finally] the Banco Hipotecario is linked to official interests in that
sector through the Compañía Salvadoreña de Café."[31] Small wonder that
between 1961 and 1975 the share of agriculture in commercial credit increased in relation to the total amount of credit available in those years. A
study by Melvin Burke uncovered evidence that during those years the coffee
sector received an average of 50 percent of all agricultural credit and 15.2 of
all commercial loans, as suggested by the data presented in Table 2-1.

There was nothing inherently conspiratorial about this. The pattern of credit
extended for commercial operations was simply the product of concentrated
and overlapping ownership and the network of relations resulting from it.
Naturally this most benefited the largest planters, who could supply collateral
and assure repayment. Burke suggests that, in general, Salvadoran finance
followed an iron law of sorts of "lending to those who own something."[32]

Burkes's figures, on the other hand, do not show that the other sectors were
starved for credit but merely that agriculture took more than its due share,
especially if one considers that the percentage of GDP contributed by agriculture began to decline in this period of time. There was credit to finance other
activities, but this was tied to the network of interests described by the
evidence presented in Figures 2-1 and 2-2.

In the late sixties, at the time when Aubey collected his data, the industrial
sector of the Salvadoran economy employed 64,722 workers in 4,220 enterprises owned by 3,389 proprietors.[33] These figures would work out to about
15 workers per firm, hardly the type of establishment characteristic of a robust
industrial sector. On the other hand, David Raynolds may have been correct
in arguing that the number of "decisive" economic actors increased from
4,000 in the thirties to 24,000 in the early sixties, but it is hard to see how he
could conclude that the system was not closed to new entrants and that even
better opportunities would open up to those not yet participating in economic
decisions.[34]

The late sixties marked the time when the bourgeoisie, dominated by the industrialists, established an important foothold in the commerce of the Isthmus with an aggressive export policy. This new avenue was beginning to make them somewhat stronger and more independent of the traditional oligarchy, since it provided them with profits that were not so enmeshed in the complex network of domestic economic relationships described above. But the 1969 "soccer war" with Honduras effectively closed that avenue.[35] There remained the possibility of association with transnational capital interested in diversification. But the country did not provide a very large market, and foreign capitalists did not need Salvadoran associates to invest elsewhere in the Isthmus. At any rate, neither of these would have made Salvadoran industrialists more independent, and the bulk of transnational capital went to Guatemala anyway. Therefore, the balance of economic power "shared" by the traditional agro-financial oligarchy—or "agrarian front"—and the agro-industro-financial bourgeoisie remained in favor of the former. (To simplify matters I will use the term *oligarchy* to refer to the faction that dominated finance and export agriculture, reserving the term *bourgeoisie* for those upper-class elements whose presence was stronger in commerce and industry.)

A bourgeoisie did indeed emerge in El Salvador, but it remained bound to the traditional groups or at least dependent on them for the finance of major projects. The bourgeoisie remained unable to secure the resources necessary to embark on the type of economic projects that would have made it socially and politically hegemonic. A democratic regime would not have been the inevitable result of bourgeois dominance, but without that dominance a new coalition could not be formed to challenge the traditional oligarchy from a solid economic footing. In short, a new alliance and a new social pact were not forthcoming, and lacking that firm economic base, the more progressive element of the Salvadoran upper classes remained unwilling to attempt more drastic options, such as a populist alliance with the lower class, much less a reformist government based on civilian supremacy.

The deterioration of the material conditions of life of most families in the Salvadoran countryside was a direct result of the oligarchy's magic square of economic domination. Despite a nominal tenfold increase between 1952 and 1979, the salaries of agricultural workers remained at or below subsistence (see Table 2-2). In 1975 the level of subsistence for an average family of six was estimated to require an income of 1,760 colones per year, with 1,332 colones just to cover nutritional requirements. During the 1970s, a majority of the rural families saw their situations grow progressively worse, following the massive return migration produced by the war with Honduras. Between 1971 and 1975 the proportion of agricultural families without land increased from 29 to 41 percent of the total, compared to 12 percent in 1961.[36] This is reflected in the figures presented in Table 2-3.

Of course barter and other ingenious schemes in the informal economy of the poor can provide some relief in situations like this. The well-documented symbiotic relationship in which *minifundia* provide subsistence—and some basic staples for the domestic market—for poor agriculturists employed seasonally in the *latifundia* can also serve to ensure the loyalty of the peasants to a dominant group. Thus, those most directly affected by the domination of the magic square, the massive number of unemployed and underemployed Salvadoran peasants providing the "redundant labor" indispensable to Salvadoran export agriculture, may not have been ready to revolt against their exploiters.

Meanwhile, the proprietors of the farms engaged in the production of export crops got a very nice bargain. El Salvador was a predominantly rural country with a very high rate of population growth and a slowly expanding industrial sector incapable of absorbing increasingly larger proportions of the work force. There was a fixed, guaranteed demand for employment that kept labor costs very low, and planters had to worry about salaries during only three or four months.

Inevitably, a demand for the redress of this historical grievance became a permanent feature of the political process, made more urgent by deteriorating conditions in the countryside. The corollary is that, if forced by the government, the planters had a sufficient cushion to assimilate reform. Given the buffer that their surplus and their profits provided, one could imagine that the traditional oligarchy would eventually reconsider and yield somewhat. But this was not to be.

Following the *matanza* of 1932, political conditions in the Salvadoran countryside were tightly controlled through a combination of paternalism, unfulfilled promises, and repression. The particular blend at any one time depended on the ups and downs of the export market, the orientation of the incumbent government, and the degree of agitation about reform. The peasantry remained outside the political process, unable to evolve autonomous organizations that would give it an independent voice. Instead, independent organizational attempts were resisted ferociously, and the government tried to bring the peasantry into its Salvadoran Communal Union (UCS).

When conditions deteriorated so far that even the government decided that some action was necessary, the oligarchy resisted and thwarted the initiatives; this happened in both 1973 and 1976. Government arguments that "reform now was a life insurance for the future" failed to convince the traditional oligarchy. To them, reform was "appeasement"; their own assumption seemed to be that, if necessary, they could repeat the "lesson" of 1932.

Like the bourgeoisie, the peasantry and the Salvadoran working class needed an ally, some group which could join forces with them and dislodge the monolith represented by the magic square. It can be argued that the post-1972 developments in Salvadoran politics have been either a series of failed and short-lived initiatives to build new alliances or contrived and short-sighted attempts to provide temporary respite from cyclical crises. The oligarchy has weakened somewhat, but it remains capable of taking bold initiatives to save itself.

Oligarchic domination in contemporary Salvadoran society rested on a scheme of "shared economic power" in which the more traditional (oligarchy) faction continued to dominate a weaker modernizing faction (bourgeoisie). The concentration of land, production, exports, and finance benefited the two, but preserved the power of the oligarchy over the bourgeoisie with this magic square of domination as the centerpiece. The armed forces, who had assumed control of the government, refrained from too much tampering, so that the private sector, led by the oligarchy, could continue to provide foreign exchange, revenue, and prosperity for some, although probably not too many.

The point is frequently made that the fatal flaw of socialism is that it concentrates too much power in the state, creating an economic monolith that suffocates freedom. In El Salvador, the agents of concentrated economic power, who managed to stifle political freedom and thus prevent the breaking down of their monolith, masqueraded as defenders of "free enterprise." From the standpoint of the established order, which offered no genuine avenues of redress, any effective solution had to be "subversive," since it had to come from a new set of actors. To understand this is to understand what is in crisis in El Salvador, and to identify solutions to this crisis is to identify what deserves to be saved, the pretense of free enterprise or the real thing.

Chapter 3

Parties and Politics in El Salvador, 1948–1977

The Cycle of Salvadoran Politics

According to Italo López Vallecillos, contemporary Salvadoran politics has
followed a cyclical pattern that is related very closely to the cycle of export
commodities. López Vallecillos sees the period between 1948 and 1977 as
divided into two stages of roughly twelve years each: one from 1948 to 1960,
and the other from 1962 to 1975.[1] Neither dogmatic nor deterministic, this
perspective is simply a recognition of a basic feature of Salvadoran political
economy, and is probably shared by Salvadorans of very diverse ideological
stripes. The nexus between economic crisis and political conflict is relatively
straightforward.

> Economic crises trigger events with political and military significance
> in which middle sectors and factions of the dominant classes intervene,
> [seeking to introduce] new modalities of expression into the system.
> [However] not always are economic crises a decisive factor of change or
> readjustment, although . . . mass movements are pressure elements
> [comparable to economic crises] especially when articulated with classes
> gaining ascendance; . . . The cyclical nature of our economy . . .
> reinforces the power of the agro-financial faction [of the oligar-
> chy] which is the only one that, during economic crises, can wield for-
> eign exchange to show the need to maintain [a] capitalist model
> based on agriculture.[2]

These considerations are very pertinent and worthwhile as a preface to any
discussion of contemporary partisan politics in El Salvador, for given the
characteristics of the military model and the outcomes that such a model could
allow, it may seem somewhat esoteric to speak of party politics in that country. Moreover, the majority of the parties to be identified in this chapter were
not really political parties. Finally, and most important, the fatal flaw of the
Salvadoran system inaugurated in 1948 is that in trying to prevent partisan

and electoral politics from disrupting the established order, the military precipitated a more direct confrontation between Salvadoran classes.

Yet the stubbornness with which the oligarchy resisted the institutionalization of a party system and competitive elections in El Salvador suggests that it clearly understood the socioeconomic implications of such a development. Since the system of political domination that prevailed in El Salvador between 1948 and 1972 was based on an exclusionist and unstable alliance between the military and oligarchy, since the regime enjoyed relatively low legitimacy, and since it was managed by an actor which had control but not hegemony, it was a foregone conclusion that elements left out of the official coalition would eventually mature and evolve their own avenues of political participation. It was also inevitable that those elements would challenge the system, taking advantage of cyclical crises to force the government to respond or repress the challenge.

The institutionalization of a party system would have reduced tensions and introduced the types of incrementalist strategies that are characteristic of a political process that includes regularly scheduled and truly competitive elections. Class interests would have become intertwined with electoral alliances, and the oligarchy could have spread the inevitable reductions in its position over a relatively long period of time. To be sure, there is no guarantee that this would have been the case, but the oligarchy and the military refused to enter into a game that entailed any degree of uncertainty and set out to pursue a partnership in which the latter would "maintain order" while the former managed the resources that sustained that order. Apparently, the military believed that it would be able to follow the Mexican model and consolidate a system of one-party domination. The oligarchy, for its part, seemed resigned to leaving the governing to the military, provided it did not embark on dangerous experiments. Both seemed to understand the functional requirements of their alliance, including the measures necessary to keep it afloat during times of crisis, although it is hard to imagine that they believed in their unyielding ability to prevent change.

The Party System of El Salvador

As a point of reference for the discussion to follow, Figure 3-1 traces the trajectories of the more relevant parties in the Salvadoran system. These include the two official parties, the Partido Revolucionario de Unificación Democrática (PRUD), which lasted from 1950 to 1960, and its successor, the Partido de Conciliación Nacional (PCN), which was unveiled in September 1961 and, although apparently moribund, is still active two decades later. The splinters of the PRUD-PCN are also included in the figure.

Some of the longer lasting and more representative parties of the opposition include—in chronological order of their founding—the Partido Communista Salvadoreño (PCS), the oldest party in the country; the Partido Acción Renovadora (PAR), which underwent a very curious metamorphosis which led to a split and its eventual disintegration in the mid 1960s; the Partido Demócrata Cristiano (PDC); and the Movimiento Nacional Revolucionario (MNR). This list would have to include the Partido Popular Salvadoreño (PPS), formed by the more conservative members of the PAR, which sought to articulate a different type of opposition from that represented by the first four.

The emergence and evolution of these parties were tied to the cycle of Salvadoran politics described by López Vallecillos, and while it is difficult to identify the constituencies that they represented with absolute accuracy, their fortunes tell us a lot about the major events of contemporary Salvadoran politics. In addition, their trajectories also reflect the limited success enjoyed by the official party and the degree to which political actors excluded from the official coalition were able to challenge its real or presumed dominance.

The track of the official party can be divided into two periods: one from 1950 to 1960, and the other from 1961 through 1977. The mini-revolution of 1960 was a watershed. It brought about a fundamental change in the context in which the party operated and limited its ability to serve as intermediary and arbiter, functions which a dominant party is supposed to fulfill. In both 1950 and 1961 the party was organized to serve as a political vehicle of the civil-military coalition, and not as an instrument of the ambitions of a personalist military leader.

The PRUD-PCN was not a mass party. It did not thrive on mobilizing the population, except to express support for government policies. The party did not have a permanent organizational structure; nor did it have much to do between elections. None of its deputies in the unicameral legislature or its municipal officials "elected" under the banner of the official party turned to it for guidance during his term of office. In reality, there was nothing to turn to: no party program or platform, no sectoral leadership to consult. While the official Salvadoran party incorporated public employees, retired military, and agricultural workers into its ranks, its de facto leadership came from the High Command of the armed forces and high government officials.

Compared to the minuscule bands that tried to present themselves as parties in order to serve as conduits of the electoral ambitions of a maverick officer or two, the official party was an impressive machine of patronage and electoral mobilization. Created to serve the ends of official policy, the party reflected the inclinations of the government in power, and this tended to create splinter groups, as represented in Figure 3-1. By contrast, the ephemeral and ad hoc groups, such as the Partido Auténtico Nacional (1956), the Partido Institucional Democrático (1956), the Partido Demócrata Nacionalista (1956), the

FIGURE 3-I
Evolution of the Salvadoran Party Spectrum, 1930–1977

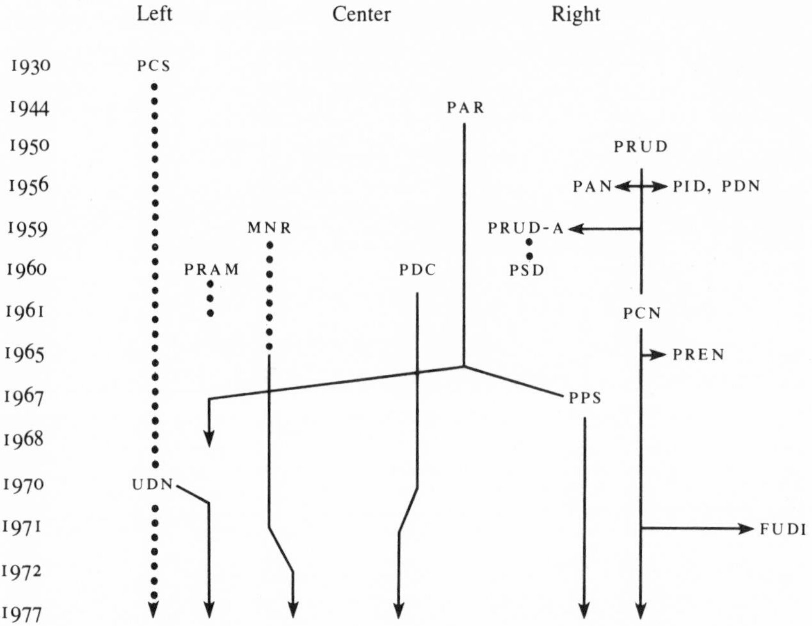

Note: Parties are arranged on a Left-Right continuum according to their position on the issues of civilian supremacy and reform of the existing socioeconomic structure. Solid lines represent periods during which the parties enjoyed legal recognition and were able to participate in elections. Broken lines represent periods during which the parties were being organized or when they did not meet one or both of the aforementioned conditions.

Partido Republicano de Evolución Nacional (1965), and the Frente Unido Democrático Independiente (1971), were organized to promote the candidacies of Colonel Luis R. Flores, Colonel Rafael Carranza Anaya, Major José Alvaro Díaz, Colonel José Alberto Funes, and General José Alberto "Chele" Medrano, respectively.

The fact that these mini-parties were organized reflects the diversity of opinions within the military institution, as well as the fact that there was always a generous supply of, for the most part, extreme conservatives outside the official party smarting at the "sell-out" by government reformism. A good example of both is the case of Chele Medrano, who, in spite of the support of the Salaverría family and the votes of the members of ORDEN, did not make much headway in the bitter election of 1972. Medrano's failure, which included arrest for conspiring against the government, suggests that the dominant party provided the military with a mechanism that preempted the actions of mavericks like Medrano.

The official party, the PRUD, was the creation of Colonel Oscar Osorio, who had lived in Mexico and had the opportunity to observe the operation of the Mexican system. Osorio had led the "majors' revolt" that deposed General Salvador Castaneda Castro on 14 December 1948. But the dominant Salvadoran party could no more be "revolutionary of democratic unification" than Mexico's PRI could become "institutional revolutionary." At bottom, neither really wanted to emphasize "revolutionary." Thus the Salvadoran emphasis on unification and the Mexican emphasis on institutions.

During his term (1950–56), Osorio adopted the reformist rhetoric of the Revolutionary Council of 1948 and pursued some of its policies as well. This emphasis may have been genuine, but Monteforte Toledo probably went too far when he included the PRUD-PCN among the social democratic parties of the time in Central America.[3] To be sure, Osorio's fallout with Lemus resulted in the formation by the former of the PRUD-A (*auténtico*), which later became the Partido Social Demócrata. But names alone will not do. Neither will the fact that although he may have harbored social democratic ideas, Osorio failed to champion *the* cause of one of the most important contributions of social democracy to Latin American politics, namely, civilian supremacy.

Osorio's reforms concerned some aspects of the social situation, primarily the problem of agricultural labor and the creation of the Social Security Institute (ISSS), the Urban Housing Institute (IVU), and the Rural Settlement Institute (ICR). But Osorio's reformism was epitomized by a series of infrastructural works—continued by his successor—which reflected the developmentalist approach of his government. Most notable among these were the works coordinated by the Acajutla Port Authority (CEPA) and the Río Lempa Hydroelectric Authority (CEL). Apparently, this kind of project, as well as the economic policies of his government, strengthened the interests of the oligarchy.[4] This emphasis on the development of infrastructure made the PRUD attractive to some of the more dynamic elements in the society, and it was able to depend on the elite sectors for its leadership and to attract the support of middle-class elements recruited into the expanding government bureaucracy.

In spite of his reformism, Osorio reached an accommodation with the oligarchy. The economy was prosperous, and part of his scheme was to create incentives for investment and diversification. The course of the Guatemalan Revolution made him especially vulnerable to accusations of softness toward leftism, and he left the peasant sector alone. The inclusion of industrialists in his coalition, as well as some middle- and working-class elements, could imply the kind of populist coalition typical of the contemporary Latin American systems, but the presence of the oligarchy in the coalition helped to keep Osorio's populist tendencies in check.

In the elections of 1950 and 1956 the PRUD had to contend with the opposition of a party that initially appeared to be the electoral vehicle of a figure representing the more progressive faction of the military, Colonel José Asencio Menéndez. Originating in the *huelga de brazos caídos* (slowdown strike) that contributed to the creation of the appropriate climate for the overthrow of Martínez in 1944, the Partido Acción Renovadora (PAR) is one of the more interesting of the time. This party supported a return to civilian rule, although it endorsed the laissez-faire approach to economics favored by the oligarchy. The PAR could have been a viable alternative in 1944 had the junta headed by General Andrés Ignacio Menéndez not been overthrown by the coup of Colonel Osmín Aguirre, which was instigated by the more reactionary elements of the oligarchy. General Menéndez wanted a free and open election, an election that could have been won by physician Arturo Romero.

All this is pure speculation, but it does give an indication of the kinds of individuals that banded around the PAR at the time. In 1950 the party obtained a respectable 43 percent of the presidential vote, while government manipulation of the 1956 presidential race assigned to the PAR candidate, Enrique Magaña Menéndez, a mere 3 percent. Magaña and the successful PAR candidate to the mayoralty of San Salvador, economist and bank president Gabriel Piloña Araujo, were part of the bourgeoisie. Therefore, it seems possible to conclude that the PAR played the role of opposition in these elections, serving as a vehicle for and an alternative supported by the more progressive elements of the oligarchy and the bourgeoisie.

The PAR was joined in the election of 1956 by another party, the Partido Acción Nacional (PAN), organized around a civilian figure, Roberto Edmundo Canessa, a wealthy planter who financed his own campaign and who had served as minister of justice and of foreign relations under Osorio. Canessa's candidacy was disqualified on "technical grounds," and he was one of the noisiest protesters of the electoral fraud perpetrated by the PRUD in that year.

If Osorio turned to repression at the end of his term to counteract the spillover of the Guatemalan process in El Salvador, his successor, President José María Lemus (1956–60), turned to repression to quell the unrest that accompanied the deterioration of the economy beginning with a drop in coffee prices in 1958 and the increasing agitation produced by the example of the Cuban Revolution. Enthusiasm for the Cuban model of 1959–60 crystallized in the formation of the Partido Revolucionario Abril y Mayo (PRAM), which drew its leadership from the university community. The PRAM was denied legal status in July 1960.

The disruption and unrest in 1960 indicated that the PRUD had failed to form a broad coalition and that the existing party system did not provide outlets for all the relevant and viable political options. In an effort to reequilibrate his government, neutralize student and labor agitation, and reorganize the governing coalition, Lemus announced a program of reforms in late July. He organized a demonstration in August, attended primarily by campesinos trucked into San Salvador. The church hierarchy lent support to his initiative, but both the church and the government were caught in a bind, preaching reform and denouncing Communism at the same time.

The problems that Lemus encountered near the end of his term and his reactions to them are not unlike the situations that other military rulers faced in their terms as they tried to settle problems of succession. Typically, these problems were influenced by or were a part of other factors, including attempts by the oligarchy and the bourgeoisie to influence the selection of the new president or to float their own candidates if dissatisfied with the official choice and opposition calls for a free and fair election, which, in some cases, would have been lost by the official party.

Thus, Salvadoran military presidents approaching the end of their terms often increased the populist content of official rhetoric, launched a "new" program of reforms, cracked down on the liberal opposition and staged an outright electoral fraud, or provoked a confrontation with the traditional oligarchy and the conservative elements of the bourgeoisie. These are typical of most of the crises of succession from 1948 to 1977, aggravated, in some cases, by the commodity cycle, as López Vallecillos has pointed out.

The Mexican system has also confronted crises similar to the one that confronted the Lemus government in 1960, but when attacked by conservatives, threatened by former presidents and their cliques, and beset by economic difficulties, a Mexican president can normally count on the support of political actors who may not love the government and its party but who, like him, share the center of the Mexican political spectrum. A president who represents that center position has the support of a party organized as a broad coalition of middle- and working-class elements, as well as of progressive elements of the industrial bourgeoisie, and can count on the legitimacy of the Revolution. In the Salvadoran scheme, however, the Right was the center of the political spectrum, there was no permanent coalition and no party to fall back upon—nor could these be organized overnight—and there were no historical loyalties to bind substantial sectors of the public to the dominant party. There was just an electoral machine that operated intermittently and a patronage network which fed on itself.

Part of Lemus's problem may have been that, according to some accounts, he had begun to contemplate the prospect of staying in office for another term. This was not allowed for in the system that Osorio had crafted so carefully, and the latter organized an "authentic" PRUD to emphasize that fact. Lemus's predicament then became desperate. He was threatened by Osorio, had lost the confidence of the oligarchy, was detested by the Left, and was unable to woo the middle class. He lashed out at some of the traditional adversaries of the military, including the General Association of Salvadoran University Students (AGEUS), the newly emerging General Confederation of Salvadoran Workers (CGTS), the PRAM, and opposition figures like Canessa, who died as a consequence of a severe beating, but he was nevertheless overthrown on 26 October 1960. His departure marked a new opportunity to bring about a process of peaceful transition to democracy—and the repetition of a familiar pattern in which such a process was derailed by obstructionists.

The Junta of 1960

In contemporary Salvadoran politics, the formation of a junta is the somewhat inevitable sequel to the overthrow of a military executive. The junta that came to power to replace Lemus was the third provisional executive of this century in El Salvador, and one of the more diffuse and contradictory, combining relatively junior officers and professionals with university affiliations. The junta's intentions and possibilities were unclear as it took power, which may have prompted the United States to withhold recognition until December. To assuage the Left and the moderates the junta assured them of its intention to conduct a free and open election soon. It also moved to try to gain the support and confidence of the military, but on 25 January 1961 the junta was replaced by a *directorio cívico-militar* (civil-military directorate), which justified its coup as a "necessary reaction to the dangerous political tensions that had built up as a consequence of the [previous] Junta having allowed extremist forces to run around wild in the country."[5] Thus, a group of genuine *aperturistas* working toward a transition were replaced by obstructionists who favored a controlled blueprint and a return to business as usual.

The coup probably served two objectives. The first was to assure that none of the "radical" actors who had coalesced around the junta had even the remotest chance of victory through elections. The coup came two days after a congress in which nine parties—including the PRAM, the recently formed (December 1960) Partido Social Demócrata (PSD), which Oscar Osorio had helped organize, the PAR, the Partido Acción Nacional (PAN), founded by the late Canessa, the Partido Auténtico Constitucional (PAC) and the Partido Institucional Democrático (PID), which had supported military candidates in the presidential race of 1956, the Partido Unionista Centroamericano (PUCA), which had existed for some time but had never presented its own candidates, and the recently formed Partido Acción Democrática (PAD) and Partido Demócrata Cristiano (PDC)—and six professional organizations met to draft a new electoral statute.[6]

A second and more important objective was simply to prevent the consolidation of an alternative coalition that, in or out of power, could begin to attract military support and thereby divide the institution. Some of the members of the prospective coalition came from the oligarchy, but they were primarily individuals who could put together a populist coalition and try to bring about a program of reforms outside the blueprint for control envisaged under the 1948 model. Basically, the motivation of the military was to retain control of the government, since, from its point of view, only the armed forces could guarantee the integrity and continuity of the "republic." Attempts to institute a process of transition through elections went against this blueprint and, therefore, had to be neutralized.

The PRAM was persecuted, and Osorio, a potentially disruptive influence but certainly not a radical, was exiled. The remaining parties were invited to form a council to draft the new electoral statute. But, for the most part, the actions of the parties gave the military no reason for alarm. The PID and the PAD were simply ignored. The PAC and the PAN were really vehicles for the personalistic ambitions of certain military officers, and the PUCA was insignificant. Only the PAR and the PDC had the possibility of making some inroads in the legislature.[7]

Apparently, the military had something in mind in addition to electoral reform. According to PDC leader José Napoleón Duarte, colonels Julio Adalberto Rivera and Aníbal Portillo, both members of the *directorio*, sought the support of his party in exchange for all seats in the one-house legislature. This overture might have been an attempt on the part of the military to co-opt some of the *doctores* and middle-class professionals that Colonel Rivera wanted to enlist in the official party. Since there was an agreement between the eight principal leaders of the PDC not to collaborate with governments that came to power illegally, however, Duarte rejected these entreaties.[8] Rivera made similar moves toward the PAR, hoping perhaps to capture the support of dissident bourgeois elements that had gravitated in that direction, but he was equally unsuccessful. He coupled these private overtures with vague public warnings about dangers from the Left and the Right. Dr. Feliciano Avelar, another member of the *directorio*, spoke of the need to set up a dictatorship if a civil-military alliance was not forthcoming. This may have been an indication that the military was under pressure quickly to define the nature of the new regime, or it could have been the military's way of bringing the oligarchy back to the fold by threatening that its place could be taken by others.

Colonel Rivera became the leader of the *directorio*. Token civilian participation was discontinued when most civilian members resigned in April. His provisional government enlarged the scope of state regulation of the economy with the nationalization of the Banco Central de Reserva and of the Banco Hipotecario de El Salvador and some legislation concerning rural labor; short-term measures adopted included restrictions on the export of capital and reduced rents.[9] To justify and legitimize these measures the *directorio* identified them with the objectives of the Alliance for Progress. This tactic may have been designed to give the government some respite from ideological blackmail by the oligarchy, but the oligarchy criticized it anyway, since it did not care much for the Alliance for Progress in the first place.

The year 1960 marked another opportunity for a genuine process of democratic transition in El Salvador. If it had succeeded, the system probably would have stabilized at the center-right, not the right, lower- and middle-class loyalties could have been engaged with the prospect of a possible electoral victory at some future date, and the moderate Left could have been incorporated. Instead, deciding to give their model one more chance, the military conspirators of 1960 made Rivera the new military president, and this time they tried to consolidate their one-party domination with a fairly broad and representative coalition. The populist option had been liquidated with the junta, however, and since the search for new partners was confined to what they perceived as centrist alternatives, the effort was largely futile. Neither the PAR nor the PDC was interested, and even these parties were a far cry from the mass-based multiclass party that the military needed to effect a genuine copy of the Mexican model.

Moreover, any gains in widening the base of support could have come only at the cost of more strained relations with the oligarchy. The military's, or at least Rivera's, attempt to consolidate the official party was a contradiction in terms because, in the final analysis, the military seemed to be trying to strengthen a mechanism for which it did not have much use in the first place. Its desire may have been, at bottom, for an official party that could win elections without fraud, but certainly no more than this.

The search for alternatives did not last long. The decision to resurrect the official party was announced on 2 September 1961, and the *directorio* scheduled elections for a constituent assembly for 17 December. Reacting to this sudden call, the PDC, the PAR, and the PSD formed a united front, the Unión de Partidos Democráticos (UPD), to contest the election. The candidates of the official party, now called the National Conciliation Party (PCN), campaigned on the record of the *directorio* and accused the UPD of "reaction." The PCN won the majority of the seats in the assembly by a margin of 37 to 17. The assembly quickly produced a somewhat altered version of the Constitution of 1950, declared an amnesty, and scheduled presidential elections for 29 April 1962. Rivera was nominated in February 1962, and he ran unopposed, since the opposition parties abstained.

Rivera did not want obstruction from an opposition entrenched in the legislature, and he made his peace with the oligarchy. He enjoyed favorable coffee prices and was able to follow a pragmatic and fairly progressive course, relaxing the electoral statute in 1964 and continuing with some reforms, which, however, always fell short of damaging the interests of the oligarchy. While Rivera was in power, the opportunities offered by the Central American Common Market enabled the industrial bourgeoisie to expand its economic base. Between 1953 and 1962 the number of corporations registered in El Salvador jumped from about 80 to 482, a sixfold increase.[10] Between 1961 and 1965 the average annual variation of GDP was 6.9 percent, while average annual growth in value added by the manufacturing sector was 10.7 percent.[11] Between 1960 and 1966 the value of industrial production went from $53.3 to $154.4 million.[12] This was Rivera's good fortune and not a result of planning.

But the relative success of the PCN under Rivera could not last. First, the Alliance for Progress collapsed eventually. In El Salvador this meant that tax reform and agrarian reform went nowhere, neither at that time nor later, and the progressive record of the PCN would yield increasingly diminishing returns, bringing back the old question of legitimacy.[13] Second, Rivera could not pass his popularity on to his successor; nor could he guarantee that his relatively successful effort in building multiclass electoral support for the government party would continue. Third, the bourgeoisie remained in a relatively weak position with respect to the oligarchy.[14] Fourth, the commodity cycle eventually brought back the phantoms of low prices, unrest, and renewed repression. And fifth and most important, the spurious openness of the system could be maintained only so long as no opposition party or coalition of parties could mount a successful challenge and force the PCN to alter election results or engineer a preventive coup.

The Elusive Electoral Game

It is difficult to determine whether the Christian Democratic Party (PDC) became the dominant party in El Salvador in the late 1960s and early 1970s. It is unlikely that in the space of a decade a political party could build lasting bonds between itself and substantial sectors of the electorate. What is clear is that the PDC became the principal antagonist of the PCN and that its electoral success made it a threat to the Salvadoran military and the oligarchy. Their reaction to this perceived threat contributed to the collapse of the scheme of government that had prevailed since 1948.

Like most Christian Democratic parties of Latin America, the PDC grew out of the deliberations of a study group of Catholics from conservative backgrounds. Through their reading of papal encyclicals and their own observation of their society they became concerned about problems of social inequality and felt the need to articulate a political alternative between Left and Right. The study group began to meet in 1958, and the party was registered in 1960.

Initially, the PDC seems to have attracted conservatives disenchanted with the official party, as well as professionals and petit bourgeois elements who had been relatively inactive in politics. During the 1960s the party maintained a line of moderate reformism which may have caused alarm in certain circles but which, according to one critic, was really "neoliberal."[15] What was a matter of greater concern to the obstructionists in the oligarchy and in the armed forces was the party's ability to organize and mobilize support. The PDC was able to enlarge its base in an essentially middle-class constituency to include lower- and working-class elements from the urban areas.[16] Given that the parties of the Left were illegal, the PDC may have benefited from the support of voters whose preferred alternatives were not available.

The PDC is not likely to have benefited greatly, however, from the splintering and disintegration of other Salvadoran parties during the late 1960s and early 1970s. For example, the disintegration of the PAR could not have resulted in much additional support for the PDC. The conservative faction of the PAR left the party following a takeover by a younger and more radical faction led by Fabio Castillo, a member of the 1960 junta and a former university rector. In 1965 that conservative faction created the Partido Popular Salvadoreño (PPS), which sought to offer an electoral outlet for the weaker faction of the bourgeoisie. The new PAR was declared illegal in 1968, and most of its followers gravitated to Guillermo Ungo's MNR (see Figure 3-1). Therefore, the growing electoral strength of the PDC must be attributed to the use of patronage to develop a political machine that engaged the support of the urban lower class.

Even though the PAR won the mayoralty of San Salvador in 1956, no opposition party has utilized that office—as well as other positions captured by the PDC through the election of 1972—with the efficacy displayed by José Napoleón Duarte during his tenure as mayor, 1964–70. Duarte created a powerful political machine based on Acción Comunitaria, a program of community self-help that organized residents on a neighborhood basis and tried to articulate their demands and serve their needs. Eventually, Acción Comunitaria became another department of the municipal administration. This record of service to the lower- and working-class residents of the city paid off handsomely on the two occasions on which Duarte ran for reelection and in his 1972 presidential campaign.

Support for the PDC also grew out of the logic of a competitive electoral process in which the strongest member of the opposition could present itself as a viable alternative, exploiting the shortcomings of military reformism. Armed with a record of service in the municipalities under its control—thirty-seven in 1964–66, eighty-three in 1966–68, and seventy-eight in 1968–70—and with the accomplishments of the independent session of the national Legislative Assembly in 1968–70, the Christian Democrats began to mount a more direct and effective challenge to the rule of the PCN. During that session of the assembly the PDC joined with MNR deputies, eight progressive deputies from the PCN, and one maverick from the PPS to form a majority. Committee rules were changed, drafts of progressive bills were reported quickly by the committees, and reformist legislation was passed. This was added cause for alarm among rightist elements, especially when President Fidel Sánchez Hernández (1967–72) attended the opening session of a congress on agrarian reform organized by the assembly and declared that agrarian reform was a necessity in El Salvador.[17]

In 1967 each opposition party had presented its own presidential candidate and the official candidate, Sánchez Hernández, had been elected with 54 percent of the vote. His election had not been tainted by blatant manipulation, and he was, therefore, able to extend some bridges to the progressives. But President Sánchez felt increasing pressure on his right flank. The growing strength of the PDC made matters worse, since he had to put some substance behind the nominal reformism of the military in order to compete with the PDC—which would incur the wrath of the oligarchy—or move quickly to turn aside the PDC challenge by other means. The 1969 war with Honduras gave Sánchez a respite by conferring on his administration an aura of legitimacy and forcing the opposition to adopt a low profile. This was a very temporary respite, however. The economic consequences of the war were very somber: the loss of a market of $23 million per year, the closing of land access to Costa Rica and Nicaragua, and the loss of a safety valve that allowed the export of surplus labor.

Even though he reached the accommodation with the oligarchy that all military presidents before him had found indispensable, relations between Sánchez and the conservative backers of the PCN were strained. The Right was alarmed by its legislative losses in 1968, unhappy that Sánchez interpreted the virtual sweep of the PCN in the elections of 1970 as an endorsement of his reformist policies, disturbed by the fact that Minister of Agriculture Enrique Alvarez, a "black sheep" of one of the fourteen families, had formed a committee to study the question of agrarian reform in 1969, and enraged by the introduction of draft legislation concerning irrigation, drainage, and the use of marginal lands. It was most unhappy that Sánchez had, in September 1970, put himself behind these initiatives and actually signed the bill into law in November.

The conservatives were able to thwart the implementation of the irrigation and drainage law, unleashing a vociferous campaign of agitation through the media, which got worse when the government announced its intention to organize agricultural workers. The continuing decline in coffee prices put the planters in an even more belligerent mood, but they failed in their not too subtle effort to provoke a confrontation between President Sánchez and his colleagues in the armed forces. These events convinced the conservatives that they would be better served by their own candidate, one whom they could support and who would stop the dangerous experiments in the agricultural sector. They found it in General José Alberto (Chele) Medrano, who had been dismissed as commander of the national guard in December 1970 amid rumors that he was plotting against the government.

The severe losses that they suffered in the 1970 assembly race had a sobering effect on the opposition parties, and in September 1971 they formed an opposition coalition, the Unión Nacional Opositora (UNO), which included the PDC, the MNR, and the Unión Democrática Nacionalista (UDN). Like the PDC, the Movimiento Nacional Revolucionario (MNR) also grew out of a study group that met during 1956–58. The MNR was not very successful as a party, however, for its platform was highly intellectualized and relatively abstract. Led by Guillermo Ungo, the son of a founder of the PDC, the MNR gradually built a following among the workers in large industrial enterprises, and while it stayed on the Left, it showed a marked tendency to collaborate with Social Democratic and Christian Democratic initiatives. Rafael Glower Valdivieso, a former economy minister under Sánchez, also joined the MNR. The party received the vice-presidential slot on the UNO ticket and filled it with Ungo.

The UDN presented itself for the first time in 1970 as an electoral vehicle for Francisco Lima, a former vice-president of the republic and ambassador-at-large to the United States, Canada, and the OAS. Lima was another PCN maverick who had resigned his post in protest over President Rivera's insensitivity to the poor. Lima tried to organize a "left" within the PCN. and was expelled from the organization, together with his brother Ramón.[18] A splinter of the official party and supported by junior army officers, the UDN was under constant pressure from the government. Both the UDN and the MNR agreed to support the presidential candidacy of José Napoleón Duarte.

Sensing some potential gains if it tried to capture some of the disaffected PCN conservatives, the PPS stood aloof from the UNO coalition and presented its own presidential candidate. José Rodríguez Porth, a lawyer and member of the oligarchy who had resigned from the 1961 directorio in protest over Rivera's reformism, had volunteered his services to prosecute the kidnappers of Ernesto Regalado Dueñas and generally represented management in labor disputes. The PPS, therefore, had great affinity with PCN conservatives. It received financial support from the oligarchy; it was—to say the least—very receptive to business demands; and it played around with terms like "silent majority," "law and order," and a host of others that were appropriate if one wished to attract conservative backing. But the PPS was not, after all, the most ideal vehicle for the more reactionary element of the Salvadoran oligarchy to vent its fury in the election of 1972. The leadership of the PPS was composed primarily of elements from the industrial bourgeoisie, and the conservatives wanted a more symbolic figure.

Their candidate, Chele Medrano, a hero of the war with Honduras and former commander of the national guard, had organized a Frente Unido Democrático Independiente (FUDI) in early 1971. According to Webre, FUDI was a conservative splinter of the PCN and an outlet for "landowner discontent with the government's coffee policy as well as its position on agrarian reform and its 'softline' approach to normalization of relations with Honduras. The FUDI appears to have drawn its leadership from the landed elite of the country's western zone, especially the powerful Salaverría family of Ahuachapán which until its defection in 1971 dominated the PCN party hierarchy in that department."[19] The connection between a former commander of the guard, reactionary oligarchs, and right-wing paramilitary groups was not coincidental; nor was it confined to the electoral campaign of 1971–72.

Medrano was neither a civilian ultraconservative like Rodríguez Porth nor an astute traditional liberal like Miguel Ydígoras of Guatemala. Medrano was the man who had pacified labor in 1966–68, a man who understood the operation of the political economy of export agriculture in El Salvador, a man who understood why it was necessary to keep labor organizers out of the Salvadoran countryside, and a man who could take initiative during times of crisis. Quite literally, he represented an opportunity to return to the golden past when Salvadoran presidents did not have to talk about reformism, when junior officers were easily put in their place, and when there was no need to appease so many professionals and intellectuals who, the conservatives insisted had never met a payroll in their lives, did not know how to read a balance sheet, and did not understand how Salvadoran society "worked." The implication was that Medrano would rule through an unadorned state of exception, that is, one above the law, without opposition parties, without labor unions, and without interest groups except those representing the oligarchy.

Hemorrhaging from a substantial loss of conservative support, confronted by a coalition of moderates and progressives with a common presidential candidate who could very likely win the popular vote, and unable to emphasize its moderate reforms to attract middle-class support, the PCN was very likely to lose the 1972 election. The campaign was bitter and full of mutual recrimination. Early totals from outlying areas had Colonel Arturo A. Molina, the PCN presidential candidate, ahead with 54 percent of the vote, but as returns from the urban areas started to pour in, the UNO closed the gap and apparently went ahead. The government stopped announcing partial results and declared its candidate the winner the day after the election—21 February

1972. The opposition protested the outcome and released its own figures of the final result (see Table 3-1 for the contrast between the government's and the opposition versions). Duarte and Ungo announced that they would challenge the election and organize a general strike if necessary.

On 25 February a hastily convened Legislative Assembly elected Molina, who had only obtained a plurality of the vote, over the objections of opposition deputies, who walked off in protest. The UNO then asked voters to deface their ballots in the upcoming legislative assembly election of 12 March. This paid off in San Salvador, where the number of null votes from defaced ballots exceeded the combined total for the PCN and the PPS. Under Salvadoran law the election had to be nullified, and the departmental electoral board ordered a new election on 22 March. The atmosphere remained very tense.[20]

It is difficult to determine the ideological orientation of the officers who staged the army rebellion of 25 March 1972. The revolt sprang from the artillery barracks of El Zapote and the San Carlos garrison. Apparently, the extreme Right was not involved. Colonel Benjamín Mejía led the revolt, and he sought the support of moderate leftists and the Christian Democrats. Glower Valdivieso and Duarte took turns in radio broadcasts to urge the country to support the rebellion. No mass appeal was made to take arms, and apparently no effort was made to distribute them, although Duarte urged his supporters to obstruct the advance of government forces. The revolt was put down by loyal units from outside the capital, the national guard, and the air force.[21]

The elections of 1972 and the military revolt represent a drastic discontinuity in the operation of the Salvadoran model of one-party domination. The system intended to maintain the domination of the armed forces in an alliance with the more significant economic groups of the country. The original blueprint excluded the possibility of defeat and assumed that the official party would be able gradually to include the more dynamic sectors of the middle class. The latter evolved their own independent mechanisms of political organization, however, and remained aloof, but their ability to participate in elections and share in the control of some sectors of the government, albeit in limited form, did create the incentives for continued participation and neutralize the more radical segments of the opposition.

The figure and actions of the main loser in the 1972 fiasco, Duarte, illustrate some of the unwritten rules of the pattern of government that was crumbling at the time. Although supported by one military faction, which came out against the fraud by force of arms, Duarte refused to try to mobilize his supporters. He may have refrained from a direct appeal to the masses for fear of turning military opinion against him and his party; given the treatment that both received after the rebellion was suffocated, it is hard to imagine how a more decisive stance would have brought them greater disgrace. On the other hand, despite his populist tactics and his progressive policies as mayor of San Salvador, Duarte may have been a practitioner of the game of controlled democracy which excluded direct appeals to the masses. Therefore, his fear of revolution or civil war may have been stronger than his fear of certain retribution.

But, after all, Duarte was not the only loser in 1972. President Fidel Sánchez was in a position somewhat similar to that in which Lemus had found himself twelve years before, and he was passing the government on to his successor under very difficult circumstances. Whatever claim the PRUD-PCN may have laid to a social democratic or reformist orientation effectively ended at that time. The equilibrium of forces within the party was upset, the chances for "reform" were compromised, and the linchpin that had held the system together all along, the "pacified countryside," was about to come loose. Duarte and the reformists may have been hoping all along that, as they had done elsewhere in Latin America, the armed forces would eventually resign themselves to a civilian president elected by a popular vote. But they did not.

As is usually the case when examining authoritarian situations, it is difficult to gauge the true alignment of forces and the real strength of each actor, but the summary included here prepared by López Vallecillos describing the salient characteristics of the more prominent actors in the Salvadoran system of parties is probably an accurate portrayal of the situation in 1972, and perhaps as late as 1977 (see Figure 3-2).

The political defeat of the moderates in 1972 compromised reformism and destroyed the new center emerging in Salvadoran politics, leaving a radical situation with two basic characteristics. One was the disappearance of political intermediaries between the government and major social groups and classes; the other was the more direct confrontation between the latter and a military increasingly unable to manage social conflict peacefully.

With their electoral options preempted by systematic fraud, opposition political parties could make only token participatory attempts in elections that were increasingly meaningless. Their main purpose was no longer to try to reach power through elections but to demonstrate the dictatorial nature of the government. This diminished their relevance and sent them into a tailspin of disorganization and internal debate, from which they have yet to recover. Lacking effective avenues to represent their interests and given the military's attempt to "depoliticize" the society, the more progressive sectors of the bourgeoisie and the lower and popular classes had to find different political roles. Social organizations filled the vacuum of partisan activity for the latter, while middle-class elites went into inactivity or began to contemplate more drastic alternatives. The Catholic hierarchy and lay organizations became in-

FIGURE 3-2
Characteristics of Salvadoran Political Parties

Class composition	PCN	PDC	MNR
leadership	middle class, petite bourgeoisie, officers	petite bourgeoisie and professionals	intellectuals, professionals, technocrats
membership (cadre)	professionals, public and white-collar employees, traditional labor leaders	faculty, students, syndicalists, employees, workers	workers, university students, employees, teachers, syndicalists, small merchants
constituency	weak in urban areas, mostly rural workers	professionals, teachers, white-collar employees, urban workers, some rural workers and farmhands	professionals, students, employees, teachers, urban workers
Ideology	developmentalism, elitist democracy, neoliberalism	Catholic social doctrine, Christian humanism, representative democracy	social democracy, nationalism, radical populism
Program	defense of policies of incumbent administration	reformist capitalism, redistribution through profit sharing	radical reformism, evolutionary socialism
Tactics	electoral mobilization, controlled mobilizations in support of the government	mobilization and politicization, electoral mobilization, opposition	development of cadre, opposition, politicization, electoral mobilization
Alliances	high-ranking officers and middle-class sectors	progressive factions of the bourgeoisie, petite bourgeoisie, urban proletariat, religious activists	petite bourgeoisie, urban proletariat, larger mass-based parties
International linkages	PRI (Mexico)	International Christian Democracy and affiliates	II Socialist International, AD (Ven.), PLN (Costa Rica)

Source: López Vallecillos, "Fuerzas Sociales," pp. 568–69, 578–79

UDN	PCS	FUDI/FDN
syndicalists, agrarian leaders, faculty	intellectuals, petite bourgeoisie, syndicalists, faculty and teachers	landowners and conservative professionals
urban workers, university students, teachers, peasant activists	university students, urban workers, some peasant activists	rural *caciques*
urban workers	not a direct participant in elections	rural workers
socialist	Marxist-Leninist	authoritarian, reactionary capitalism, caudillism
evolutionary socialism, autonomous capitalism	transition to a socialist system	defense of traditional system of agrarian exploitation
development of cadre, penetration of mass organizations, political agitation, electoral mobilization	development of cell structure and cadre, opposition, mass propaganda	electoral mobilization, mobilization for armed confrontations with peasant organizations
PCS for elections and UNO activities, petite bourgeoisie, UNO, Foro	petite bourgeoisie, leftist intellectuals, moderate parties	none previously
socialist organizations	Communist International (Soviet line)	Latin American anti-Communist movements

creasingly militant and critical and began to confront the government with the results of its repression—such as the peasant massacre of La Cayetana in November 1974 and the student massacre of July 1975—and to articulate the demands of the lower and popular classes.

The role of student, peasant, and worker organizations became more important, as they started to collaborate with each other, to organize protest demonstrations, takeovers, and sit-ins, and to engage in civil disobedience in order to make their demands heard and to defend themselves from increasing attacks by the paramilitary Right. This last, meanwhile, was becoming a very effective vehicle for the expression of oligarchic dissatisfaction with the status quo. This polarization mirrored the developing confrontation between the oligarchy and the church and other civic organizations, at the elite level, and between the right-wing paramilitary groups and popular organizations like the Bloque Popular Revolucionario (BPR), created in 1975; the Frente de Acción Popular Unificada (FAPU), created in 1974; the Federación Cristiana de Campesinos Salvadoreños (FECCAS); and the Unión de Trabajadores Campestres (UTC). Urban terrorism, clashes between these rival groups in the countryside, and assassinations of priests, popular leaders, and oligarchy figures became frequent. Finally, the *vía armada* became a more realistic option, and insurgent groups, which had been operating intermittently, became larger, better organized, and more capable of becoming *the* opposition.

The military believed that it could continue to operate in these new conditions with only minor alterations in its basic formula of domination. It assumed that the opposition would eventually calm down, that some concessions would be forthcoming from the oligarchy, and that its own version of reformism would carry the day. It was wrong on all counts.

The opposition became more defiant and effective. The Right reacted with more violence. The oligarchy clung to its narrow and selfish version of free enterprise. And the Salvadoran military's version of the old Porfirian scheme (*pan o palos* [bread or the stick]), repressive reformism, became simply repression. In the words of José Simán, a Catholic intellectual and a progressive member of the bourgeoisie, "A horizon of death came to replace the horizon of life."[22]

Chapter 4

The Deterioration of the Salvadoran Regime

From Repressive Reformism to Militarized Capitalism

Although Salvadoran scholars disagree over when a state of exception emerged in El Salvador and what exactly that entailed, nearly all agree that the Salvadoran system of controlled democracy underwent a profound transformation in the mid-1970s. This disagreement is fairly common in the literature of authoritarian regimes. For example, despite a relative consensus on the definitional characteristics of the "new" authoritarian regimes of South America, identified most frequently as "bureaucratic authoritarian" regimes or "national security" states, among a host of alternative labels, students of those regimes differ on which of their characteristics is most relevant.[1]

At least in the case of El Salvador, one cannot treat this purely as a question of semantics. An accurate diagnosis of the present Salvadoran crisis requires an informed understanding of the differences between the administrations of Arturo Molina and Carlos Humberto Romero, and between these and the governments organized after the coup of 15 October 1979.

Authoritarian regimes share a similar formula of political domination. In essence, this consists of a dictatorial government, maintaining a *régime d'exception*, that is, one above the law and beyond the constraints of intermediary institutions. Such a scheme depends on the ability of the government to exclude some sectors of the society from the political process and to prevent the opposition from becoming effective. Regimes differ in how they go about fulfilling these requirements, who the principal actors are, who their closest allies and main adversaries are, and how much violence they have to utilize in order to maintain power.

At first glance the term *bureaucratic authoritarian* appears applicable to El Salvador. The Salvadoran military institution has controlled the political process since 1948. The regime had to rely on an increasing level of violence between 1972 and 1979. Military officers occupied more positions in the government.[2] The military closed ranks in an attempt to maintain control of an increasingly polarized political process. In addition, the Salvadoran regime, especially during the Romero administration, began to resemble the post-1968 government of Brazil, the regime of General Pinochet in Chile, and the Argentine military regime of the late 1970s more than it did the Salvadoran regime of the Rivera and Sánchez administrations.[3]

But let us not carry the analogy too far. The bureaucratic-authoritarian regimes of the Southern Cone came to power to replace socialist or populist governments that had become too threatening to some sectors of the society. Once in power these counterrevolutionary governments had to disarticulate many political organizations—primarily political parties, labor unions, and other voluntary associations—that were only beginning to emerge as actors to be reckoned with in El Salvador. With varying degrees of success, these governments tried to implement new economic models that would bring about more advanced forms of capitalism grounded on a more sophisticated industrial infrastructure. This was all but impossible in El Salvador, where the basic economic problems were how to dismantle the "magic square" of economic domination by the oligarchy and how to minimize the adverse effects of the commodity cycle.[4]

The term *national security* does not fare much better, because in El Salvador, as elsewhere, a characterization of the regime that makes use of only one aspect of the ideology of one of the dominant factions is not sufficiently comprehensive. Tomás Campos shows how the doctrine of national security gained currency with elements of the military during the 1970s.[5] According to Campos, the doctrine emphasized anti-Communism, state autonomy, and the need to subordinate the exercise of civil liberties.[6] More important, application of this doctrine, particularly during the Romero administration, unhinged the "normal" relations between state and society in El Salvador that had existed since 1948. It appears, however, that we must search for some other label to characterize the regime that emerged as a result of the application of the doctrine of national security. Otherwise, we might find ourselves examining a "crisis of the national security state," which would be an inappropriate focus since it was not the national security state but the model of 1948 that was in crisis.[7]

The Salvadorans have come up with some terms of their own to try to define the kind of regime produced by the turmoil of the 1970s. For example, Italo López Vallecillos talks about a *caciquismo conservador* (conservative bossism) to characterize the authoritarian, exclusionary, and autocratic regime implemented by Molina.[8] The term is adequate, but it describes only a style of leadership and not really a type of political regime. Moreover, Molina's attempt to play the reformist option one last time and the failure of this attempt made him a lame-duck president, enabling an even more conservative coalition of military and oligarchy actors to put Romero in power. Rafael Guidos Véjar refers to the last period of the Molina government as a "regency."[9] During this regency, according to Guidos Véjar, the political organizations of the oligarchy became more important than the PCN.[10] This view supports the argument that there was an important change in the composition of the government coalition from Molina to Romero.

Under the regimes of Colonel Arturo Molina, who began and ended his term under a state of siege, and his successor, Romero, an expert in counterinsurgency who served as Molina's minister of defense, the military increased the distance between itself and civil society in general in an attempt to reassert its control and to protect its own institutional integrity from leftist subversion and rightist attempts to control the government. This effort was in vain, however. The armed forces could not replace the moderate political parties as the center of Salvadoran politics, they could not move the system in a new direction without redefining the nature of the state, and during the Romero administration, the oligarchy managed, once again, to penetrate the government thoroughly. After twenty years in power, the best solution that the Salvadoran military could come up with was a more repressive version of the system that had prevailed since 1948.

Under the banners of "definition," "decision," and "firmness," Molina moved against the university, abrogated its autonomy, nominated a rightist rector, sent dissident faculty into exile, and sought to destroy the student organizations.[11] The electoral campaigns of 1974, 1976, and 1977 were unabashedly fraudulent, with *tamales*—stuffed ballot boxes—transported in military vehicles and intimidation dispensed through the Organización Democrática Nacionalista (ORDEN). Molina continued the "reformist" line of the PCN: he nationalized the International Railroad of Central America (IRCA) concessions and turned over IRCA operations to the Acajutla Port Authority, increased the minimum wage for agricultural workers, initiated a timid program of agrarian reform in 1975 by setting aside 150,000 acres of government-controlled land in San Miguel and Usulután, and created the Instituto Salvadoreño de Transformación Agraria (ISTA).

The creation of the ISTA brought about one of the most intense confrontations between the reformist faction of the military and enlightened elements of the industrial bourgeoisie, on the one hand, and the traditional oligarchy, operating through and assisted by the Asociación Nacional de la Empresa Privada (ANEP), the most important private sector organization, which included the *cafetaleros* (coffee growers), the Salvadoran Chamber of Commerce, the American Chamber of Commerce of El Salvador, and most of the agricultural associations, on the other. Therefore, this was not merely a conflict between civilians and the military but a contest between the two factions of the upper classes, each trying to take advantage of the fluid situation to move the military government in the direction of a model which was more attuned to their economic interests, as well as to their ideological preferences.

There were, to say the least, quite a few precedents for the political conflict that accompanied the raising of the land question in El Salvador. The most notorious in this century would, of course, be the *matanza* of 1932.[12] Another would be the long period of 1932–73, during which the government considered the topic subversive. The PAR was declared illegal in 1967 on the grounds that its platform included a plank inadmissible in the established constitutional order—agrarian reform.[13] A 1972 initiative by the PDC to discuss a project of agrarian reform did not even reach the floor of the legislature for debate. Other examples include the timid initiative of 1973–74, the creation of the ISTA in 1975, and the creation of the first district of agrarian transformation in 1976.[14]

The ISTA initiative received mixed reviews from leftist democrats in the opposition. Rubén Zamora, for example, called the initiative "an attempt to modernize the capitalist structure of Salvadoran agriculture [which could] create a relatively ample strata of small and medium proprietors."[15] By contrast, Luis de Sebastián saw the law as "a bourgeois reform . . . whose objectives included the suppression of *latifundia* and all the large estates . . . and the creation of a fairly egalitarian property structure . . . without confiscation [and in which] landowners must change their assets, that is, the source of their income."[16] Guillermo Ungo saw the ISTA project as one aspect of a process in which the military government sought to change the appearance of the existing system, modernizing it at the expense of the dominant faction, or agro-financial sector, of the oligarchy.[17] This was another initiative from above, without grass-roots participation, as well as another attempt to steal the thunder from the opposition without converting the reform into a political program. However, Ungo believed that the new legislation marked the beginning of a new stage and a new normative orientation that went beyond previous ones, which had benefited only the oligarchy.[18]

More radical critics were less impressed. Oscar Menjívar and Santiago Ruiz saw the Agrarian Transformation as part of the Plan of National Transformation that the armed forces had vowed to implement "energetically," so that the necessary changes would not disturb public order and "Communists" would not be able to take advantage of the situation. In short, to Menjívar and Ruiz, the transformation was a combination of structural change and military dictatorship to strengthen the capitalist model of development.[19]

Judging from the reaction of the "agrarian front," it would appear that this most reactionary sector of the oligarchy, the government, and its opposition critics were talking about entirely different things altogether. In spite of the fact that the model adopted in the transformation was Taiwan's—and not Cuba's—that most of the land involved was government property, that the United States Agency for International Development (AID) would provide the money for compensation, and that the "agrarian reformers" were wearing a uniform that had always defended their privileges, the traditional oligarchy and much of the Salvadoran private sector went on the warpath. The ANEP played a key role in the campaign orchestrated by the private sector to resist these measures.

The ANEP, the organ through which the oligarchy and the bourgeoisie reconciled their differences and articulated their interests, published a declaration against the new agrarian legislation—Law-Decree 31 of 29 June 1976 creating the First Project of Agrarian Transformation—on 9 July 1976. The ANEP's contradictory stance purported to welcome the transformation but decried "an orientation predicated on a negativistic state intervention in the economy."[20] Furthermore, the ANEP expressed dismay over the "surprise and haste" with which the government had passed the legislation: in twenty-four hours, ignoring public opinion, and trampling on the dignity of the Legislative Assembly.[21] Finally, the ANEP argued that the lands affected by the decree were being worked intensively and efficiently, at a high rate of productivity and labor utilization.[22]

On 10 July the government responded with a communiqué of its own, stressing the fact that the enabling legislation—Law-Decree 302 of 30 June 1975 creating the Salvadoran Institute of Agrarian Transformation (ISTA)—had been in place for a whole year. In addition, the government expressed its own surprise that the ANEP had overlooked "clear and concrete announcements made by the President," beginning with his inauguration.[23]

The ANEP's rejoinder of 13 July underlined the dire consequences that the measure would bring about—production and export shortfalls that would affect the standard of living of the population—and the impossibility of making everyone residing in the affected area a landowner, given its high population density. The bottom line, it said, was that the Salvadoran economy could not "withstand experiments in agrarian policy" and that the ANEP was against this project because it undermined the very bases of the economy.[24]

A 14 July rebuttal by the government attacked the second declaration of the ANEP by singling out its instigators as a small, intransigent group and citing the endorsement extended to the project by a group of experts from the Simeón Cañas University and the government's awareness "of the situation in which most Salvadorans live . . . as well as of its causes." Finally, the rebuttal rejected the ANEP's contention of haste and improvisation.[25] Surprisingly, the government's document alluded to the problems created by those who neglected their fiscal obligations and warned that, if "unable to reconcile the interests of the majority without means with the interests of a minority in possession of everything, [the government] reiterated its historical compromise with the former."[26]

The ANEP's final note to the government protested its "totalitarian stance" and "absolute intransigence," and reminded the government of its "obligation to listen.'' The ANEP stated that the organization would continue to air its views without fear.[27] On 16 July a very detailed and bitter response by the government included seven points: (1) only the government was responsible for the political direction of the country, (2) the ANEP's leadership was intransigent and selfish, hiding behind a facade of social concern, (3) the project strengthened private property, (4) the government would listen, "but the act of listening should not be confused with the action of obeying,'' (5) the ANEP's preoccupation with verbal violence should turn into a preoccupation with the explosive situation that its closed and unjust opposition could create, (6) many of the ANEP's leaders had occupied government positions and had failed to take any action, and (7) the government would not default on its 1 July 1972 commitment to serve the majority.[28]

It is difficult to think that President Arturo Molina acted alone on this matter, without at least consulting the more senior military officers. It appears that the military had been discussing the issue during Molina's term, as witnessed by a national seminar on agrarian reform prepared for officers of the armed forces and conducted in August 1973, as well as by the substance of Molina's declarations in a series of speeches delivered during his term of office.[29] Moreover, shortly after the announcement of the first ISTA project, the government organized what was, according to Rubén Zamora, one of its largest public gatherings of the last fifteen years, bringing to San Salvador between 70,000 and 100,000 peasants of ORDEN.[30] This took place on the occasion of the fourth anniversary of Molina's coming to power and on the eve of the angry exchange between the government and the ANEP in July. Finally, Molina launched a two-pronged campaign to explain the Agrarian Transformation to the armed forces staff, line officers in the various garrisons, and government bureaucrats during July and to stir up support through the media during August.[31]

Although the majority of the organizations appearing as signatories of the first proclamation of the ANEP were associated with the "agrarian front," a number of organizations from other sectors were also included in the manifestos.[32] Both the oligarchy and the bourgeoisie seemed united in their objections to the First Project. In its position as junior partner the latter may have gone along reluctantly, in the hope of serving as a mediating force between a government embarking on a project that could help the industrialists in the long run and the traditional oligarchy, which saw little if any gain from it. However, as Zamora argues, the Salvadoran bourgeoisie has been consistent in its opposition to any restriction or limitation on property.[33]

The timing of the execution of the transformation is not hard to understand. The government was one year away from another general election and, as usual, preoccupied with the electoral prospect. More to the point, there was a real likelihood that a repeat of the fraud of 1972 would be necessary, with the inevitable loss of prestige, public unrest, and general discredit of the military. From a longer perspective, and not unrelated to this, the government had to offer some tangible benefits to the PCN constituency, namely, the small and medium-size cultivators integrated in ORDEN, the agricultural laborers, who might still find the UCS attractive, and other sectors of the peasantry which were beginning to move away from the PCN. The political activation of these groups outside the government-controlled channels was a subject of concern for the agricultural entrepreneurs, but for the government such an activation posed a problem of public order and required "energetic response." Apparently, Molina opted for reform, trying to take advantage of available AID support for his initiative.

But like his predecessors, Molina lacked a true political party to support his policies in time of need, especially if opposed by the oligarchy. At the outset, he had institutional support from the military, the governmental bureaucracy, and the "official peasantry." He may have hoped to bring some of the uncommitted aboard, but the PDC was still smarting from the fraud of 1972, the fledgling popular organizations did not trust the government, and the institutions of the progressive element of the bourgeoisie were silent or nominally on the side of the ANEP.[34] To be sure, the ANEP continued to air its objections "without fear."

Beginning on 19 July the ANEP and its affiliates saturated the media with a barrage of propaganda. The tone and tenor of this campaign was one of hysterical anti-Communism; in addition, the exclusion of the peak private sector organization from a policy decision was made no less an issue than the substance of the transformation itself.[35] The ANEP was joined in its campaign by a chorus of phantom organizations—the Civic Committee, Western Agriculturalists, Committee for the Defense of Human Rights, Eastern Agriculturalists, Uncommitted Catholics Group, Cereal Growers of El Salvador, Committee for the Defense of the Social Function of Private Property—which came out of nowhere to attack the government. Most prominent among these was the Frente Agrario de la Región Oriental (FARO), which adopted a militant posture, instructing landowners on how to resist the implementation of the transformation through dilatory tactics. Gradually, the target of these attacks became the "planning group at CONAPLAN" (the National Planning Council), the Jesuits at the university, and unpatriotic Salvadorans.[36]

It is interesting that throughout this crisis none of the figures who were viewed as representatives of the private sector holding portfolios in the government resigned his position. This may have been an indication of a breakdown of consensus within the ANEP or of individual support for the transformation or it may simply have been a means of maintaining a presence for the private sector within official circles to channel demands and mediate the dispute. The more recalcitrant element of the "agrarian front," however, felt compelled to form its own organization, the FARO, and take more resolute action. Given the heterogeneity of the economic interests and political viewpoints expressed within the ANEP, the traditional oligarchy, feeling more threatened by the transformation than were the industrialists, may have embarked on a new course of action by itself.

The fact remains that by October 1976 the government had lost the initiative. The transformation was being shelved, and in spite of his unwavering commitment to the majority of Salvadorans, Molina was retreating. The retreat was greeted by those who had supported the transformation with ill-disguised contempt for those who were really "at the service of Salvadoran capital."[37]

The question whether this was a personal defeat for Molina, who had to govern as a regent during the rest of his term, unable even to extend official protection to those who had supported him, a defeat for the reformist faction of the armed forces, or a defeat for the military institution itself remains open to debate.[38] The safest hypothesis would make Molina the goat, but, after all, his presence in power was the result of a blatant electoral fraud, so his commitment to reformism was always in question. On the other hand, the reformist faction of the military, whatever its actual size and political influence at the time, had been in no position to dominate its own institution; nor had it seemed to have "captured" the Molina government. At best, that faction could have advocated or joined in the initiative, which was, after all, Molina's, who could be blamed for its failure.

If López Vallecillos is right, however, the loser in the crisis of 1976 was the military. López maintains—and he is not alone in this—that in 1931 the armed forces were given the task of managing the state institutions, a role that was expanded under the social pact of the Constitution of 1950 to include some participation in the development of the country.[39] The defeat of 1976 was one more in a series of episodes in which the military tried to include the popular sectors in redistributive schemes, making some advances in times of prosperity but beating a pell-mell retreat at the end of a twelve-year cycle.[40] In this line of reasoning, therefore, the military—and not Molina alone—exceeded its assigned role and had to be put in its place by the traditional oligarchy. The ANEP played a role in this campaign, but the traditional oligarchy assumed the leadership of the movement, creating the FARO and distancing itself somewhat from the more moderate and heterogenous ANEP.

The very useful comparison between the ANEP and the FARO offered by López Vallecillos is reproduced below, albeit with some minor alterations (see Figure 4-1). In practically every category of comparison the FARO comes out as more radical and specific. It was not only more homogeneous in constituency and leadership but also more specific in its goals and programs and more radical in its tactics. Concerning the latter, it is apparent that the FARO was

FIGURE 4-1
Peak Private Sector Organizations in Late 1976

	ANEP	FARO
Leadership	oligarchy and bourgeoisie (all factions)	traditional oligarchy
Constituency	entrepreneurs	landowners and cattlemen
Ideology	social market economy; private sector supremacy; politically heterogeneous but mainly right of center; divided on question of democratic capitalism	social market economy; complete control of agriculture by private sector; for authoritarian political control (order and peace); opposed to democratic capitalism
Program	articulation and promotion of private sector interests; check state interventionism; participate in public policymaking; prevent urban labor from becoming effective politically	defense of latifundia; defense of traditional export agriculture; opposition to any communal form of agriculture; prevent unionization of agricultural workers; maintain low salaries
Tactics	use of media to attack government irresponsibility and promote its own civic image, and rationality and efficiency of private enterprise	use of media (alarmist and defamatory campaigns, accusations of Communism against its adversaries); violence (not included in the López scheme)

Adapted from López Vallecillos, "Fuerzas Sociales," pp. 576–77.

more prepared to use violence than were many of the organizations and entrepreneurs represented in the ANEP. Although the evidence is sketchy, it appears that the FARO was one more attempt by traditional conservatives to regain the degree of political power that their cause had once enjoyed, and that had been deteriorating since 1948. For example, a comparison between the FARO and Chele Medrano's FUDI (see Figure 3-2 above) reveals an impressive number of similarities between the ideology, programs, tactics, and clientele of the two organizations. But the FUDI, like the PCN, was only an electoral mechanism, and in a moment of crisis, such as that of the ISTA, the oligarchy wanted a more reliable and decisive instrument of pressure and mobilization. Apparently, it got it in what Guidos Véjar—referring to the FARO— called "a sort of corporation and political party of large landowners which successfully led the campaign . . . against the Agrarian Transformation."[41]

But let us not exaggerate the "subordinate role" of the Salvadoran armed forces. The oligarchy maintained its class superiority by "inviting" a select few to join its ranks after they had retired from the military, and few in the military were welcomed with open arms into the more exclusive clubs of San Salvador. This does not mean, however, that the military was the errand boy for the oligarchy or that a majority of the officers saw themselves in that capacity. For example, as astute an observer as Zamora could not detect a single instance of criticism against the military institution among the proclamations of the ANEP against the transformation. By contrast, a reading of the government manifestos shows frequent references to armed forces support for the transformation and *direct attacks* against "a few selfish individuals."[42]

In short, the behavior of the private sector vis-à-vis the government seemed an attempt to undermine support for Molina and his initiative, but not to question the legitimacy of the military's presence in power. The complaint was based on a perceived transgression of the pact of 1948, in which the military institution gave itself the right to rule and pledged not to interfere with the basic mechanisms of capitalist accumulation. Therefore, as had happened before, the oligarchy, aroused by an attempt to modify the traditional division of jurisdictions, was able to put the military on the defensive by implying that the government was subversive.

There are several versions of the nature of the crisis in El Salvador. Most authors allude to a gradual divergence between the interests of the traditional oligarchy and of the modern sectors of the bourgeoisie. There seems to be agreement that the latter could not dominate the former but that, somehow, they managed to control the military government. It is one thing to prevent government interference, that is, to resist government initiatives, however, and quite another to force the government to do something. Apparently, the Salvadoran private sector had sufficient *influence* to do the former but not enough *power* to do the latter. This probably suited the bourgeoisie fine, since the process of change would ultimately give it the opportunity to become the dominant group. But in order to maintain itself, the traditional oligarchy had to force the government to take action to defuse the process of change that was undermining its economic and political influence.

It would be simplistic to aver that the Salvadoran oligarchy precipitated a civil war. One important lesson that contemporary Salvadoran politics teaches is that in such a complex process no single actor, no matter how powerful, can dictate outcomes. It is apparent, however, that the traditional oligarchy of El Salvador tried to move the government in the direction of a system which included aspects of the traditional authoritarian model, with some elements borrowed from the national security or bureaucratic authoritarian regimes of the Southern cone. The experience of the ISTA crisis may have signaled to the traditional oligarchy that if it was going to save itself, it had to take much more drastic action. Therefore, it tried to break a "catastrophic balance," not between itself and the industrialists, which it could still dominate, but between itself and the armed forces in an attempt to restore itself to power. Using their extensive contacts and summoning all the influence they could muster, the members of the traditional oligarchy tried to make the conservative faction of the military the dominant group within the institution, to initiate a process of exclusion and extermination of their class enemies, and to utilize reactionary despotism to bring about their resolution of the crisis that El Salvador had suffered since 1931. These attempts contributed to the country's drift toward civil war.

The fact that the traditional oligarchy failed in its short-lived attempt to "restore" reactionary despotism does not invalidate this interpretation of the nature of the organic crisis of hegemony in El Salvador. Instead, the oligarchy's failure to consolidate this restoration is one more indication of the complexity of the crisis and of the difficulty that any one coalition of actors faces in trying to produce a stable and viable system of domination based on an exclusionist authoritarian model.

Finally, it is clear that the ISTA crisis contributed to the polarization that was eroding the prospects for a reformist solution. The failure of the Agrarian Transformation of 1975–76 only aggravated the lawlessness of the Salvadoran state. The new administration of General Carlos Humberto Romero took office already stripped of any reformist pretenses and ready to do battle with the opposition.

From Molina to Romero

Molina sowed so much discontent that during his term the popular organizations grew dramatically and the climate for guerrilla operations improved
markedly. New patterns of violence emerged, elements within the Catholic
church increased their demands for change, and the regime became the target
of constant criticism from human rights organizations.

Romero simply made matters worse. He dropped all pretensions of reformism and made an open alliance with the extreme Right in order to face the
common enemy, which grew stronger and bolder. Under Romero, a hardline
anti-Communist, the government and the right-wing paramilitary organizations drew closer together. The "official" paramilitary organization, ORDEN,
was used constantly to counteract the efforts of the popular organizations, and
especially of the peasant organizations. ORDEN had been created by Colonel
Rivera in 1966 for precisely those ends, but never before had its use been so
peremptory. The coordinator of ORDEN responded to the executive directly
and was not, in a strict sense, in the chain of command of the military. The
cadre and the rank of the organization, however, came from army reservists
and retired security officers. The organization grew to become a militia force
of between fifty thousand and one hundred thousand armed peasants used to
maintain "order" in the countryside.

In the mid-1970s the activism of priests and religious in organizing peasants
created a dilemma for the Romero government. To counter this, new "unofficial" groups of right-wing terrorists appeared. In 1975 the Fuerzas Armadas de Liberación Anticomunista de Guerras de Eliminación (FALANGE)
emerged, promising to exterminate all "Communists" and their allies and
denouncing bishops, priests, deputies, and even military officers. The hierarchy, clergy, and lay people of the Salvadoran Catholic church played a very
important role in undermining the Romero government.[43] Inspired by revi-
sions of Catholic social doctrine—primarily the Declaration of Medellín of
the Latin American Conference of Bishops (CELAM) and the assumptions of
"liberation theology"—Salvadoran Catholics became formidable adversaries
of the regime through their campaigns of "consciencitization" and political
organization. It was only a matter of time before the military decided to take
action.

In March 1977, Fr. Rutilio Grande, S.J., an organizer of peasants in Aguilares, was killed.[44] In May, Mauricio Borgonovo, who had served as Molina's
foreign minister and was a figure in the oligarchy and a business partner of
former president Arturo Molina and of Anastasio Somoza, was assassinated.
He had been kidnapped by the guerrillas. In revenge the Unión Guerrera
Blanca (UGB) took the life of Fr. Alfonso Navarro, a diocesan priest. The

UGB had emerged in April, during the crisis over the Borgonovo kidnapping; in June it issued a death threat against all Jesuits residing in El Salvador.

The escalating conflict between the church and the government had very profound consequences. First, the deepening rift was one of the proximate causes in the deterioration of the Romero government. The newly inaugurated archbishop of San Salvador, Oscar Arnulfo Romero, repeatedly denounced government repression and terrorism and refused to adopt a more conciliatory attitude unless the government stopped its persecution of the church and its repression against the Salvadoran people. When one conservative bishop decried the "radical" attitude of the Salvadoran church, he was quickly rebuked by the Vatican for ignoring "the genuine, brave and heroic ministry that many priests and catechists were developing in the country." In sum, church criticism eroded the little legitimacy that the government of Romero had left.

A second important consequence of the repression against Catholic activists was the public outcry abroad. The UGB's death threat against the Jesuits led the Carter administration to express grave concern and forced Romero to extend government protection to them and to allow a number of inquiries into the human rights record of his administration to be conducted by such international groups as the Inter-American Committee on Human Rights, the International Commission of Jurists, and a British parliamentary delegation. The reports produced by these inquiries were uniformly critical of Romero, whose government came to be regarded as "one of the world's worst violators of human rights."[45]

In March 1977 relations between El Salvador and the United States reached a low point when the government of Molina rejected U.S. attempts to link military assistance to observance of human rights, refusing the aid altogether. This made El Salvador's the fifth Latin American government to follow that course of action, joining a group that included the most repressive regimes of the Southern Cone. The findings of the human rights inquiries suggested that the Salvadoran government had more in common with those governments than a mere refusal to subordinate arms deliveries to self-restraint. In sum, the inquiries found that the rule of law no longer governed the "normal" treatment of opposition by the Salvadoran government.

Foreign pressures did not deter Romero from enacting a tough public order statute in November 1977, which received scathing criticism in the report prepared by Donald Fox, a New York attorney, for the International Commission of Jurists.[46] Findings like these forced the Carter administration to take its pledge to human rights seriously in the Salvadoran case, contributing to the increasing international isolation of the Romero government and sapping it of what little legitimacy it still enjoyed, having come to power as a result of another electoral fraud and having quickly accumulated such a dismal record of systematic violations of human rights.

According to Guidos Véjar, the Law for the Defense and Guarantee of Public Order, passed on 24 November 1977 by the Romero administration, responded to a series of demands by the private sector to deal more firmly with the opposition.[47] The ANEP and the FARO appealed to the military, not the government, to deal with the growing pressure of the mobilization of the popular sectors, which included labor demands as well as a demand for the cessation of the increasing repression directed against them.

The law was relatively ineffectual in dealing with labor unrest, however, since between November 1977 and February 1979, the period during which the statute was in effect, there were more than forty illegal labor strikes in El Salvador.[48] In addition, popular organizations, primarily the Bloque Popular Revolucionario (BPR) and the Frente de Acción Popular Unificada (FAPU), tried to create a "labor front" which would press labor demands through a combination of legal and illegal methods.[49] By July 1979, although the three dominant federations remained intact—the Confederación Unitaria de Trabajadores Salvadoreños (CUTS), formerly under the control of the Communist Party; the Confederación General de Sindicatos (CGS), with the closest ties to the regime; and the Federation of Unions of Construction and Transportation (FESINCONSTRANS), which had been the most successful in gaining concessions since 1968 and maintained some linkages with other government unions, such as the UCS—their links with the political parties seemed to be eroding, and as a result, the government's ability to control labor unrest was diminishing.[50]

The Public Order Law was practically a license to kill. Of course government violence against the opposition in El Salvador was not invented by the Romero administration, but there was a stunning increase in acts of violence against an opposition which the Public Order Law had put in the category of subversive. Under Romero, government violence reached epidemic proportions. Considering only government-initiated violence, political assassinations increased tenfold, prosecutions of "subversives" increased threefold, and the number of disappeared doubled (see Table 4-1). In addition, four Catholic priests were killed by security forces or their proxies.

The guerrillas, for their part, also increased their use of violence. The number of their actions doubled, their killings of security and paramilitary personnel increased twofold and threefold, respectively, and the number of political kidnappings doubled. The Fuerzas Populares de Liberación Farabundo Martí (FPL-FM) engaged in a series of political assassinations through 1978, including Borgonovo's (10 May), former Consejo Central de Elecciones (CCE) secretary René Guzmán (1 July), former police chief in charge of the *matanza* and provisional president Osmín Aguirre (12 July), the rightist rector of the University of El Salvador Carlos Alfaro Castillo (16 September), and former president of the legislature Rubén Alonso Rodríguez. The Fuerzas Armadas de Resistencia Nacional (FARN) kidnapped two foreign business-men in 1978, Fujio Matsumoto and Kjell Bjoerk; Matsumoto was killed when the government refused to negotiate, while Bjoerk was freed in August after his company paid for the publication of a guerrilla manifesto in Central American and foreign newspapers. The Ejército Revolucionario del Pueblo (ERP) engaged in a series of bombings of government offices, industrial plants, the Nicaraguan embassy, and other installations of some symbolic value to the guerrillas. It is important to emphasize that the Salvadoran guer-rillas were practically nonexistent until the mid-1970s, when a climate more conducive to their activities was created by the repressive policies of the government.

This political mobilization was not a result of a Communist conspiracy; nor was it a direct result of the difficult social circumstances of the popular classes. It is true that 90 percent of a work force of 1.75 million Salvadorans were paid, when employed, salaries below minimum wage and that they faced very harsh economic conditions. But persons do not become politically activated or change their styles of political participation unless they realize the futility of *individual* action. To these Salvadorans, their only strength was in their numbers. Therefore, the reason for the success of the Federación Cris-tiana de Campesinos Salvadoreños (FECCAS) and the Unión de Trabajado-res Campestres (UTC) among some sectors of the peasantry and the ability of the popular organizations to mobilize thousands of persons must be sought in the new organizational strategies through which they proposed to redress grievances.

Unlike the professionals and members of the middle class who tried to expand the franchise, create effective suffrage, and begin a process of demo-cratic transition in the 1960s and early 1970s, the members of the popular organizations could not go back to their professions and simply wait for a better opportunity. They bore the brunt of the most profound contradictions of Salvadoran society, and they found themselves on the receiving end of repres-sive political measures designed to maintain an order which excluded them from the market and, by implication, excluded them from citizenship. It was only natural that they would react in similar fashion and begin to use political means to change their economic plight.

It is important to point out the differences between the guerrillas and the mass organizations. "Mass organizations" are the broad fronts of popular organizations that emerged in El Salvador in the mid and late 1970s: the Bloque or BPR, FAPU, the Ligas Populares 28 de Febrero (LP-28), and the smaller and much more recently created Movimiento de Liberación Popular (MLP; 1979). These organizations were subversive under the formula of

FIGURE 4-2
Guerrilla Groups in El Salvador

	FPL-FM	FARN	ERP
Origins	splinter of PCS (1970)	division of ERP (1975) after assassination of Roque Dalton	proponents of the *foco* theory (1971)
Leadership	workers, peasants, teachers, students	workers, students, peasants	workers, students, peasants
Tactics	*ajusticiamientos* of figures linked to the oligarchy, the regime, and ORDEN	kidnappings of prominent politicians and businessmen; actions against ORDEN	military actions against government installations; *ajusticiamientos*
Strategy	*guerra popular prolongada*	popular insurrection	guerrilla warfare
Ideology	Marxist-Leninist	Marxist-Leninist	Marxist-Leninist
Alliances	PCS (although denying hegemonic role), BPR	Resistencia Nacional, FAPU	Partido de la Revolución Salvadoreña, LP-28
Program	revolutionary government; socialist society	socialist society	popular-democratic government of peasants, workers, and other oppressed groups
Comparative features	largest; most orthodox; best organized	most visible; most successful in collecting ransoms	most militaristic and radical; best trained and most efficient as a fighting force

Source: López Vallecillos, "Fuerzas Sociales," pp. 574–75; our own evaluation from sources identified in the text and personal interviews with Salvadoran exiles.

domination prevailing in El Salvador, which would not grant them legal recognition. Unfortunately, attempts by the Romero government, by the private
sector, and by the local media to identify them as "terrorist" were successful,
since the international media adopted this label uncritically. But their ideological affinity and organizational links to the guerrillas should not overshadow
the differences between the two types of organizations. These could be illustrated by comparing the information presented in Figures 4-2 and 4-3.

It appears that only the LP-28 could be considered a satellite of a guerrilla
organization, the ERP, which seems to have created the former to have its
own political vehicle. As the most radical and militaristic guerrilla organization, the ERP may have felt the need to create the Ligas in order to combat
leftist criticism of its militarism and to serve its attempts to control the opposition. Since the FAPU was created before the FARN, and since it includes what
is perhaps the most powerful labor federation in El Salvador—the Federación
Nacional Sindical de Trabajadores Salvadoreños (FENASTRAS)—as well as a
wide variety of other popular and labor organizations, it is unlikely that the
guerrilla organization can dominate the FAPU completely. Finally, the connection between the BPR and the PCS is real, but there are a number of
organizations included in the Bloque, such as the FECCAS and the UTC,
which are not Marxist in orientation and which respond to radical Christian
Democratic leadership.

According to Charles Anderson, the "price of admission" into the Central
American political arena has two installments: first, a demonstration of a
"power capability" and, second, a willingness to abide by the existing rules.[51]
In the 1970s these conditions no longer held in El Salvador, since when the
popular organizations "showed off" their power capabilities—mainly the
strength of their numbers—through acts of civil disobedience, which were the
only ones available at that time, the government unleashed ORDEN, the UGB,
and the FALANGE on them. In short, the popular organizations emerged as a
result of the obsolescence and unfairness of the rules of the Salvadoran formula of domination.

The specter of how they would behave if they were legalized remained, but
conservative fears about the possibility of a government primarily oriented to
them were not only ideological but also practical. Could such a government
govern effectively? Middle-class apprehensions centered on considerations
about the kind of violence that the oligarchy would utilize to prevent the
creation of such a government.[52] During 1977–79 civil disobedience, demonstrations, and takeovers of churches, government buildings, and foreign embassies were the primary violent tactics utilized by the popular organizations,
but these were met by a much more violent response from the Romero government.[53] The result was a "praetorian" climate, that is, a situation in which a
regime with a low level of institutionalization must deal with increased politi-

FIGURE 4-3

Mass Organizations in El Salvador

	BPR	FAPU	LP-28
Origins	7/30/75, following student massacre	September 1974	early 1978, political arm of ERP
Class composition: leadership	petite bourgeoisie, radical workers	petite bourgeoisie, radical workers	petite bourgeoisie, radical workers
cadre	students, workers, peasants, teachers	workers, students	workers, peasants, students
militants	rural and urban proletariat	urban workers	urban and rural proletariat
Strength (10/79)	60,000–80,000	8,000–15,000	about 5,000
Affiliates (10/79)	FTC (FECCAS and UTC), Universitarios Revolucionarios 19 Julio, Unión de Pobladores de Tugurios (UPT), Comité Coordinador de Sindicatos José Guillermo Rivas (CCS), Movimiento Estudiantil Revolucionario de Secundaria,	FENASTRAS, Movimiento Revolucionario Campesino, Vanguardia Proletaria, Unión Nacional de Jornaleros (UNJ), Asociación Revolucionaria de Estudiantes de Secundaria, Organización Magisterial Revolucionaria, Frente Uni-	Ligas Populares Obreras de Estudiantes de Secundaria, Ligas Populares Universitarias, Ligas Populares Campesinas

	FUR-30, Asociación de Educadores Universitarios	...dor Allende	...Marxist, with Leninist tendencies
Ideology	Marxist-Leninist with radical tendencies	Marxist	Marxist, with Leninist tendencies
Tactics	mobilization, propaganda, strikes, occupations, demonstrations	urban mobilizations, strikes, occupations, protest marches	street actions, support of labor strikes, occupations
Program	establish a socialist revolutionary government with proletarian hegemony without PCS influence	establish a revolutionary government with democratic-popular predominance	establish a revolutionary-socialist government, with many diverse sectors from the oppressed classes
Alliances	tends to shun them although more willing during 1980	with political parties of similar ideological orientation	with urban popular organizations

Source: Campos, "Seguridad Nacional," pp. 924–25; López Vallecillos, "Fuerzas Sociales," pp. 572–73, and "Rasgos Sociales," pp. 870–71, 873; Viron Vaky, Testimony before U.S. Congress, House, Committee on Foreign Affairs, Subcommittee on Inter-American Affairs, *Foreign Assistance Regulation for Fiscal Years 1980–1981*, part 5, 96th Cong., 1st sess., 1979.

cal mobilization. Two outcomes were possible: more repression to crush the opposition or a change of government.

The threat initially posed by the popular organizations fell considerably short of a Marxist takeover—the "another Nicaragua," which began to cause so much consternation in late 1979. The basic problem of the people that these organizations served was a living wage, and their best weapon was to organize. Once they were organized, the exclusionist formula had to be changed or they had to be crushed, à la 1932. The reasons were simple. The Salvadoran oligarchy did not want to readjust its living standards or to share economic power. The Salvadoran military saw any attempt to organize outside the control of the government as inherently dangerous and popular class organizations as simply subversive. Under the model with which it was working, the military could not allow the popular classes to become a political actor. The system that had prevailed from 1948 to 1972 precluded the popular classes' enjoying full-fledged citizenship, and the changes, the *endurecimiento*, in that system following the debacle of 1972 had been made to make sure that this remained the case. In essence, political exclusionism and exceptional, that is, coercive, capitalism were the two basic ingredients of the Salvadoran model of the late 1970s, which is best described as reactionary despotism. This model was intended to prevent democratic reformism, not to fight Communism. The electoral fraud of 1977 and the Public Order Law of November of that year made this more explicit.[54]

But Molina's defeat of 1976 in the ISTA affair and Romero's closer collaboration with the traditional oligarchy should not obscure another, and perhaps more subtle, change that took place during the late 1970s. This must be sought in the greater distance that the Salvadoran military tried to interpose between itself and civil society in general. The close collaboration between the extreme Right, acting through its paramilitary organizations and the FARO, and the more reactionary elements of the military and the PCN is a matter of record and needs little further elaboration.

This alliance did not extend to all issues in the public agenda, however. For example, a rift developed between the Asociación Salvadoreña de Beneficiadores y Exportadores de Café (ABECAFE), a bastion of the oligarchy, and the Compañía Salvadoreña de Café (COSCAFE), a state enterprise, over the matter of export sales. In 1978 the COSCAFE found it necessary to restrict exports in an attempt to counteract a fall in coffee prices. This provoked the wrath of the ABECAFE, which was controlled by the thirty-six family groups who monopolized exports. Despite this formidable opposition, the COSCAFE maintained the ban until August 1979, when prices were more favorable and export sales were resumed.

Given the bloody conflict going on at the time—and what was yet to come—historians and students of El Salvador may overlook this contradiction between the interests of the state and those of the oligarchy. It is clear, however, that the reactionary coalition between the traditional oligarchy and the conservative military broke down in matters as significant as trade policy.[55] This does not deny in any way the existence of a defensive alliance to maintain order and prevent the mobilization of the peasantry and the popular classes. But it emphasizes the ideological nature of that reactionary alliance, which, given the changes in Salvadoran society, was very unstable and could not be maintained for very long, regardless of the amount of violence used to consolidate it.

This is an exceedingly important point if one is to understand the nature of the relations between the military institution and the oligarchy following the coup of 15 October 1979. This apparent reappraisal by the military of the interests of the Salvadoran state—as different from those of the traditional oligarchy—was not carried to its full implications after the coup, but it provided a rationale for a different relationship between the military, as an institution serving the interests of the state, and the oligarchy, which had monopolized the interpretation of those interests up to that moment.

It goes without saying that Romero's strong-arm methods did not neutralize the praetorian situation; nor did he provide the basis for a comprehensive settlement of the large questions facing Salvadoran society. Romero had to repeal the Public Order Law in February 1979 under intense pressure from the Carter administration, the Catholic church, international organizations, and even some elements of the Salvadoran private sector and military. In May the government organized a National Forum in a desperate attempt to ease tensions and tried to point to the next scheduled elections as a possible solution to the crisis. But the nation was still mindful of the most recent electoral fraud, which had robbed the candidates of the opposition coalition—Ernesto Claramount, a retired army colonel, and Dr. José Antonio Morales Ehrlich, his Christian Democratic running mate—of a certain electoral victory in 1977. Perhaps more important, the fall of Anastasio Somoza in Nicaragua and the emergence of a popular government with socialist inclinations in that country prompted the Carter administration to seek an alternative to Romero in order to prevent a repetition of that kind of outcome in El Salvador.

The bloodless coup of October 1979 was an attempt to inaugurate a government based on a new political model in El Salvador. However, this attempt excluded the popular organizations, and this, viewed in the context of the last thirty years of Salvadoran politics, constituted a major strategic mistake, since it compromised the chances that the process of transition initiated then could result in a genuinely democratic outcome. The new coalition could not be consolidated, nor could the Salvadoran political system regain its equilibrium, unless the economic power and the political influence of the oligarchy were neutralized and the role of the military institution redefined. This required the fulfillment of two broad objectives: a restoration of the rule of law and a redefinition of Salvadoran political economy. Given historical precedent, these two objectives would meet the obstinate opposition and obstructionism of the oligarchy and the conservative elements in the armed forces. In light of the experiences of previous juntas and transitional governments in El Salvador, any government that committed itself to those two goals had to be built on as wide a base of popular support as possible. It had to be established on a new alliance that would bring together the petite bourgeoisie and organized labor, already represented by the PDC and the MNR, and the popular classes and the peasantry, whose only outlet at the time was the popular organizations but who were, in reality, the natural constituency of the MNR or other Social Democratic parties. In short, a formidable force—represented by this kind of coalition—was required to displace the immovable obstacle of oligarchic power and military control.

The execution of this blueprint implied undeniable risks and not a small amount of intense conflict. The basic dilemma confronting the conspirators of October and those whom they invited to participate in their government was whether to run that risk—and to be prepared to pay the costs that it entailed—or to take short cuts and play a safer game in which a pluralist solution would somehow seek to accommodate the oligarchy and the army, leaving the popular organizations out of the picture. It is a basic premise underlying the analysis to follow that neither the restoration of the rule of law nor a program of socioeconomic reform could take place in a pluralist context if this implied the maintenance of an effective veto for the oligarchy and the military. Nor could a democratic outcome be forthcoming without the implementation of a program in which all actors willing to abide by the law would be invited to participate, irrespective of ideology or social status.

Part Two

American Fantasies

Before 15 October 1979 the United States was a powerful actor in Salvadoran politics. It would be no exaggeration to say that the American ambassador to El Salvador enjoyed a level of prestige and influence approaching, if not surpassing, that of the Salvadoran president. Yet the public record suggests that United States attempts to use its power to dictate or even shape decisively the course of domestic Salvadoran politics were few and far between. In addition, these were not always successful.

The United States used its influence to obtain outcomes compatible with what it interpreted as its national interests in the overthrow of Martínez in 1944; in the consolidation of military rule in 1948; in the reequilibration of the military's "controlled democracy" in 1961 after a brief challenge by the short-lived junta that came to power following the overthrow of Lemus; in restraining the excesses of the Romero administration in the late 1970s; and finally in the overthrow of Romero in 1979. On the other hand, the United States did not play a discernible role in the *matanza* of 1932 or in the electoral frauds of 1972 and 1977, except by default. Finally, the United States was not able to make much headway through the Alliance for Progress in El Salvador; nor was it able to sell socioeconomic reforms to the oligarchy, especially during the Agrarian Transformation fiasco of 1975–76.

Thus it appears that the bottlenecks of domestic Salvadoran politics were seldom a matter of much concern in official circles in Washington and that, for better or for worse, the Salvadorans were able to manage by themselves. All of this changed following the October 1979 coup.

One of the American fantasies about El Salvador is not peculiar to that country. This fantasy is very much the result of an assumption that is shared equally by liberals and conservatives, although applied to the pursuit of diametrically opposed goals in some instances: that is, the assumption that, given its status as a superpower and the resources at its command, the United States can dictate the outcome of a crisis like that in El Salvador. Part 2 of this book is, in a way, a somewhat polemical exercise which tries to dispel this. The

reader should not seek for any adversaries other than this assumption when-
ever there is some shadow boxing in the analysis.

More specifically, the three chapters to follow explore the degree to which
the United States could influence the Salvadoran crisis according to its own
agenda: a controlled process of political transition that was somehow supposed to result in a democratic outcome. Albeit through a different blend of
initiatives and actions, the Carter and Reagan administrations were pursuing
two contradictory goals: the inauguration of a democratic regime and the
denial to the Left of any important role in the process. This agenda gave
priority to the legitimation of a provisional revolutionary government through
a series of reforms that would widen the base of popular support of that
government. This plan, however, relegated the restoration of the rule of law
to a second priority, which would take place at some unspecified point in the
future. As events would show, the repressive apparatus remained largely intact, and the only moves toward a more lawful state were the removal of certain officers who had ties to the paramilitary Right.

Contemporary social science must share the blame for this perversion of
priorities, for it has offered a series of paradigms in which the insights of
ordinary people amount to nothing and objective indicators are the measure of
progress. But the true and only possible centrist coalition that could have
emerged in El Salvador fell apart not because socioeconomic reforms were
not coming fast enough but because a sector of Salvadoran society remained
at the mercy of arbitrary violence, which the government could not control.
The resolution of this problem is crucial to any solution that promises to lead
El Salvador out of civil war and into a peaceful transition to democracy. In
essence, the provisional government became a continuation of the repressive
reformism of the military that had created the crisis in the first place.

Another American fantasy, and one made more precarious after the departure of the moderate leftists from the provisional government in December
1979, was the attempt to bring together the Christian Democrats and the organizations of the Salvadoran private sector. A long and painfully detailed
section is dedicated to the exposure of the futility of this attempt in chapter 7.
Although less violent and subversive than the disloyal Right—described and
discussed in chapter 6—the conservative element of the Salvadoran bourgeoisie turned out to be equally obstructionist, and its actions were really aimed at
the restoration of a military or extremely conservative regime.

Some aspects of the civil war are reviewed to challenge another fantasy: the
idea that it is possible to conduct a "clean" campaign of counterinsurgency
that, somehow, will pacify the countryside. This is the aspect of the crisis
more reminiscent of Vietnam and the one that has stirred passions on both
sides of the controversy about El Salvador in the United States. It would take
much less than another Vietnam for the United States to really complicate

things in El Salvador, however, for much of the problem has resulted from an inability—remember the original assumption about American omnipotence—to put the Right and its paramilitary allies in their place.

The "guys with the guns" on the other side are discussed in a short section in the last chapter. This study disputes the contention that they could not survive without Cuban and Nicaraguan assistance and gives full credit to the efficacy of counterinsurgency in turning peasants into guerrillas. But I treat the guerrillas as one more actor and make no attempt either to fulminate against them or to elevate them to heroic status. The real heroes of the Salvadoran crisis are those who have tried to resolve it by peaceful means and have, in many cases, paid with their lives for their attempts.

To keep things in perspective I invite the reader to compare the sources and references that support the analysis in this section with those of the previous one. Part 1 relied on the Salvadorans to talk about themselves. Part 2 depends very much on American opinions about El Salvador, which is appropriate in a section that purports to investigate American fantasies about El Salvador. Each has its own validity, but, ultimately, the best we can do for Salvadorans is not to impose our own dilemmas on them. This is not an isolationist but a truly libertarian aspiration, and my own fantasy, namely, that the Salvadorans can give themselves something better than what we believe they are capable of.

Main Events of the Salvadoran Transition (15 October 1979–28 March 1982)

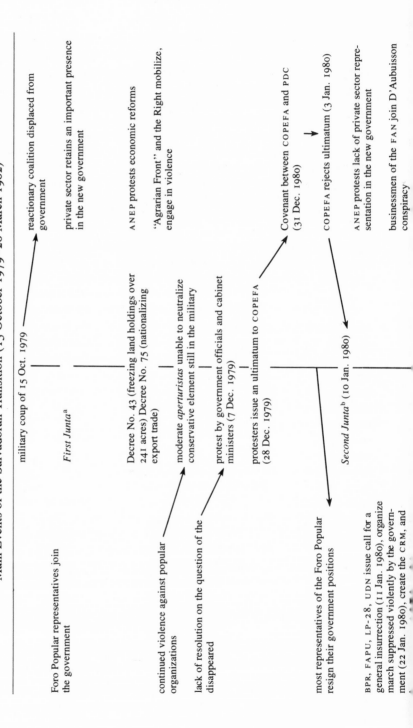

(25 Feb. 1980)

PDC Junta member Héctor Dada resigns (3 Mar. 1980)

Third Junta[c]

7 Mar. 1980: Decree No. 128 (exchange controls) Decrees No. 153 and 154 (agrarian reform) Decrees No. 158 and 159 (nationalization of banks) Decree No. 155 (state of siege)

rightist elements try to resist Agrarian Reform through violence

Archbishop Romero assassinated (23 Mar. 1980)

D'Aubuisson conspiracy gaining momentum

resignation of some PDC cabinet ministers (27 Mar. 1980)

FDR created (1 Apr. 1980)

Decree No. 207: Land to the Tiller (28 Apr. 1980)

May 1980 crisis: D'Aubuisson incarcerated briefly, Col. Majano demoted

Col. Majano tries to maintain contact with the Left

FDR fails in its attempt to organize a general strike (early Aug. 1980)

most supporters of Col. Majano removed (1 Sept. 1980)

FAN, AP try to link themselves to Reagan presidential campaign in the United States

Col. Majano removed

disloyal Right encouraged by Reagan victory unleashes violent campaign

PDC note to the junta protesting violence (25 Nov. 1980)

Six FDR leaders assassinated (27 Nov. 1980)

Three American nuns and one religious worker assassinated (3 Dec. 1980)

United States suspends military aid (5 Dec. 1980)

PDC ultimatum to military (6 Dec. 1980)

U.S. presidential inquiry commission meets with junta (8 Dec. 1980)

new D'Aubuisson conspiracy neutralized (mid-Dec. 1980)

Carter administration restores military aid (14 Jan. 1980)

White Paper released (23 Feb. 1980)

D'Aubuisson attempt to destabilize the government (Mar. 1980)

Sustained campaign by the private sector to reverse economic reforms and gain control of the government (Summer 1981)

United States efforts to reconcile PDC and private sector (Summer 1981)

D'Aubuisson announces formation of ARENA (29 Sept. 1981)

Rightist parties demand removal of PDC from the CCE. Finally succeed by voting them out 4–2 (5 Nov. 1981)

Col. Majano ousted from the government (10 Dec. 1980)

Fourth Junta[d] (13 Dec. 1980)

removal of hard-line officers associated with D'Aubuisson (31 Dec. 1980)

ISTA President Viera and 2 AIFLD officials assassinated (10 Jan. 1981)

Pres. Duarte accuses private sector of being principal enemy of his government (1 July 1981)

Duarte visits the United States (19–29 Sept. 1981)

Ban on political parties lifted (31 Oct. 1981)

Col. García visits the United States (4–11 Nov. 1981)

CCE sets date of election, will clarify details of electoral statute (11 Nov. 1981)

FMLN replaces DRU as joint guerrilla command (late Dec. 1980)

guerrillas launch unsuccessful final offensive (11 Jan. 1980)

Ambassador White removed (1 Feb. 1980)

Mexico and France recognize FDR (28 Aug. 1981)

FDR leaders urge talks (Fall 1981)

U.S. Senate votes to condition military and economic aid to performance of the Salvadoran government (24 Sept. 1981)

guerrilla offensive: sabotage economic infrastructure, increase territory under their control, and create joint field command in Usulután (Fall 1981)

Guerrilla commanders declare willingness to negotiate in secret interview (late Nov.

Two FDR representatives received at the Dept. of State (15 Dec. 1981)

United Nations vote in favor of a political settlement in El Salvador (16 Dec. 1981)

Large guerrilla force in control of most of Usulután province (Jan. 1982)

Guerrillas stage successful raid against Ilopango air base (27 Jan. 1982)

Guerrillas attack and hold briefly the cities of San Miguel, Santa Ana, and San Vicente (10 Mar. 1982)

Guerrillas launch attacks to disrupt election in areas under their control (27 Mar. 1982)

CCE reshuffled: PDC, ARENA, PCN, and AD representatives out (9 Jan. 1982)

Electoral statute published amidst rightist protests (Jan. 1982)

PDC offer to delay election, given the upsurge in guerrilla attacks, rejected by rightist parties (9 Mar. 1982)

Pres. Duarte suggests elections as a way to control army (16 Mar. 1982)

Constituent Assembly elections (28 Mar. 1982)

Salvadoran election (8 Dec. 1981)

Salvadoran troops sent to the United States to receive training (Jan. 1982)

Reagan administration certifies El Salvador for continued aid (28 Jan. 1982).

Secretary Haig meets with Mexican Foreign Minister Castañeda to discuss Salvadoran crisis (early Mar. 1982)

Ambassador Hinton suggests that a rightist electoral victory might imperil U.S. aid (16 Mar. 1982)

Four Dutch newsmen slain by army in ambush (17 Mar. 1982)

---

a. Composed of Guillermo Ungo, Román Mayorga, Col. Jaime Abdul Gutiérrez, Col. Adolfo Majano, and Mario Antonio Andino.

b. Composed of Héctor Dada Hirezi and José A. Morales Ehrlich for the PDC, Col. Gutiérrez, Col. Majano, and José R. Avalos Navarrete.

c. Dada was replaced by José Napoleón Duarte.

d. Col. Majano was not replaced. Duarte was named president of the junta and given decree powers, Col. Gutiérrez was named vice-president of the junta. Morales Ehrlich and Avalos remained in the junta.

Chapter 5

The Breakdown of Reactionary Despotism in El Salvador

Transition toward What?

In January 1979, General Carlos Humberto Romero took a trip to Mexico City. Romero's situation was desperate, and he was attempting to polish up his tarnished international image, break the increasing isolation of his government, and seek guaranteed delivery of twenty thousand barrels per day of Mexican crude. Seldom has a political trip undertaken by a Latin American head of state turned out as disastrously as did Romero's. The reception of his hosts was cool, and he could get only a tentative agreement on oil delivery. Worst of all, the details of a report on the situation in El Salvador by the Inter-American Commission on Human Rights were leaked to the press in Mexico City during his stay. He was bombarded at a press conference with questions about the report. Romero averred that ORDEN was a "civic association" created to defend El Salvador's democratic institutions, and he maintained that his government held no political prisoners. Nobody believed him. To add to his distress, the FAPU occupied the Mexican embassy in San Salvador during Romero's trip, attracting additional international attention to the domestic situation.

President Romero's visit coincided with a visit to Mexico by Salvadoran Archbishop Oscar Arnulfo Romero, a leading critic of the military government, who was attending a meeting of the Latin American Conference of Bishops (CELAM) in Puebla. The archbishop had just been nominated for the Nobel Peace Prize, and the contrast between the two men was not lost on observers. The trip may have convinced General Romero that he would have to make some changes if he wanted to remain in power. In February he relented to pressure and repealed the Public Order Law, announced a series of reforms that were completely out of line with his previous record and personal inclinations, and replaced the head of the national guard, Colonel Ramón Alvarenga. This apparent "rectification," however, may have had more to do with a pending loan application with the Inter-American Development Bank (IDB) than with any desire to seek reconciliation with those who sought a democratic solution to El Salvador's troubles. Repression continued unabated, and Romero may have been trying merely to mollify critics in the Carter administration and to make the job of his foreign minister, Antonio Rodríguez Porth, a little more bearable. In a convenient turnabout of the enthusiastic support it gave to the Public Order Law in 1977, the Asociación Nacional de la Empresa Privada (ANEP) also began to call for a "rectification of past errors."

Labor grew more militant. In March, La Constancia and La Tropical soft drink bottling plants, which belonged to the Meza Ayau family, were occupied by workers. This was the first in a series of labor conflicts that the government tried to suffocate with its repressive apparatus. On 20 March a sympathy strike organized by the workers of the Río Lempa hydroelectric plant (CEL) virtually paralyzed the country, at a cost of $24 million. However, the few decisions rendered by labor courts that went in favor of the workers were ignored by management.[1] Labor tensions reached a critical juncture in August. Management started to shut down plants, and some transnational firms abandoned the country altogether.

In early May the BPR occupied the French, Costa Rican, and Venezuelan embassies, as well as the Metropolitan Cathedral. The Bloque was seeking the release of five of its leaders who had been taken into custody and "disappeared." On 8 May police opened fire on a peaceful demonstration outside the cathedral, killing twenty-three persons. This prompted a scathing attack on the government by Archbishop Romero, recently returned from a visit to Rome.

In an attempt to engage the moderate opposition in a "dialogue" with civilian members of the government, like National Assembly chairman Leandro Echevarría and Minister Rodríguez Porth, Romero lifted the state of siege on 24 July. Earlier in the summer, Echevarría had visited Washington, where he had a breakfast meeting with President Carter to discuss a formula for "decompression." But Romero refused to meet the conditions of the opposition, which included the dissolution of the death squads, a general amnesty, the return of exiles, an end to repression, and, in sum, a return to the rule of law. Neither the PDC, the main quarry in Romero's campaign, nor the church hierarchy participated in the "dialogue," which was confined to a caucus that included the ANEP, the Salvadoran Industrialists' Association (ASI), the Chamber of Commerce, and the Bar Association.

The fall of Anastasio Somoza, on 17 July 1979, marked a turning point in the Salvadoran crisis. Shortly thereafter, Romero's government began to disintegrate. Having failed in the attempt to bring the PDC and the more progressive sectors of the bourgeoisie together, the United States increased pressure on the Romero administration and began to seek an alternative to the faltering general. In late July, Assistant Secretary of State for Latin American Affairs Viron Vaky flew into San Salvador for secret talks with government officials. Apparently, Vaky made no effort to contact any opposition figures other than representatives of the PDC. U.S. Ambassador Frank Devine revealed the concerns of the Carter administration with a direct allusion to the need "to avoid a repetition of the tragic events that had occurred in Nicaragua." Deputy Assistant Secretary of State William Bowdler visited the country in August for follow-up discussions, but Romero remained steadfast, stating that his government enjoyed the confidence of the private sector and offering, as his only concession, to allow the return of exiles. In September, Assistant Secretary Vaky went before the House Inter-American Affairs Subcommittee and testified that El Salvador might be near insurrection, a view which was shared by a representative group of Salvadoran intellectuals.[2]

In August, following the failure of Romero's attempt at dialogue, the opposition organized its own caucus, the Foro Popular, which attracted the participation of an impressive array of organizations of different ideological persuasions (see Figure 5-1). The Foro was significant in that it demonstrated the possibility of an alliance between the moderate petit bourgeois elements of the larger opposition parties and the popular organizations. The platform of the Foro (summarized in Figure 5-1) called for, among other things, a democratic *and* popular project to find a replacement for the existing system of governance.

The platform could be termed "radical" only from the perspective of the reactionary conservatives lined up behind Romero or of someone totally unfamiliar with El Salvador.[3] Flores Pinel correctly points out that the Foro was but the seed of a possible alliance between the middle and lower classes.[4] The prospect of such an alliance must have been one of the deciding factors behind the military's decision to oust Romero, however, since the Foro could have evolved into a grand coalition in the style of Nicaragua's Frente Amplio de Oposición, which was instrumental in the defeat of Somoza. The Salvadoran military was fearful that such a broad-based and popularly supported group could reorganize the military institution or simply do away with it—as had happened to the Nicaraguan national guard.

But a repetition of the Nicaraguan experience was unlikely. El Salvador had no Somoza, and, therefore, class conflict was a more explicit and ominous component of the struggle there. A unified opposition was still only a remote possibility, and some of the governments that had supported the opposition against Somoza were still studying the Salvadoran situation and waiting to commit themselves. This implies that there was still time for solutions that would have avoided civil war. Finally, the balance of force was overwhelmingly in favor of the government and its paramilitary organizations. All

Somoza had was his national guard. In El Salvador, by contrast, the opposition had to reckon with ORDEN and other paramilitary groups in addition to the regular army, and these could not be defeated overnight.

Vaky's prediction may have been premature, but the Department of State and the Carter administration seemed to share his assessment. The primary concern of the administration seems to have been the prevention of "another Nicaragua." According to its view the real enemy in El Salvador was a Left that could emerge stronger from a protracted conflict, ready to pick up the pieces of reformist failure and rightist intransigence. This lumped together all the organizations of the Left, ignoring or overlooking differences in their ideologies and tactics, as well as linkages to "middle-class" organizations, that continued to divide them. Perhaps more important, this reading of the situation was shared by the more progressive of the military factions actively involved in conspiracies against Romero.

Concerned with the rapidly deteriorating situation and mindful of the damage that Romero's continuation in office could inflict on their institutional prestige, different factions of the military competed in their plans to replace him. The officers who staged the coup of 15 October 1979 appeared to be oriented to a progressive solution. They were prepared to address the land question, but they did not deal with the issue of the participation of the popular organizations in the new order that they were advocating.

The Coup and the First Junta

A *juventud militar*, the junior officers—majors, captains, and lieutenants— organized the coup of 15 October 1979 that brought down the government of General Romero. Theirs was an institutional action different from previous military insurrections and does not appear to have been a preventive coup.[5]

The military conspirators issued two proclamations on the day of the coup. The first was a formal announcement describing the rationale for the coup. According to this proclamation, Romero had been overthrown by the military institution because (1) he had shown himself unable to deal with the anarchy created by extremist elements, (2) he had repeatedly violated fundamental principles, such as the right of the population to participate in major decisions of national interest, (3) he had persisted in the use of violence to deal with political problems, and this was leading to a confrontation between the "Armed Force" and the people, and (4) he had allowed the public administration to become corrupt. While this rationale voiced the anxiety of the military about its own institutional integrity, the proclamation also promised that the Armed Force would establish the appropriate climate for real and dynamic democracy and would hold free elections.[6]

FIGURE 5-1
The Foro Popular: Participants and Platform

Participants:

Partido Demócrata Cristiano (PDC)
Partido Unión Democrática Nacionalista (UDN)
Partido Movimiento Nacional Revolucionario (MNR)
Partido Unionista Centroamericano (PUCA)

Ligas Populares 28 de Febrero (LP-28)

Confederación Unitaria de Trabajadores Salvadoreños (CUTS)
Federación Unitaria Sindical Salvadoreña (FUSS)
Federación Nacional Sindical de Trabajadores Salvadoreños (FENASTRAS)
Federación de Sindicatos de Trabajadores de la Industria del Alimento, Vestido, Textil, Similares y Conexos del Salvador (FESTIAVTSCES)
Federación de Sindicatos de la Industria de la Construcción, el Transporte, Similares y Conexos (FESINCONSTRANS)
Asociación de Trabajadores Agropecuarios y Campesinos de El Salvador (ATACES)
Central Campesina Salvadoreña (CCS)
Sindicato Textil de Industrias Unidas, S.A. (STIUSA)

Summary of the Common Platform:

No more repression; dissolution of ORDEN, FALANGE, UGB, and Mano Blanca; general amnesty, freedom of political prisoners.

Inclusionary political participation and ideological pluralism; effective freedom of organization; recognition of the right to strike.

Short-term economic measures to stop inflation, improve wages; control of prices of articles of popular consumption; rent control.

Long-term economic measures guaranteeing access of peasants to the ownership and use of land.

Inauguration of a democratic regime *before* elections.

Effective participation of the popular organizations to guarantee a process of real democratization and the consolidation of a new political regime.

Source: *Estudios Centro Americanos* 34, 371 (September 1979): 843–45.

Students of the Salvadoran process have elaborated their own inventories of the reasons that prompted the military coup (see Figure 5-2). Some of these reasons are sociohistorical, namely, the need to form a new alliance between the middle class, represented by the Christian Democrats, and the industrial bourgeoisie, as well as the crisis of an economy based on the export model. The political bankruptcy of the Romero government, representing the attempt to restore the political supremacy of the traditional oligarchy, and the high level of polarization also figure prominently among the immediate causes of the coup.

The second proclamation of 15 October indicates that the military was hoping to implement a *reformist* program. It proposed first to stop violence and corruption—by dissolving ORDEN and eradicating corrupt administrative practices. Second, it promised to guarantee human rights—creating the climate for free elections, allowing the organization of political parties of all ideological stripes to strengthen the democratic system, granting political amnesty to all exiles and political detainees, recognizing the right of labor to organize, and promoting free speech. Third, it planned for a more equitable distribution of national resources through agrarian reform and a reform of the financial sector that would extend more protection to consumers, promote development programs to create employment and increase national production, and guarantee private property and its social function. Finally, the proclamation promised to implement a more positive foreign policy by reestablishing diplomatic relations with Honduras, strengthening ties with Nicaragua, and promoting better relations with Guatemala, Costa Rica, and Panama.[7]

Of course too much should not be made of a document of this nature, which must be sufficiently ambiguous to maintain the conspiratorial coalition intact and sufficiently ample and specific to attract as much support as possible from different sectors of the public. Yet the second proclamation is a useful benchmark for the initial objectives of the Salvadoran transition process that began on 15 October 1979.

Of course the implementation of these objectives would provoke a very obstinate and certainly violent resistance on the part of the oligarchy. This reformist platform—which was relatively similar to that of the Foro Popular (see above, Figure 5-1)—was interpreted as *revolutionary* by the oligarchy. This being the case, it is difficult to imagine how the Provisional Revolutionary Government could have consolidated a coalition that would have included both the popular organizations, considered "subversive" by many in the military, and the oligarchy, which had no interest in the role of "loyal minority" in a democratic regime. On the other hand, given the historical context and the relative weakness of the middle class, the exclusion of the popular organizations and the possible alienation of organized labor would have only made the new center that the military hoped to create more vul-

FIGURE 5-2
Causal Factors in the Overthrow of the Romero Government

Flores Pinel[a]	López Vallecillos[b]	UCA[c]
Conflict between factions of the dominant class	Political bankruptcy of the Romero government	Crisis of the export model and crisis of oligarchic domination
Alliance between the Christian Democrats (petite bourgeoisie) and the modernizing faction of national capital (industrial bourgeoisie)	Disenchantment of the private sector with government inability to neutralize the guerrillas (kidnappings) and popular organizations (plant occupations)	Inability to sustain the high level of repression

Political polarization

Government corruption and incompetence |
| | Opposition of the Catholic church | |
| Promotion of the alliance by the United States | United States pressures | Economic crisis |
| Willingness of the military to play the pivotal role in the alliance | Economic crisis: inflation, decapitalization, crisis of liquidity | Lack of legitimacy and of credibility of the government

Role of the Catholic church

Role of the popular organizations

Increasing concern of the military with their institutional integrity |

a. "Golpe de Estado," p. 894.
b. "Rasgos Sociales," pp. 876–77.
c. *Estudios Centro Americanos* 34, no. 372/373 (Oct.–Nov. 1979): 850.

nerable to subversion by the oligarchy and other disloyal rightists, including those still in the military. As it turned out, neither the oligarchy nor the popular organizations participated in the first junta or in the Provisional Revolutionary Government. Two years after the coup they remained outside the regime and very much opposed to it, although for very different reasons.

Despite this contradiction the moderate elements in the military seemed to have made an effort to be as inclusionary as possible. The first proclamation appealed to both the extreme Left and the extreme Right to abandon violence and participate in a process in which the Armed Force would guarantee the will of the majority. While these offers were being made, however, the more recalcitrant factions of the military showed, from relatively early in the process, that they were more alarmed by the "extremist elements" mentioned in the proclamation than interested in the conditions for a peaceful transition. Which extremist worried them more was palpable in the harshness with which the security forces dealt with the popular organizations during the first three weeks of the first junta.

The junta attracted the support of a fairly heterogeneous group, including most of the participants in the Foro Popular, with the exception of the Ligas Populares (LP-28). The Foro was represented by Guillermo Ungo and Román Mayorga, a former president of the Universidad Centroamericana Simeón Cañas (UCA). Both men had relatively good relations with the popular organizations and wanted to include them in the government's blueprint for transition. The more progressive element of the private sector was represented by Mario Antonio Andino. The two other members of the first junta—and undoubtedly the most influential—were Colonel Adolfo Arnoldo Majano and Colonel Jaime Abdul Gutiérrez, identified in the first proclamation as "enjoying the confidence of command vested upon them by the Armed Force."[8] The coalition supporting the junta included the Social Democrats of Ungo's MNR and the Christian Democrats, reformists from the private sector, organized labor, many technocrats, and the UDN, which had been dominated in recent years by orthodox Communists.[9] Although this was a coalition and not an alliance, many of its members had a relatively long history of collaboration in the UNO. The stability and continuity of their participation depended upon the depth of the military's commitment to the reform program, which Colonel Gutiérrez believed impossible to "be carried out in one day," and upon the government's ability to prevent systematic abuse of human rights.[10]

The first junta and its supporting coalition moved relatively quickly to put together and implement the reform package contained in the second proclamation and in the Foro platform. On 6 November 1979 the junta issued Decree No. 12, disbanding ORDEN and rendering illegal any action taken in its name.[11] Decree No. 9, issued on 26 October, had organized an independent Special Investigative Commission to look into the thorny question of the "disappeared," and produce a complete account of the whereabouts of those persons.[12] The junta's success in dealing with this extremely sensitive issue would be used by many, including the popular organizations, who had been the recipients of much of the repression during the Romero era, as a measure of the willingness and ability of the provisional government to restore a state of lawfulness to El Salvador. An uneasy truce arranged by Ungo and Mayorga prevailed between the government and the popular organizations at the time; the latter were waiting to see the outcome of the investigation of the Special Commission.[13]

The first junta also addressed the socioeconomic issue. The existing statute of commercialization and price regulation was amended by Decree No. 14 to give more muscle to the fight against inflation, and the minimum wage was increased for *jornaleros* (day laborers) working in the sugar and cotton harvests of 1979–80.[14] More important, Decree No. 43 froze all holdings over 100 hectares—about 247 acres—until a new agrarian statute could be enacted.[15] This meant that title to those farms could not be altered, whether by inheritance or commercial transaction. In addition, Decree No. 75 nationalized the coffee export trade and created a new organization, the Instituto Nacional del Café (INCAFE), to assume the functions of the Compañía Salvadoreña de Café (COSCAFE).[16] Agriculture Minister Enrique Alvarez Córdova went on national television to defend the decrees and explain the government's rationale for agrarian reform. Alvarez made a very simple point: 99 percent of the 280,000 agricultural proprietors in El Salvador shared 51 percent of the land, while 0.7 percent held 40 percent of the land.[17] In a letter to his subordinates the minister pledged a continued effort to break with this past.[18]

The intentions, therefore, were good, and the commitment was real. But the ability to implement these measures was lacking. For example, the minister of the presidency, Rubén Zamora, could not really bring about the dissolution of ORDEN because he lacked the cooperation of senior military officers connected to the Romero administration who had managed to survive the coup and were now entrenched in the security apparatus. The measure was also resisted by local *comandantes* of the national guard. These had traditionally served the interests of large landowners, and some were now engaged in a campaign of violence and intimidation.[19]

The popular organizations remained very apprehensive. The BPR charged that the coup was an *autogolpe* (preventive coup) orchestrated by Yankee imperialism and the bourgeoisie.[20] The LP-28 suspected the junta since it had taken power "behind the backs of the people," who had every right to doubt the sincerity and intentions of the junta.[21] The FAPU viewed the coup as the result of class contradictions and denounced it as an attempt by the State Department to form a coalition between the *aperturista* faction of the bour-

geoisie and the moderate parties and to leave intact the repressive organs of
the state.[22] This intransigent rhetoric connotes a somewhat simplistic appraisal
of the very complex, unstable, and difficult relations between the armed
forces, the *juventud militar*, the junta, and the security apparatus, but the
popular organizations had reason to complain: the level of violence directed
against them exceeded that reached under Romero.[23] Even commentators
sympathetic to the junta concurred in this appraisal and voiced their disap-
proval of the manner in which the workers occupying the Lido, Arcos S.A.,
Duramás, and Apex plants had been maltreated.[24]

Judging by this evidence, one can assume that the leadership of the security
apparatus was still in the hands of hard-liners who could not be controlled or
who were acting with the at least tacit approval of some government officials.
Apparently, these elements coalesced around the defense minister, Colonel
Guillermo García, who reportedly had authorized the use of army units to
attack mass demonstrations and break up labor conflicts in the cities. Ambiguity about whether these actions constituted "official" policy or not could
only be tolerated for a while by the Left. The truce could last only as long as
the government was perceived as trying to bring the Right under control.

Colonel García, who had been brought into the coalition at the last moment,
was the "swing man" between conservative and progressive officers. García,
and his deputy, Colonel Nicolás Carranza, represented, if not the hard-line
element within the junta, at least the determination not to allow the Left to
derive any advantages from reform—the same mentality displayed by Molina
in his proclamations on the Agrarian Transformation of 1976 and made explicit in the proclamations of 15 October 1979.

Presumably, the moderate officers loyal to Colonel Majano, a member of
the junta and a leader of the conspiracy, shared the colonel's desire to build
bridges to the Left. They were handicapped in this, however, by their poor
connections with and lack of control over the intelligence services of the
armed forces. Foremost among these was the ANSESAL, which controlled
and coordinated the G-2 and S-2 intelligence agencies of the armed forces.
This organization was a bastion of national security advocates bent on stop-
ping the Left at any cost. Even though the more notorious collaborators of
General Romero had been retired after the coup, the hard-liners retained considerable influence. They could play the card of Communist insurgency to discredit the moderates, and they were quick to remind everyone of the precedent
of Nicaragua. Finally, control of promotions and transfers was in the hands of
García, as defense minister, and of Colonel Jaime Abdul Gutiérrez, the other
military member of the junta.

Thus, the progressive members of the military and their civilian allies had
no effective control in the crucial area of abuses by the security forces. The
majority of the direct contacts between the "government" and the popular

organizations were through a security apparatus—including the intelligence
branch of the armed forces, the National Police, the Treasury Police, and the
national guard—that was controlled by elements who saw those organizations
as the enemy. Furthermore, the question of the *desaparecidos* (disappeared)
could not be resolved without the collaboration of that apparatus, which of
course included persons who had been implicated in previous abuses and had
reason to obstruct the inquiry of the Special Commission. The commission
was frustrated in its attempts to compile a full account, giving leftist opponents of the junta more reason to doubt its legitimacy.

In general, in cases where the military decides to collaborate in a process of
transition to a democratic regime, the question of earlier abuses is carefully
sidestepped. Seldom, if ever, are officers implicated in such abuses or in any
wrongdoings during a period of military rule brought to justice. Even in the
most favorable circumstances imaginable, the military is reluctant to allow
any inquiry into these matters and is, needless to say, able to prevent an
effective and independent inquiry. As a matter of fact, it would appear that a
very important component of the bargain made between moderates and hard-
liners in the military in these cases is an agreement, tacit or otherwise, that no
such inquiry will be forthcoming. Usually, the question of a general amnesty
for all political offenses—which is often one aspect in a restoration of a state
of lawfulness—is understood to cover cases of military abuse.

In El Salvador, particularly given the situation confronting the country in
late 1979, the satisfactory resolution of the issue of the *desaparecidos* was
impossible short of a complete victory of the moderates and the *aperturistas*
over the conservatives and obstructionists. In December 1979 that victory
could have come only from an armed confrontation between rival military
factions, but neither faction—assuming there were only two, which is not
entirely realistic anyway—was really interested, since both realized that this
would imperil the integrity of the military institution. In addition, many
officers felt that the guerrillas were also to blame for acts of violence and that
if these went unpunished, there was little they could do to sell to their colleagues the need to satisfy the popular organizations on this score.

The inability of the junta to resolve the issue of the disappeared was interpreted by the Salvadoran Left as a clear sign that the moderates were not in
full control. The Left may or may not have been willing to maintain its distance from the junta and allow the program of reform to get started. But the
fact remains that the obstructionists were determined to stop not only the inquiry but the very process of transition itself and to make sure that the Left
was not given any participation in the process. Violence against the Left was
the issue that, more than any other, contributed to the polarization of opinion
within the government and that finally led to the collapse of the first junta.

On 7 December 1979 a group of government ministers, justices of the

Supreme Court, and directors of state enterprises confronted the junta with the demand for a clear definition of objectives that would state the antioligarchic aims of the revolutionary government and a halt to the ongoing repression of "extremists" aimed exclusively at the Left.[25] On 28 December the demand was made again in an ultimatum to the Consejo Permanente de la Fuerza Armada (COPEFA), an armed forces council which represented the officers and served as a mechanism of consultation on major policy questions. The COPEFA was asked to respond by 30 December.

Reading the document prepared by these moderate civilians, one can understand the difficult predicament in which they found themselves. They very candidly admitted that their participation in the new government had been based on "the conviction that the *juventud militar* had sufficient military power to implement their own proclamation [and on] the possibility of incorporating the people to the process."[26] In an allusion to their 7 December demand, which had been addressed to the junta, the signers of the ultimatum declared that they had reached a consensus on the reasons for the shortcomings of the government. They stated that a change had taken place in the command structure of the military which had displaced many of the initial participants in the movement and had allowed the defense minister and some of the garrison commanders to exercise their powers independent of the junta. As a result of this, they charged, the process of transition had made a turn to the right.[27] To rectify this departure from the original intentions of the movement they asked the COPEFA to issue a public statement identifying the oligarchy and its allies as the more fundamental enemies of the process of transition and to support the following proposals:

(1) that the junta really assume the leadership of the Armed Force;
(2) that the COPEFA become the only intermediary between the Armed Force and the junta;
(3) that any order of the day issued by the Defense Ministry involving personnel changes be approved first by the plenum of the junta;
(4) that the junta be reduced to colonels Majano and Gutiérrez, representing the military, and Mayorga and Ungo for the civilians;
(5) that the army stop intervening in labor disputes;
(6) that a dialogue be opened between the government and the COPEFA, on the one hand, and the popular organizations, on the other, to clarify the aims of the Military Proclamation of 15 October and to lay some ground rules that would avoid further confrontation; and
(7) that the COPEFA publicly endorse a constitutional statute that would establish a legal framework for the process of transition.[28]

Essentially, the COPEFA was being asked to accept the leadership of the junta and to help remove the obstructionists from the government coalition, to as-

sume the leading role within the armed forces, and to sanction a new coalition
that would include the popular organizations.

Discounting the specifics of the Salvadoran situation and looking at the behavior of the military institution in cases of peaceful transition to democracy
in other countries, this demand may have come too early to allow the *aperturista* faction of the Salvadoran military to overcome the obstructionists.[29]
On 3 January 1980 the military responded, arguing that the COPEFA "was
not a political organization [and] could not be diverted from its *institutional*
mission by *extremist* attempts; [the COPEFA] was a special organ created to
maintain the unity of all its constituent elements" (emphasis added).[30] In
essence, this response "passed the buck" to the junta for all matters involving
policy, but it was emphatic in asserting that

> [the] Proclamation of the Armed Forces does not at any time estab-
> lish strategic alliances with *extremist* sectors and clearly enunciates that
> the structural reforms are aimed to break up the power of the oligarchy,
> with the intention of benefiting the great majority of the Salvadoran
> people. . . . [Furthermore] minority extremist organizations, [whether]
> ultra-right or ultra-left, refuse to participate in and obstruct the [transi-
> tion] process, [and] must be considered counterrevolutionary, and it
> is the duty of the people and of its Armed Force to defend their conquest
> and avoid the destruction of the Republic and, by implication, of the
> armed institution [emphasis added].[31]

In late 1979 the military *aperturistas* could not come to terms with the
question of the popular organizations; nor could they create the necessary
consensus that would welcome popular participation in the process of transition. Their tactics aimed at putting some reforms in place, thus gradually
persuading their colleagues and the Salvadoran people of the seriousness of
their commitment. Apparently, they were being outmaneuvered inside the
military, and they lacked the strength necessary to confront the hard-liners
directly.

On the other hand, a majority of their colleagues in the military followed a
moderate line which, in practice, worked to the benefit of the Right. At
bottom, this moderation implied an attitude of detachment from "political
questions." The reasons for this attitude among members of this pivotal group
must be sought in the atavistic nature of contemporary Salvadoran politics, in
the relative simplicity of military attitudes regarding "political" issues, and in
four decades of anti-Communist rhetoric. Moreover, there was the ever-
present concern with the integrity of the institution. They seemed more willing to take their chances with the existing arrangement than to run what they
perceived to be the greater risk of collaborating with (leftist) "extremists."

The COPEFA's refusal to change the status quo and redefine its role brought about a major reshuffle in the governing coalition that witnessed the exit of the Social Democrats. The reasons submitted by departing government officials underscored their desire to give definition and content to the process of transition (see Figure 5-3). The timing of their ultimatum was obviously related to their inability to resolve the question of the disappeared, to what appeared to be a campaign mounted by the Right to win the "battle of the streets," and to the increase in rightist terrorism. Viewing, as they did, the incorporation of the popular classes in the process of transition as a top political priority, these officials were in a position with respect to the popular organizations similar to that in which military moderates found themselves with respect to their civilian allies. They could promise, but they could not deliver, at least on the question of the protection of basic rights.

It would be a mistake to consider the men who abandoned the government in January 1980 an inexperienced group of idealists or "fellow travelers." Most of them had paid their dues in Salvadoran politics and subscribed to Social Democratic or Christian Democratic principles.[32] They may have made a tactical mistake in trying to produce a confrontation with the obstructionists at a time when they did not hold a sufficiently strong hand, but they were essentially correct in trying to consolidate the transition process in a new coalition that would include the popular sector. Their inclusionary model held more promise for democratic stability than did a new attempt to reequilibrate the regime under an elitist solution or an additional dosage of repressive reformism. Their formula excluded rightist participation in the government— but not in the political arena. This reflected their clear understanding of the role that the oligarchy had played in Salvadoran politics since 1948, derailing every attempt to bring about socioeconomic reform and a peaceful transition to democracy.

The Attempt to Stabilize the Transition Process

The former mayor of San Salvador José Napoleón Duarte, considered by many the most astute Salvadoran politician of his generation, may have made a mistake in accepting the military offer for the PDC to become the government. His party had lost much of its mass appeal, and although he could extract some concessions from the military, he could not force the *aperturistas* to weed out their obstructionist colleagues, especially after the crisis of the new year. The military proclamation of 9 January 1980 can be read as a concession to the Christian Democrats, and as a late response to the Social Democratic ultimatum. This proclamation reaffirmed the military's commitment to the goals of the first two proclamations, but it was much more specific concerning the reforms that the government was contemplating. These in-

FIGURE 5-3
Reasons for the First Cabinet Crisis

Samayoa, Alvarez, Barahona, Sevilla, Tona Velasco[a]	Zamora, Valiente, Dada Hirezi, Badía, Méndez, Velásquez de Avilés, Hart, Navarrete, Menjívar, Silva, Soriano, Guerra y Guerra, Oquelí, Villacorta, Quiñónez, Dada Rinker, Arene, Acosta, Cerna Torres, Simán Jacir, Buitrago, Siri[b]	Mayorga Quirós, Ungo[c]
Continued repression of popular organizations.	Lack of clear definition of objectives being pursued, and of the means to be used to guide the transition.	Military adoption of an attitude of "neutrality" and "apoliticicism" incongruent with Military Proclamation.
Neutralization of *juventud militar* by reasons of hierarchy and institutionalism. Autonomy of the minister of defense and army commanders. Ability of the oligarchy to renew the formula of PCN: reformism with repression.	Disagreement with an interpretation of "pluralism" that allowed reactionaries in the government while the repression of popular organizations continued unabated.	Unwillingness to rupture the 1948 model. Ability of the rightist minority to regain its strength.
Inability to pass a statute for the process of transition. Flawed interpretation of the situation by military.	General drift to the right as a result of this.	Rightist drift.

Source: Texts published in *Estudios Centro Americanos* 35, no. 375/376 (Jan.–Feb. 1980), as follows: a. pp. 120–21, b. pp. 121–22, c. pp. 122–23.

cluded the nationalization of banking and foreign trade, the unionization of peasants, and a constitutional statute for the transition period. The January proclamation also admitted the need for a dialogue with the popular organizations in order to include them in the process and suggested that the crisis of the new year had clarified the need to be more specific about the objectives of the Salvadoran transition.[33]

On 10 January a new junta was formed with the addition of two prominent Christian Democrats—Héctor Dada, who had just resigned as foreign minister, and Dr. José Antonio Morales Ehrlich, the president of the PDC—and a third civilian, Dr. José R. Avalos. The larger presence of the PDC in the revolutionary government was not exactly welcomed by those sectors of the "loyal" Right that the United States had hoped could establish a closer collaboration with the junta. The industrialists' association (ASI) complained that the PDC had managed to exclude the private sector from the new junta,[34] while the foremost association of the private sector, the ANEP, disputed the PDC's claim that it represented a majority of Salvadorans, dismissing it as "gratuitous."[35] On 20 January the ANEP cut all formal ties with the government. The PCN may have outwitted itself in describing the cabinet crisis as "the fall of the Foro [Popular] government" and as a maneuver instigated by the Communist-controlled UDN to radicalize the process of transition.[36] Chafing for being left out of the new government, the ASI, the ANEP, and the PCN continued their virulent attacks on the PDC throughout February.[37]

The reaction of the Left was equally bombastic, but it led to more visible changes in tactics. On 11 January the three popular organizations—the BPR, the FAPU, and the LP-28—and the UDN issued a joint communiqué calling for unity and armed insurrection.[38] That very week they announced the creation of an umbrella organization, the Coordinadora Nacional, which later became the Coordinadora Revolucionaria de Masas (CRM). The Coordinadora produced a programmatic platform which was made public on 28 February.[39] In a lengthier document the PCS, the FARN, and the FPL announced the formation of "an organism of revolutionary coordination" between their national directorates, called for a popular revolution, and invited "honest members of the military" to join in the people's struggle.[40] The MNR, for its part, welcomed the unity of the popular forces and maintained that senior officers had derailed the revolution and reimposed repressive reformism.[41]

The extreme Right saw things differently. On 8 February, Chele Medrano issued his own version of what constituted the gravest aspect of the crisis: Communist subversion. Unveiling previously undetected skills as a constitutionalist, Medrano argued that the junta had no power to decree a constitutional statute and that only a constituent assembly could reform the constitution—the same one he had ignored during his tenure as commander of the national guard.[42] Joined by the rising star of the Salvadoran Right, former intelligence chief Major Roberto D'Aubuisson, who had strong ties to the UGB paramilitary group, Medrano organized the Frente Democrático Nacionalista (FDN) and presented himself as the champion of the small agricultural proprietor. In reality, though, the FDN, like Medrano's previous party, the FUDI, was an outlet for disloyal reactionary conservatives like those represented by the Frente de Agricultores de la Región Oriental (FARO). Both Medrano and D'Aubuisson were the focus of constant speculation about a rightist coup, although they seemed to have drifted apart later on.

Once in power the Christian Democrats proved equally incapable of bringing the security apparatus under the control of the government. For example, on 22 January 1980 the Coordinadora staged a march in San Salvador. Although estimates of the size of the crowd vary, the Coordinadora seems to have exceeded the number of people put on the street by the Right in its *Paz y Trabajo* demonstrations of December 1979. As they approached the National Palace, police opened fire on the leftist demonstrators, killing twenty-four persons.[43] On 19 January, D'Aubuisson had joined the Frente Amplio Nacional (FAN), an organization of very conservative businessmen, in denouncing the purposes of the Coordinadora demonstration and asking "patriotic Salvadorans" to obstruct it.

On 25 February, Attorney General Mario Zamora, a PDC member and the brother of the recently resigned minister of the presidency, Rubén Zamora, was assassinated by right-wing terrorists. Major D'Aubuisson had accused Zamora of being a member of the FPL. Zamora had been trying to get the stalled inquiry into the disappeared moving again. His assassination worsened an internal crisis which had been brewing within the PDC concerning the party's collaboration with the military, the proper attitude toward the Left, and the pace and substance of the reform program. Before Zamora was murdered, Archbishop Romero had urged the Christian Democrats to withdraw from the government. The murder and the exhortations of Romero led to the resignation of several leaders from the government and the party and to the formation of a splinter group, the Movimiento Popular Social Cristiano (MPSC). Their basic grievances were very similar to those proffered by the Social Democrats when the latter abandoned the first junta.[44] The resignation of Héctor Dada brought Duarte into the junta.

On 19 February, Archbishop Romero had written to President Carter to ask him to reconsider his offer of $50 million to the junta.[45] Responding on behalf of the president, Secretary of State Cyrus Vance argued that the junta had proven to be moderate and reformist, that most of the aid was economic, and that the United States would make sure that the military aid would not be misused in the violation of human rights.[46] In his Sunday homily of 23 March the archbishop asked soldiers not to fire on their brethren. On 24 March, while saying late-afternoon mass, Romero was assassinated. On 30 March police and army units opened fire on a crowd of about eighty thousand gathered at the Plaza of the Cathedral in San Salvador for Romero's funeral. The government blamed the Coordinadora Nacional for the incident, but foreign bishops attending the funeral declared that soldiers positioned nearby had fired first.[47]

These incidents diminished the legitimacy of the government and eroded its popularity. To be sure, the PDC condemned rightist terrorism,[48] deplored the disruption of the 22 January march by the Coordinadora,[49] and launched what it claimed was a vigorous investigation into the assassination of Romero. Shortly thereafter, however, Judge Atilio Ramírez Amaya, who was in charge of the investigation, was himself the target of an assassination attempt, and he left the country.[50] Data compiled by the Salvadoran Commission on Human Rights, the Socorro Jurídico of the archbishop's office, and the press office of the archbishop showed that between 1 January and 13 March 1980 a total of 689 political assassinations had been perpetrated.[51]

One wonders why the PDC agreed to assume so much responsibility with so little power, and in a country moving toward civil war. To put the best face on things, perhaps the PDC leadership believed that it could prevent the situation from worsening, as it certainly would have if the Right had gained control of the government. Supported by the United States and Venezuela, the PDC leaders sought to consolidate their position with that of their *aperturista* allies in the military. If they could then effect some reforms, they could increase the credibility and legitimacy of the government and try to bring the Social Democrats back into some kind of collaboration with the government. Finally, after waiting for the appropriate opportunity, they could provoke, and win, a confrontation with the Right.

This scenario had one great flaw, however. A party, and the government that it organizes, cannot show itself unable or unwilling to stop indiscriminate killings by its security forces for a long period of time without having to share moral responsibility for such actions. Neither the PDC nor the military *aperturistas* could hope to gain enough leverage vis-à-vis the Right without a very strong show of popular support. But as we have seen, Majano and his supporters hesitated too long on the question of popular participation in the new government, they wasted time while their power base was eroding, and they were unable to risk an alliance with the popular sectors. In what was rapidly becoming an undeclared civil war, the disruptive capability of the Right could be matched only by the numerical strength of the popular organizations or by the unequivocal support of the military for the process of transition. And the PDC could count on neither of these in March 1980.

Yet Duarte had been unwilling to support his legitimate claim to electoral victory in 1972 with an appeal for a popular uprising. In addition, he had refused to join forces with the military during the crisis of 1960, for this would have tarnished the image of his fledgling party. What were the motives for his decision to make common cause with a former enemy in 1980? How much had the military and Duarte changed to make this possible? One possible answer is that Duarte and the PDC leaders who stayed in the government were anti-Communists willing, within certain limits, to prevent "another Nicaragua."

A "Machiavellian" explanation of the continued presence of the PDC in the Provisional Revolutionary Government assumes that the party believed that its presence in the government would give both their best chance to resist a rightist onslaught. The party would lose some prestige from its collaboration with the military, but it would be supported by the United States in its efforts to implement reforms, which the military would have to accept as the price of collaboration. In the meantime, while the party recovered its prestige through the implementation of reforms, leftist and rightist extremists would knock each other out and clear the way for the moderates. The coming to power of the Reagan administration may have made this gamble all the more desperate.

The sobering fact is that, despite its failure to control the violence, the PDC managed to push forward a limited yet real program of reforms. Yet without the restoration of a state of lawfulness, the reforms alone could not legitimize the PDC-military junta.

In late February Decree No. 153 was announced. More timid than the draft prepared by Enrique Alvarez under the first junta, this statute for agrarian reform affected only holdings above five hundred hectares, that is, the 25 percent of the land controlled by 244 landowners.[52] On 8 March Decree No. 158 nationalized the banking industry.[53] This new package of reforms, however, was accompanied by the declaration of a state of siege, on 7 March, which made the undeclared civil war official.[54]

Later on, when Dr. Morales Ehrlich addressed the nation in a televised appearance to review the accomplishments of the first six months of the Christian Democratic juntas, he would be able to enumerate some important achievements.[55] However, the significance and value of these measures were stained by the continuing repression, which the junta was unable to stop. In essence, the Christian Democrats were embarked on reformism under a state of siege.[56]

The End or the Beginning?

The coup of 15 October 1979 ended the dominance of a system that well fits the model of *reactionary despotism* described by Spanish sociologist Salvador Giner. Used by him in his analysis of the traditional authoritarian regimes of the Mediterranean area, reactionary despotism is a mode of domination char-

acteristic of capitalist economies that have developed "late," that is, since
World War II. Such governments are monopolized by reactionary coalitions
that maintain exclusionary political regimes in which actual or potential opponents are denied basic citizens' rights. The power of the state is utilized
arbitrarily to contain or disarticulate organized opposition, and co-optation
and passive obedience replace the active consent of the society.[57]

Central American regimes that fit Giner's model display quite a number of
important differences. It appears, however, that the core element of the reactionary coalition can be identified. This core element would include the largest
agricultural planters, who monopolize the control of sectoral associations,
cattle ranchers, large merchants with linkages to agricultural interests, finan-
ciers and bankers whose main creditors or factors are engaged in the export
trade, real estate speculators, former government officials and retired military
officers who used their positions in government to enrich themselves illicitly,
and individuals connected to the repressive apparatus, whether official or
paramilitary.[58]

In El Salvador this core group of the reactionary coalition was closely tied
to the "magic square" of oligarchic domination of the economy: the monopoly of land tenure, agricultural production, export sales, and finance. If
one is to understand the dynamics of the Salvadoran process of transition
inaugurated by the October 1979 coup, one important fact must be taken into
consideration. Despite the continuation of authoritarianism in El Salvador, the
condition of civil war, the continued exclusion of large sectors of the population from the exercise of citizen's rights, and the division of power between
the junta and the military, the governing coalition has changed and some basic
aspects of the mechanism of reproduction of capital that characterized El
Salvador before October 1979 have come under the control of the state.

The shortcomings of the agrarian reform carried out by the third junta are
well known: holdings between one hundred and five hundred hectares have
not been touched; the government bureaucracy has had a difficult time managing the logistics of the reform; titles have been slow in coming; and credit
has been insufficient. In addition, it remains open to question whether the
reform has been truly "redistributive"—as formulated by the late minister of
agriculture and FDR leader Enrique Alvarez—or a function of "counterinsurgency"—in the blueprint of Professor Roy Prosterman, a United States
agricultural expert responsible for the model of rural pacification in Vietnam.[59]

Nevertheless, the army moved with tremendous speed to implement the
reform. On 4 March 1980 the ISTA was reconstituted, and on 6 March
decrees 153 and 154—respectively, the Basic Statute of Agrarian Reform and
the transitory dispositions on the appropriation of lands—were passed by the
junta.[60] These were accompanied by the declaration of a state of siege—
Decree No. 155—suspending constitutional guarantees for thirty days. Ap-

parently, those responsible for drafting, announcing, and implementing the decrees had not forgotten the lessons of the crisis that accompanied the ISTA–Agrarian Transformation in 1976, and they acted swiftly. According to a leading critic of the reform of 1980, the oligarchy, "which had become convinced that the dynamics were returning to their favor, were flabbergasted at this unexpected turn of events."[61]

There is little question that the enactment of the reform marked a turning point in the countryside, as the paramilitary Right took matters into its own hands to try to frustrate the program. Numerous resignations and complaints followed the upsurge in violence, which began to take its toll among ISTA officials and peasant beneficiaries of the reform. As a matter of fact, passage of this statute may have marked the beginning of the civil war in El Salvador. As far as the largest agriculturalists were concerned, these two decrees, together with Decree No. 43—which had frozen the status of all holdings above one hundred hectares under the first junta—were a severe blow. They did not solve the land question in El Salvador, but they constituted an important *political* measure, for they weakened one of the corners of the square. Another corner of the magic square was also affected by the burst of decrees in early March that marked the entry of Duarte into the government: decrees 158 and 159 of 7 March nationalized banking and savings and loans institutions in El Salvador.[62]

Unlike the agrarian reform statute, these two decrees could be enforced efficiently and stringently, the oligarchy could evade them only with difficulty, and the PDC could closely supervise their implementation. Judging by the opposition of the private sector to the decrees—which were still in place in late 1981—they must have been relatively efficient in achieving their purpose.

One further encroachment on the prerogatives of the oligarchy had already taken place during the first junta: the nationalization of the domestic and export trade of coffee. This measure had been bitterly resisted by ABECAFE, which disputed "the argument that the concentration of economic power in a few hands is contrary to the interests of the *cafetaleros* and the country in general . . . because the coffee that we used to export was not ours."[63]

It is important to understand and discriminate among the different confrontations going on in El Salvador. This is difficult to do given the profound human drama posed by the catastrophic loss of life, the savagery of some of the killings, the contradictory reports flowing out of the country, the insistence of some on seeing the crisis as a textbook case of Communist interference and the grief of others who dread a repetition of Vietnam, and the natural tendency to reduce the roles of a host of peripatetic actors to a few stereotypes. But this much can be said: the coup displaced the reactionary coalition, and the decrees of the first and third juntas, reviewed above, seriously undermined the economic bases of the core element of the reactionary coalition.

These measures merely decapitated the dominant group, however, and aspirants to succeed it are not in short supply. For example, it is quite possible that those cultivators spared by the reform, with holdings between one hundred and five hundred hectares, could, under the leadership of someone like Chele Medrano, forge a coalition with conservative officers and restore reactionary despotism. It is also possible—and there is considerable precedent for this—that elements of the military could appropriate the land and become a new oligarchy under a facade of "state capitalism." Meanwhile, as will be made clear by the discussion presented in chapters 6 and 7, the more reactionary elements retain considerable power and have been able to neutralize any alliance between the PDC and the industrial faction of the Salvadoran bourgeoisie.

Reformism under a state of siege did not pacify El Salvador, and the reforms and the prospects for a democratic transition were in dire straits in late 1981. Yet these reforms, though enacted behind the backs of the people, were sufficiently effective to provoke the wrath of the Salvadoran Right. Assuming that these elements would continue their obstructionist tactics, one must ask whose interests were really served by the continued estrangement between Social and Christian Democrats? What additional cost could be incurred by an attempt to form a broader coalition that would include the popular organizations? How could a process of transition to democracy be effected without the neutralization of the rightist obstructionists?

During 1980 and 1981 most of the private sector of El Salvador remained opposed to the government of the Christian Democrats. The position of the *aperturistas* in the military deteriorated considerably. Duarte remained the formal representative of a state that had acquired more independence vis-à-vis the traditional oligarchy, but his government remained incapable of delivering the key element to legitimize a provisional government trying to implement a transition to democracy. This was the restoration of citizens' rights. Whatever qualitative changes had taken place in El Salvador, these were overshadowed by a conflagration that had already surpassed the toll of the *matanza* of 1932. One of the reasons to proceed with a "controlled solution" had presumably been a sincere desire to minimize violence and loss of life, but this could not be treated as a valid reason in late 1981. Perhaps in reality the coup and the controlled solution were first and foremost attempts to prevent a leftist victory. Paradoxically, this solution, this return to repressive reformism, was the situation that had created the problem in the first place.

Chapter 6

The Politics of Transition and the Possible Restoration of Reactionary Despotism

Introduction

After 15 October 1979 Salvadoran political actors became embroiled in a protracted confrontation which seems headed toward one of three outcomes: the consolidation of a reformist democratic regime, the restoration of authoritarianism, or the installation of a government committed to a socialist model. Militarily, the confrontation pitted the Salvadoran armed forces against five different guerrilla groups, while the paramilitary Right, assisted by the Treasury Police and ORDEN, waged a campaign against real or suspected adversaries. By late 1981, although neither side had managed to overcome the other, the civil war had taken about thirty-two thousand lives and left 10 percent of the population homeless.

The prospects for a political settlement looked very grim. The progressive coalition of Social Democrats, Christian Democrats, and Communists, which had banded together to contest the elections of 1972 and 1977 and which had been represented in the first junta of 1979, had split into two antagonistic camps. Efforts to reconcile these groups had failed both because of differences in their positions and because of their precarious relationships with their armed allies—the guerrillas for the opposition and the military for the Christian Democrats. These differences were exploited and deepened by the relentless violence of the Right.

While nominal control of the government remained in the hands of the PDC, there was widespread agreement among rightist and leftist Salvadorans and some foreign observers that that government remained in office only because of the support of the United States, which had its own view of the conflict and its own ideas as to how to resolve it. Finding itself unable to attract the support of the bourgeoisie, to control or discipline the armed forces, or to initiate a dialogue with the opposition, the Christian Democratic government issued a call for a constituent assembly election, through which it hoped to increase its legitimacy and neutralize some of its opponents. The crucial problem for the government, however, and the Achilles' heel of the efforts of the Christian Democrats, was its continued inability to restore the rule of law to El Salvador.

The Disloyal Right

Since the October 1979 coup the Salvadoran Right has been trying to regain control of the government. Under normal circumstances there is nothing inherently conspiratorial or subversive about a political group or faction trying to become the government. But, to say the least, circumstances in El Salvador have not been normal, even by that country's standards. The term *disloyal* is applicable to groups and individuals who, in a process of transition, engage in obstructionist tactics seeking to prevent the inauguration and consolidation of a democratic regime. In the Salvadoran case, the term *disloyal Right* refers to the core elements of the deposed reactionary coalition who have been conspiring to derail the process begun in October 1979. By the most generous standards, one could say that the disloyal Right has played the spoiler role, contributing to the climate of anarchy and indiscriminate violence. Others might argue—with considerable evidence—that it neutralized the process of transition, put into question the whole program of reforms, and opened a huge chasm between potential allies who could have created the kind of broad coalition that could stabilize the transition and see it to a successful conclusion.

The conspiratorial activities of Major Roberto D'Aubuisson exemplify the tactics used by the disloyal Right and provide a look at the individuals and groups behind these initiatives, their external allies, and the impact that they have had on the Salvadoran process. D'Aubuisson began his activities when he was relieved of the command of ANSESAL, the military's National Agency of Special Services. Between October 1979 and October 1981, D'Aubuisson's trail would take him to Guatemala City, San Salvador, and Washington, D.C.; to late-night meetings at military barracks, surreptitious appearances at gatherings of rightist businessmen, impromptu conferences with journalists at safe houses, and inflammatory broadcasts from neighboring countries. This trail would link D'Aubuisson to at least two major military conspiracies and to the assassinations of several prominent figures of the government as well as its opposition.

Shortly after Ambassador Robert White presented his credentials, on 11 March 1980, the Carter administration sent an unequivocal warning to D'Aubuisson and Chele Medrano to refrain from conspiratorial activities, since the United States would not tolerate a rightist coup. In April the major surfaced in Washington, D.C., accompanied by Alfredo Mena Lagos, a wealthy Salvadoran businessman connected with the Frente Amplio Nacional (FAN). It appears that both men were trying to create support for a right-wing government in El Salvador. Their trip was sponsored by the American Security Council, which organized their appearance before a gathering of the American Legion, as well as private meetings with conservative senators and members of Congress. D'Aubuisson used the opportunity to try to discredit members of the Salvadoran government, arguing that Morales Ehrlich had "known links" with the armed Left—technically true, since Morales had two sons who were guerrillas—and that Colonel Majano, a personal enemy of the major, was a member of the Communist Party of Mexico.

Upon his return to El Salvador, D'Aubuisson repeated his charges against Majano in a videotape distributed to most military garrisons. In late April, assisted by former deputy defense minister Eduardo "Chivo" Iraheta and by hard-line officers based in the garrisons of Usulatán, Gotera, and Sonsonate, he tried to launch a coup. On 2 May an eleventh-hour appeal during a tour of the barracks by Duarte and Majano persuaded the soldiers to remain loyal.

On the night of 7 May troops loyal to Majano surrounded an isolated farmhouse near Santa Tecla and captured D'Aubuisson as he was trying to destroy the contents of a briefcase which included documents describing the blueprint for the conspiracy. About a dozen officers in active service and some prominent members of the FAN were linked to the cabal and were detained for questioning.

A serious split developed within the military about what to do with the conspirators. Younger officers supporting Majano wanted D'Aubuisson shot for treason or sentenced to life imprisonment by a court martial. Others were content to strip him of his rank and send him into exile. A third group protested that D'Aubuisson's treatment could not be harsher than that meted out to former government officials who had made common cause with the Left and were trying to overthrow the government. For their part the Christian Democrats threatened to leave the government if D'Aubuisson and his co-conspirators went unpunished.

The major was incarcerated at a time when it appeared that the Right was gaining momentum. Former President Romero had visited the country. A campaign was afoot to force Majano out of the junta. The COPEFA had been neutralized as a vehicle for concerted action by progressive officers, and Majano was rapidly losing his base within the armed forces—which at one time had included the First Infantry Brigade, the Signal Instruction Center, the Second Infantry Brigade, and the Frontier Detachment of Chalatenango.

These impressions were apparently confirmed when, on 10 May, the senior officers spoke through the defense minister, Colonel Guillermo García, to announce that the command of the Armed Force, previously shared by Majano and Colonel Jaime Abdul Gutiérrez, would go to the latter. Colonel Gutiérrez described this as a "purely administrative matter," but the move was interpreted as a victory for the Right. The senior officers justified the decision to demote Majano on the grounds that this was the consensus of opinion within the COPEFA.

On 10 May a crowd of FAN demonstrators led by Ricardo Jiménez Castillo, a founder of the organization, laid siege to the residence of Ambassador White in San Salvador. The demonstrators were demanding the release of D'Aubuisson and, apparently, trying to link the incarceration of the Major to the ambassador's denunciations of rightist agitation and terrorism. On 28 March, during a speech to a luncheon gathering of the American Chamber of Commerce of El Salvador, White had accused some Salvadoran businessmen of financing hit squads to kill leftist activists. José Eduardo Palomo, president of the chamber, had taken exception to the speech, claiming that he had now become a possible target for assassination. The FAN demonstrators vowed to harass White until D'Aubuisson was freed, and they passed their time chanting, "White is Red," "Viva Reagan!" "Viva Senator Helms!" On 12 May U.S. marines dispersed the group, but the FAN was not to be denied.

Late on Tuesday, 13 May, Major Miguel Angel Méndez, the officer in charge of the investigation, released D'Aubuisson. Defense Minister García claimed that no one could be held without charges for more than seventy-two hours, certainly a practice which, if it had been applied systematically by the military during the 1970s, would have helped to forestall the turmoil of the 1980s. On 15 May the junta filed an appeal for the military tribunal to reverse itself and bring back the twenty-three officers and civilians arrested on 7 May, but to no avail.[1]

Meanwhile, D'Aubuisson remained unrepentant. Several journalists were picked up by armed men driving military jeeps, blindfolded, and taken to a secret destination for an interview with the major. Flanked by Alfredo Mena and other militant businessmen associated with the FAN, D'Aubuisson denied that he was conspiring, insisted that he was fighting Communism, and accused Ambassador White of threatening to support a government in exile if Majano were forced out of the junta. D'Aubuisson called his posture "nationalist," and claimed that Argentina, Chile, Paraguay, and Uruguay had given his group "ideological and logistical support." Shortly thereafter, the former intelligence boss left for exile in Guatemala.[2]

The D'Aubuisson episode illustrates several aspects of the Salvadoran situation. First, it marked the second occasion in which the *aperturistas* lost out in a confrontation with hard-liners. A number of face-saving tactics were employed to maintain a certain circumspection and dignity, but in the end *both* Majano and D'Aubuisson were punished. The former was demoted for his continued insistence on building bridges to the Left and the popular organizations—a matter of survival for the *aperturistas*. The latter was punished for "overreacting" to Majano's "softness" with subversives. Second, if we are to take García at his word and accept that the "administrative action" involving Majano was the consensus within the COPEFA, then we must conclude that by April 1980 the senior officers had managed to reinstate the Right at the center of military opinion.

Finally, the light treatment meted out to D'Aubuisson and his coconspirators suggests that some of the postulates of the doctrine of national security continued to linger on in the thinking of the military. To be sure, it was now confronted by an increasingly unified Left bent on following the *vía armada*, and it had to meet this challenge, but its lenient treatment of a violent conspirator like D'Aubuisson suggests that it perceived the need for a continued "dirty war" against subversion. Little evidence of any revision of these firmly held convictions was evident during the first year of the junta.

Looking at recent cases of transition in Ecuador, Peru, and Portugal, it is possible to identify moments at which the advocates of democratization looked defeated. In the Salvadoran case, however, one can only interpret the demotion of Colonel Majano as a very serious setback for the cause of democratic transition. Even if one interprets the demotion as a corrective measure on the part of the military to neutralize an officer faction perceived to be "too close" to the civilians in the government, the evenhandedness with which Majano and D'Aubuisson were treated could only bode ill for the prospects of democratic transition.

The disloyal Right saw D'Aubuisson as a crusader for the restoration of the reactionary despotism in El Salvador. The restoration would require resolute action in the style of Maximiliano Hernández (Martínez). This implied the elimination of the adversary in all its different forms: priests, nuns, labor and peasant leaders, moderate politicians, teachers and university professors, and the guerrillas themselves. The inability or unwillingness of members of the Right to distinguish between their adversaries underlined their fanaticism and their selfish intransigence, which was matched only by that of the more hardened guerrillas.

At the time of the demotion of Majano disloyal rightists had a firm grip on the Treasury Police and the national guard and complete control of the supposedly disbanded ORDEN and the UGB. They had numerous sympathizers among junior military officers, *jefes civiles* (mayors), and local *comandantes* paid by the Defense Ministry to head small local reserve forces. While this did not give them sufficient power to take control of the state directly, it did afford them considerable operational autonomy, as well as enable the leaders of organizations like the FAN to boast of "popular support" for their cause.

The events surrounding the conspiracy of May 1980 showed that the links between the paramilitary Right and conservative segments of the private sector were not a matter of academic speculation. Instead, the *public* association between these two confirmed their *institutional* links, their readiness to offer themselves as an alternative, and the possibility that they could put together the pieces of a fascist formula of political domination, or at least one very similar to the Guatemalan regime from which D'Aubuisson seemed to receive much encouragement and inspiration. More ominously, the leaders of this reactionary coalition were looking forward to a change of administration in Washington to create a more favorable domestic and international climate for the execution of their blueprint.

During the summer of 1980 the disloyal Right demonstrated that it could count on the support of certain sectors of North American opinion. On 30 June D'Aubuisson arrived by private aircraft in Key West from Guatemala. Although his U.S. visa had been revoked, he was allowed entry, and he flew immediately to Washington. The visit was arranged by the American Legion and the American Security Council, and, once again, the major was trying to rally support for an FAN government that would be installed in power by a coup. In a press conference attended by several members of Congress, D'Aubuisson depicted Ambassador Robert White as a guerrilla sympathizer. More important, those members of Congress did not dispute D'Aubuisson's assertion that they had told him to hang on until November and that an electoral victory by Ronald Reagan would turn things around. As he left the press conference, the visitor told a National Public Radio reporter that a Reagan victory "*es lo que estamos esperando* [is what we are waiting for]."

D'Aubuisson's second visit made the Carter administration extremely uncomfortable, since it represented an attempt by ultraconservatives in the United States to force the hand of the administration in El Salvador. They misquoted several CIA and DIA intelligence reports to charge that the Carter administration was not getting the job done.[3] The Department of State provided official reaction through spokesman John Trattner, who characterized the visit as "not in the best interests of the United States," since the FAN was suspected of violent activities in El Salvador. A few days later, Ambassador White expressed apprehension that the Salvadoran Right was anticipating a Reagan victory and making extensive preparations to overthrow the government.

D'Aubuisson left Washington under the custody of INS agents, but he remained upbeat, claiming that he had accomplished the objective of his visit, which was to link his cause to the Reagan campaign. He claimed that he had talked to several U.S. senators and repeated his conviction that with a new (Reagan) government "our luck will change."[4] He maintained this in a series of tape-recorded messages that circulated widely among right-wingers in El Salvador.

If during the summer of 1980 the disloyal Right had to content itself with symbolic victories in the battle for sympathy and legitimacy in official circles in Washington, it had more reason to be encouraged by the continued erosion of Colonel Majano's remaining base of support. During the summer, Majano continued to lose ground, in part owing to his own indecision and to his inability to prevent the removal of his associates and supporters from sensitive positions within the military. A decisive blow came on 1 September when Colonel Guillermo García, the defense minister, using his powers under the state of siege, signed a battle order removing virtually all of Majano's remaining supporters from their posts.[5] Majano tried to hang on and to cut his losses; he continued his contacts with opposition leaders, but his influence had been effectively neutralized. In spite of this the Right did not let up; on 3 November it tried to assassinate Majano while the colonel was at ISTA headquarters.

Majano saw a coup unfolding, since the Salvadoran Right felt all powerful with Reagan's victory and was anticipating a victory of its own.[6] This charge came following a meeting of 19 November, during which Majano was abused verbally by senior military officers. "The Right," he said, "has certainly increased its battering to get me out. [They] have been waiting for this moment to define the situation in their favor."[7] Majano felt the need for urgent action. On 6 December, while he was in Panama seeking the support of General Torrijos—himself a graduate of the Salvadoran military academy and a frequent mediator between Salvadoran military factions after the coup of October 1979—and discussing the possibilities of new conversations with the Left, the military removed Majano from the junta. Defense Ministry sources claimed that the COPEFA had voted 300 to 4 against Majano, who, after sending his family to the United States, returned to El Salvador to try to resist the decision. He toured a number of garrisons in an attempt to explain his position and to rally support, but it was too late. On 10 December government figures announced an imminent reorganization, and the colonel was out for good.

Majano's demise came at a moment in the Salvadoran transition when a series of events in that country combined with the victory of Ronald Reagan in the U.S. presidential election to precipitate a very serious confrontation. This confrontation led to the creation of the fourth junta, and to a new and precarious balance between the military and Christian Democrats, which persisted through 1981. The events showed that the disloyal Right remained the greatest threat to the Junta Revolucionaria de Gobierno, even though the guerrillas were increasing their leverage in the Salvadoran transition.

The Disloyal Right and the Reagan Transition

Of course the disloyral Right did not focus its efforts exclusively on progressive military figures like Colonel Adolfo Majano. From the very moment of the coup the Right had embarked on a program to eliminate important figures in both the government and the opposition camps. These efforts were intended to frustrate and demoralize the government, to make it more difficult for the

PDC to remain in the junta, and further to alienate the opposition from the government. More and more frequently, the tactic that the Right chose was the assassination of prominent figures. Although relatively successful in creating a climate of fear and uncertainty, this program fell short of its most important objective, which was to drive the moderates out of the junta. For example, the Right was unable to force José Antonio Morales Ehrlich out of the government. Unlike Majano, Morales Ehrlich had the support of a party behind him, but many of his coreligionists in the PDC and many opposition leaders were not so fortunate.

One of the first to fall was Dr. Martín Espinosa Altamirano, shot on 5 February 1980 in his office by three suspected right-wing terrorists. Espinosa was a leader of the MNR, which had just moved into opposition. Shortly thereafter, on 25 February, Attorney General Mario Zamora was murdered at his home in front of his family. One of the most popular Christian Democrats, Zamora had been accused by D'Aubuisson very recently of being a member of the FPL. The party immediately charged that D'Aubuisson was behind the assassination, but the damage was done.

Events like these not only generated divisions within the party, but prompted calls from other sectors that the PDC leave the government. For example, in February 1980, Monsignor Romero asked the Christian Democrats not to participate in the government so that their presence would not contribute to the masking of repression. On 24 March, Romero himself was murdered, plunging the party once again into a deep crisis. On 27 March three members of the PDC resigned their portfolios in protest over the government's inability to prevent rightist violence.[8]

PDC leaders tried to maintain their composure and denounced the oligarchy for complicity in subversion and indiscriminate killings, but they exonerated the armed forces.[9] Outrage inside the party prompted junta members Morales Ehrlich and Duarte to pressure the military to police itself. In his letter to the party explaining his resignation, however, Héctor Dada claimed that "the party has not been able to earn the respect of its 'partners'; on the contrary, the repeated presentation of demands which are not even rejected formally [by the military], and that are then forgotten by the [PDC] leadership has strengthened the position of those who from their leadership roles in the Armed Forces maintain attitudes contrary to the covenant."[10] Shortly before their split from the PDC, Dada and members of the "popular tendency" claimed that the 31 December 1979 covenant between the party and the armed forces was a futile attempt to govern by itself. Thus isolated, the party had few resources with which to try to control the fascist element within the army.[11]

In short, the inability to control the military led dissident Christian Democrats to demand that the party abandon the government. Meanwhile, party activists were subjected to such a rightist onslaught that in June 1980 PDC

Secretary General Juan Ramírez Rauda would state that more of its members had been killed during that year than during the Molina and Romero governments combined. This merely reflected what was happening in the Salvadoran population as a whole. According to Socorro Jurídico, 2,065 persons had died that year through the end of May.

The Christian Democrats wanted to utilize D'Aubuisson's complicity in the May 1980 conspiracy to neutralize him for good. Yet it is apparent that they were unable to do so. Party members remained convinced that the major was responsible for the assassination of Mario Zamora. Duarte himself was quoted as being "absolutely certain" that D'Aubuisson was responsible for the assassination of Monsignor Romero—*"Estoy absolutamente seguro."*[12] More important, the PDC had had the support of the American embassy in its attempt to remove the major from the scene and to neutralize the actions of the rightist military. But the embassy had little influence on the rightists, and this evaporated during the period following the election of Ronald Reagan. The Salvadoran Right was convinced that the new administration's decision to de-emphasize human rights implied an endorsement of its tactics. An alarmed Ambassador White flew to Washington in mid-November to urge the Reagan transition team to clarify its position and to restrain the Right.

A group of Salvadoran businessmen associated with the Alianza Productiva, a recently formed organization which offered qualified support to the junta, met with Reagan advisers Jeane Kirkpatrick, James Theberge, and Constantine Menges on 28 November. The visitors were assured of continued military aid, but were warned that this would not be forthcoming in the event of a rightist coup. Apparently, the Salvadoran Right was not listening, or else the rightist conspirators could not believe that they would be denied.

On 27 November a large group of about two hundred men raided the Externado San José, a Jesuit high school in San Salvador, taking twenty-five persons captive. The detainees had been holding a meeting of the Frente Democrático Revolucionario (FDR), an umbrella organization formed on 4 April to coordinate leftist opposition to the junta. The mutilated bodies of four FDR leaders were found the next day; a fifth was found the day after. Those killed included FDR president and former secretary of agriculture in the first junta Enrique Alvarez; Juan Chacón, secretary general of the BPR; Manuel Franco of the UDN; Enrique Barrera of the MNR; and Doroteo Hernández.

The killing of the FDR leaders followed closely on a 25 November note from the PDC to the junta in which the party analyzed the problem of rightist violence and demanded immediate action. Party leaders were convinced that the initiative to assassinate these opposition leaders had come from the military hierarchy itself, although they would not say so in public. The Christian Democrats felt that a new coup was in the offing, and they were demanding the removal of officers implicated in efforts to destroy the government.

The outcry and the violence generated by this incident had not died down when four American women were reported missing on 3 December. The women—Maryknoll sisters Ita Ford, 40, and Maura Clarke, 46; Ursuline sister Dorothy Kazel, 40; and lay worker Jean Donovan, 27—were last seen driving a 1978 Toyota van from the San Salvador International Airport on the evening of their disappearance. Sister Ita and Sister Maura were arriving from Managua, Nicaragua, where they had attended a regional meeting of their order. The women were headed toward the city of La Libertad. Their burned-out van was discovered the next day. On the afternoon of 4 December, Ambassador White and the U.S. consul general in San Salvador arrived at a site, some fifteen miles northeast of the airport, beside a back road some way out of the village of Santiago Nonualco. The ambassador had been notified by the vicar of the diocese of San Vicente that the four women were buried there in a shallow grave. Father Paul Schindler from La Libertad parish met the American diplomats at the site. The bodies of the women were dug out by local villagers. At three o'clock that afternoon, the secretary to the local justice of the peace arrived and authorized the removal of the bodies. All four women had been shot in the head. The face of one had been destroyed; the underwear of three was found separately. All had been shot repeatedly with high caliber bullets, and their bodies were bruised badly.[13]

On 5 December the Carter administration suspended all new military aid to El Salvador pending clarification of the murder of the four women. The administration also announced that a fact-finding mission headed by former under secretary of state William D. Rogers and William G. Bowdler, assistant secretary of state for inter-American affairs, would leave immediately for El Salvador.[14]

On 6 December Salvadoran foreign minister Fidel Chávez Mena was in Panama briefing General Omar Torrijos on the details of a forty-eight hour ultimatum that Christian Democratic junta members Duarte and Morales Ehrlich had served on the military, threatening to resign. Taking advantage of the uncertainty and turmoil surrounding these events, D'Aubuisson—who was boasting openly of having masterminded the killings of the FDR leaders—had offered the leadership of a new junta to national guard chief Colonel Eugenio Vides Casanova and to Colonel Nicolás Carranza, the deputy minister of defense. D'Aubuisson was acting through his associates, majors Mauricio Staben, Joaquín Zacapa, and José R. Blanco and captains José R. Pozo Durán and René A. Majano Araujo. The conspirators believed that they could count on the national guard, the Treasury Police, and the Third Infantry Brigade if they could find a suitable senior officer to lead the movement, and they anticipated that other units would follow.

The members of the PDC realized that a confrontation was imminent and that they had to move or be exterminated. They were aware of the conspiracy and of the fact that fourteen of their leaders had been targeted for assassination. Supported by Ambassador White, who was himself in a very precarious position, they had taken their case to Torrijos. They demanded the removal of D'Aubuisson's military associates and the demotion of Colonel Carranza and Colonel Morán, the head of the Treasury Police, which had one of the worst records of indiscriminate violence.

The presence of the presidential commission of inquiry may have helped the Christian Democrats' cause. It is also likely that General Torrijos played a role in the confrontation. On 8 December the commission met with the junta. The commission had already established that a military patrol had probably intercepted the four women and that they had been buried in a remote area under the supervision of local civilian and military authorities, even though these officials would have known that the four bodies matched the description of the missing American churchwomen. This suggested to the commission an attempt to conceal the deaths, since the embassy had not learned of the whereabouts of the bodies from official sources.[15]

Any possibility of a dialogue between the Christian Democrats and the moderate Left had been ended by the assassination of the FDR leaders; the intentions of a new administration in Washington did not augur well; the PDC's closest collaborators in the military were gone; and the Right had once again humiliated the party with impunity while it waged an aggressive campaign to destroy the government. In these ominous circumstances the Christian Democrats were trying to play their only card, the threat of resigning from the government. They asked the military to live up to its pact with the PDC and remove the officers involved in the conspiracy.

Until the crisis of December 1980 the military had shown little enthusiasm for the removal of any officers accused or suspected of political murders. It had viewed their actions as a necessary component of the "dirty war" against subversion. For whatever reasons, Duarte and his collaborators had not been forceful enough on this matter before. But now they had little choice.

The "government reorganization" that produced the fourth junta was, at best, a modest victory for the Christian Democrats. The reorganization was announced on 13 December. Duarte and Colonel Gutiérrez disclosed at a press conference that they would become president and vice-president of the junta, respectively. Duarte would assume legislative functions, and Gutiérrez would remain as commander in chief of the Armed Force. Therefore, the question of civilian supremacy remained unsolved, even on paper, since the civilian president of the junta had no authority over the military. Yet the reorganization did produce a neutralization of the new D'Aubuisson conspiracy, as both Vides Casanova and Carranza disassociated themselves from his initiative. In addition, Carranza was demoted, which earned Colonel García the wrath of the more conservative officers, who considered this a "sell out." More important, a battle order of 31 December 1981 removed the nucleus of hard-core supporters of D'Aubuisson from active service. In summary, this resolution of the crisis gave the Christian Democratic members of the government some breathing room, but it did not put an end to rightist attempts to destroy their government. The views of the incoming Reagan administration toward authoritarianism and the Salvadoran situation in particular continued to send a signal to the Salvadoran right wing that conditions were ripe for a power grab.

A Change of Emphasis

This crisis had barely subsided when the junta had to make a difficult and perilous adjustment to a new emphasis in the policies of the United States toward El Salvador. This had begun to emerge in the last few days of the Carter administration, perhaps in anticipation of changes that the new administration would make but also in response to the "final offensive" that the guerrillas launched on 10 January 1981.

Since November 1980 the Department of State had been in possession of a cache of documents, purportedly captured from the guerrillas by the Salvadoran armed forces, which seemed to indicate that the former were receiving weapons from abroad. Secretary of State Edmund Muskie had cabled the embassy to this effect. On 14 January the Carter administration announced that it would give $5 million in "nonlethal" military aid to the Salvadoran armed forces. Ambassador White defended the measure on the grounds that the United States was "under obligation" to counter the guerrilla threat.[16] At a press conference in San Salvador, White suggested that the nature of the struggle had changed because of the quantity and sophistication of the weapons that the guerrillas were receiving from Nicaragua. He added that during the guerrilla offensive about one hundred well-armed guerrillas had come across the Gulf of Fonseca from Nicaragua. On 18 January, President Carter authorized an additional $5 million in combat equipment and supplies.[17]

Carter's action renewed the flow of aid that had been suspended as a result of the assassination of the four American women in December. Ironically, this military aid represented the first direct shipment of such aid to El Salvador since 1977, and it was approved after the Salvadoran army had defeated the guerrilla offensive. This change in policy was met with skepticism by some members of the government. An unidentified member of the cabinet told reporters wryly that the only change that had taken place was that in the United States, since the weapons had been coming to the guerrillas for over a year.[18] The Christian Democrats were concerned that the new emphasis on a military solution or on the military aspect of the crisis would help to strengthen the position of the hard-liners in the army and of the rightist element in general. White shared this view, which he aired frequently throughout 1981.

The issue of the resumption of military aid was joined to the issue of human rights in El Salvador, making the latter a source of considerable embarrassment to the PDC, since the United States Congress would insist on a certification of progress on this front as a condition for aid. On this occasion, the murders of the nuns had stood in the way, and the Department of State had issued a statement on 17 January, while Carter was still in office, to the effect that the Salvadoran government had taken "positive steps" in the investigation of the killing. Ambassador White disputed this contention and argued that while the aid had been justified, there was no need to obscure the fact that the junta had done very little to investigate the murders.[19] This public disagreement precipitated the removal of White, who had been targeted for removal by conservatives in the U.S. Senate anyway. The issue was joined, however, and American public opinion was invited to look at El Salvador through either the distorted lenses of a new group of policymakers bent on showing the world that America would not be pushed around anymore, or those of the horrified opponents of this new group, who saw a familiar scenario unfolding.

The early weeks of the Reagan administration were marked by a hardening attitude toward the Soviet Union, and the administration also set out to demonstrate that El Salvador was a "textbook case of Communist aggression." The case was to be made by the secretary of state, who perceived his role as the president's "Vicar" for foreign policy.

On 10 January 1981, less than a week after American Institute for Free Labor Development (AIFLD) officials Michael P. Hammer and Mark D. Pearlman and José Rodolfo Viera, president of the ISTA, were gunned down by rightist terrorists in the coffee shop of the Sheraton Hotel in San Salvador, General Alexander M. Haig, Jr., in testimony before a Senate Foreign Relations Committee hearing on his nomination as secretary of state, complained that recent American pressures on El Salvador over human rights violations might be said to diverge from the spirit of the OAS charter.[20] On 1 February Haig fired Ambassador White. Although spokesmen for the Department of State hastened to declare that this did not necessarily imply a change in U.S. policy toward El Salvador, they did indicate that a policy review was under way. More important, White's removal produced consternation within Christian Democratic circles in the junta and rejoicing among those who had characterized him as a "guerrilla sympathizer" and as a man "sending the wrong signals to a troubled nation."[21]

White may have anticipated his downfall, which may explain his indiscretion, but given the ideological bent of the new administration and of its supporters in the Congress, the outgoing ambassador may have wanted to do his part to counter what several observers were seeing as a drastic change in policy. Conservative supporters of Reagan, in particular Republican Senator Jesse Helms of North Carolina, the new chairman of the Subcommittee on Latin American Affairs of the Senate Foreign Relations Committee, were determined to put their own people in sensitive positions within the foreign policy apparatus. This brought about considerable delays and negotiations over ambassadorial appointments, as well as over assignments to top policy positions at the Department of State.[22] In the summer of 1981 most senior positions at the department's Bureau of American Republics were still vacant, and, needless to say, morale was low and the design and conduct of policy very uncertain and contradictory.[23] In the meantime, the embassy in San Salvador, temporarily headed by Frederic L. Chapin, a career foreign service officer who was appointed to the post on 23 February, appeared to be under cross-pressures from human rights activists and die-hard conservatives.

The guerrilla documents captured the previous November became an important part of the case assembled by the team reviewing the Salvadoran situation. This evidence fit well into Haig's attempt to redefine the situation. Jon D. Glassman, an American diplomat stationed in Mexico City, was dispatched to San Salvador to retrieve a second batch of documents captured during the January offensive. Together, these documents provided the essential ingredients of a report that the review team was preparing to bolster the secretary's view of the conflict. As one official familiar with the circumstances in which the report was prepared would state later, this was "a hasty job, under a lot of pressure, and it was sloppy in some ways."[24]

Segments of the report were leaked to the press in early February. On 14 February the administration announced that Lawrence S. Eagleburger, assistant secretary of state for European affairs, and General Vernon A. Walters would be sent to Europe and Latin America, respectively, to present the administration's case. The Special Report was released on 23 February in two installments: an 8-page summary presenting the conclusions drawn from the evidence and a 180-page book of documents of more limited circulation.[25] The summary concluded that "over the past year the insurgency in El Salvador has been progressively transformed into another case of indirect armed aggression against a small Third World country by communist powers acting through Cuba."[26]

This conclusion was grounded on five major inferences:

1. that Fidel Castro and the Cuban government had played a direct role in late 1979 and early 1980 in bringing together the diverse Salvadoran guerrilla factions into a united front;
2. that outside assistance and advice was given to the guerrillas in planning their military operations;

3. that Salvadoran Communist leaders and key officials of several Communist states had had a series of contacts that had resulted in commitments to supply the insurgents with nearly 800 tons of the most modern weapons and equipment;

4. that a covert delivery to El Salvador of nearly 200 tons of those arms had been made, mostly through Cuba and Nicaragua, in preparation for the guerrillas' failed "general offensive" of January 1981; and

5. that the Communists had made a major effort to "cover" their involvement by providing mostly arms of Western manufacture.[27]

Reaction to the Special Report was predictable. On 6 February, anticipating its release and responding to early commentary by the media, Shafik Jorge Handal, secretary general of the Communist Party of El Salvador (PCS), issued a rebuttal from Mexico City. Handal made the following points:

1. it was false that an agreement had been reached between Soviet Bloc governments and the PCS to deliver weapons to the guerrillas;

2. the allegation was really a maneuver by the United States to justify the growing supply of U.S. arms and military personnel to the junta;

3. the Salvadoran people had been pushed toward a war of survival and national liberation by government massacres and repression;

4. the PCS did not want future hostile relations with the United States; and

5. the fact that the Department of State, and not the Salvadoran junta, had assumed responsibility for the publication of the report provided further evidence of the blatant way in which the United States government was intervening in the internal affairs of El Salvador.[28]

After the Special Report was published, Dr. Rubén Zamora, an FDR leader and also secretary of the presidency under the first junta and the brother of the slain attorney general, Mario Zamora, countered that the U.S. charges were based on false documents; that the guerrillas were getting their weapons from sources in Costa Rica, Honduras, and Nicaragua, but without any involvement on the part of the governments of those countries; and that the United States had presented the documents as a cover-up for continued backing of the Salvadoran junta.[29]

Although more detailed and devastating criticism of the Special Report would not surface until the summer, the political offensive mounted by the Reagan administration got relatively little mileage out of the report. In addition, adverse reaction in the United States to the tone and messages that the administration sought to sustain with the report forced Reagan to abandon the campaign almost as suddenly as it had been started.

Eagleburger's contacts with and representations to Western European governments generated only mild support. Britain, France, Italy, and West Germany were "convinced" and condemned Communist support for the guerrillas as "unacceptable interference." EEC countries even agreed to delay granting humanitarian aid to the victims of the fighting, under pressure from the Reagan administration, who insisted that most of the aid wound up in the hands of the guerrillas. However, most European governments continued to oppose a military solution to the Salvadoran conflict.[30]

General Walters's mission to Latin America produced responses that varied from skepticism and annoyance to outright opposition and dismay. Argentina and Venezuela, whose governments approved of United States support for the junta, expressed disagreement with the idea of an inter-American peace force. The Brazilians received their old friend warmly, but they repeated their opposition to any type of intervention in El Salvador. Finally, Mexican President José López Portillo, who had already met with President Reagan, provided the most stinging response, declaring that Cuba was the Latin American country dearest to Mexico, warning against "unscrupulous arrogance of military power," lamenting the elevation of Central America to the undesirable rank of strategic frontier, and condemning as "unnatural and unreasonable" the foreign powers' espousal of Latin American conflicts as though they were theirs.[31]

Many observers shared the impression that El Salvador was being used by the Reagan administration as a test case to show American determination to fight Communist subversion. Congressional sources believed that the administration had evolved a short-term strategy toward El Salvador consisting of four different desiderata: (1) build up the military capabilities of the junta, (2) reduce international support for the guerrillas, (3) rally support in Latin America and Europe for the U.S. position, and, most important of all, (4) stem the flow of weapons reaching the guerrillas.[32] The administration was relatively successful on the last score, at least temporarily, but part of this success was owing to the fact that the actual tonnage of weapons reaching the guerrillas had been overestimated greatly.[33] The second and third goals were simply not met.

The administration's drive to secure congressional approval of increased military aid to the junta was probably not dependent on the acceptance of the Special Report. Although the report may have been instrumental in switching a few votes in the key committees of Congress, President Reagan's personal powers of persuasion would have probably sufficed, for the president seemed capable of achieving victories in Congress on even the most hopeless issues during his first year in office. Congress, however, remained skeptical and committed to the principle of linking the aid to the performance of the junta on human rights.

On 24 March, exactly one year to the day after Monsignor Romero was assassinated, the Foreign Operations Subcommittee of the House Appropriations Committee approved the additional $5 million in "lethal" aid initially proposed by Carter. This approval did not come easy, however, as ex officio members Jamie Whitten (D.-Miss.) and Silvio Conte (R.-Mass.), respectively, the chairman and ranking minority member of the committee, had to take the relatively infrequent action of joining in a subcommittee vote to produce a majority for the administration. Most of the subcommittee members who voted in favor of the measure justified their action on the grounds that it was necessary to support the president so that he would not look weak.[34]

The month lapse between publication of the Special Report and the subcommittee vote had witnessed an increasingly adverse public reaction to any military involvement in El Salvador and considerable media scrutiny of the situation. These put the administration on the defensive. The Foreign Operations Subcommittee became a forum for constant discussion of the situation. On 25 February former ambassador White testified before the subcommittee. He disclosed that during the last days of the Carter administration he was under constant pressure from his military attaché, Colonel Eldon Cummings, to request additional military aid and advisers. Cummings confided to the ambassador that the Pentagon wanted these in place before the Reagan inauguration. White added that social reform and political reconciliation were the best means to defeat the guerrillas, who, in his view, lacked popular support, and that the new equipment would be used to assassinate and kill in uncontrolled ways. In a dramatic gesture, White turned to the Republican members of the subcommittee and asked them, "Do you want to associate yourselves with this kind of killing?"[35] The ousted diplomat may have been trying to defend his actions and his views, but his testimony managed to raise the central question for United States policy in El Salvador. In addition, White's testimony occasioned much editorial comment questioning the wisdom of the administration's blueprint.[36]

Public opinion was also reacting to stern warnings delivered by Presidential Adviser Edwin Meese and Secretary Haig to the effect that the administration did not rule out any action to halt the flow of arms. The president tried to allay the mounting concern over his apparent desire to "win one in El Salvador." On 24 February he declared that he had no intention of involving U.S. troops in the fighting, although on 26 February he protested that the "Vietnam syndrome" should not deter the United States from helping countries endangered by a Communist insurrection. The weekend of 28 February–1 March witnessed extensive coverage and commentary on El Salvador by most major newspapers.[37] On 3 March, Reagan realized how deep the concern ran when retiring CBS news anchorman Walter Cronkite opened an interview with the president with seven consecutive questions about El Salvador. Reagan was forced to repeat that he did not plan to send U.S. troops to El Salvador and that Haig's statement about "going to the source" of the weapons did not imply that Cuba would be assaulted.

In summary, reaction to the tough administration rhetoric pushed the Salvadoran crisis to the forefront, confronting Reagan with an issue that, he now concluded, was taking too much time and overshadowing his domestic economic program. Shortly thereafter, the administration began to downplay the issue.

The debate on El Salvador did not die down, however. The press continued to scrutinize the situation and ask embarrassing questions,[38] officials and critics of the administration continued to defend their views on the situation,[39] and administration officials continued to issue hard-line statements, although less frequently. In addition, Congressional committees kept the issue alive. Meanwhile, the situation in El Salvador followed a logic of its own which had little to do with the content or the tone of the ongoing debate in the United States.

The Salvadoran Right, for one, remained convinced that the situation had turned to its advantage and that the time had come for a decisive challenge to the hapless junta, whose already low legitimacy had been eroded further by the geopolitical machinations of the Reagan administration. Salvadoran rightists had been encouraged by the tough talk coming out of Washington, and they were emboldened by the apprehension reigning among the Christian Democrats. Washington had ignored Duarte's protestations that the most pressing problem was the economic one and had issued the Special Report, which had interpreted the civil war going on in El Salvador as "Communist aggression"—an interpretation challenged by Salvadoran Foreign Minister Fidel Chávez, who insisted that the conflict was, first and foremost, domestic. White had been fired, and the new administration did not seem to care much about human rights. Finally, more military aid seemed to be on the way. All this only confirmed the impression long held by Salvadoran rightists that Reagan was one of theirs.

On 3 March, Roberto D'Aubuisson resurfaced in El Salvador, calling for the removal of the junta and stating that a "totally military" government would be acceptable to Reagan. D'Aubuisson claimed that talks he had conducted with two members of the Reagan transition team, Roger Fontaine, formerly of Georgetown's Center for Strategic and International Studies, and Lt. General Robert Graham, had given him the impression that Reagan would support such a government in El Salvador.[40] Fontaine confirmed that he had spoken to the major the year before, but he characterized D'Aubuisson's conclusion as "pure fiction."

Fact or fiction, D'Aubuisson was conducting this new attempt to destabilize the junta at a time when Duarte seemed to be entertaining an offer made by

West Germany to bring together the democratic forces on both sides of the
Salvadoran conflict. Duarte was desperate to recover some of the ground lost
by the civilians in the government. The major was trying to exploit what was
perhaps the most divisive issue separating the military and the Christian
Democrats, as he accused Duarte of setting the stage for negotiations with the
Left.

News of another rightist cabal in El Salvador failed to produce much reac-
tion from the Reagan administration at first, since this was happening just as
Reagan had decided to try to move El Salvador off of the front page. On 4
March White House press secretary James Brady announced that Reagan had
no views on the coup, while Department of State spokesman William J.
Dyess refused to comment on internal Salvadoran politics. That same day,
however, Chargé d'Affaires Chapin, who was much closer to the action, and
Secretary of State Haig, who had been chastised for his failure to react strongly
to news of an unfolding coup d'état in Spain in February, warned that a military coup would have "serious consequences" for United States aid. Two
days later, answering one of five questions on El Salvador at a White House
press conference, Reagan said that a rightist coup would be a matter of grave
concern to his administration,[41] and Dyess declared that the United States
supported President Duarte's attempt to solve the crisis through elections.

On 4 March occupants of a passing truck fired on the American embassy,
prompting Chapin to link the shooting to the conspiracy. Apparently, the
Salvadoran Right had served notice of its disillusionment with the Reagan
administration in characteristic fashion. On 6 March the junta put out word
that D'Aubuisson was being sought for his complicity in the abortive coup
but, to no one's surprise, the major was not apprehended. On 17 March two
gunmen repeated the attack one half-hour after Representative Clarence Long
(D.-Md.) had ended a press conference at the embassy building expressing
opposition to United States military involvement in El Salvador.

To the chagrin of the administration El Salvador remained very much in the
news through the year. The civil war, which most senior members of the administration continued to view as a case of Communist insurgency, lingered
on. Critics remained unconvinced and dismayed by the new emphasis displayed by officials. Duarte and his associates survived the Reagan transition,
but it remained to be seen whether their ineffectual government could find the
means to turn the process of transition toward a political settlement; if anything, this looked more and more remote. Their precarious situation was
made worse by the instincts and personal convictions of the formal allies of
the Christian Democrats. These seemed ready to end the conflict with a
military victory, but that victory had so far failed to materialize.

It is too early to give a full appraisal of what difference, if any, the Reagan administration made on the Salvadoran situation. For our purpose, which is to determine whether the actions undertaken by the United States helped or hindered the Salvadoran process of transition, the Reagan policy seemed to strengthen the position of the obstructionists. To be sure, the wilder right-wingers did not get their wish, but they did get away with murder, literally. The more moderate rightists, on the other hand, were encouraged by what they saw and heard, and they felt little need to cooperate with the Christian Democrats, who appeared to be out of favor with the new team in Washington.

The role of United States conservatives like Helms deserves brief mention, in that they consciously or unwittingly helped to legitimize the actions and programs of the more violent rightist element in El Salvador. These conservatives wanted not only to "draw a line" in El Salvador but to dictate a geo-political approach to the problem, which could only result in a regionalization of the conflict. These elements did not appear as interested in a peaceful solution to the problem as they did in the use of this "textbook case" as a pretext for "getting tough" with Nicaragua and Cuba.

President Reagan sensed the depth of opposition to his initial approach and adopted a more cautious one. Therefore, he failed to live up to the direr predictions of his opponents. He had come to office with a reputation as a hawkish anti-Communist, and many had anticipated that his actions would result in a complete neutralization of the chances for peaceful transition in El Salvador. After the first year of Reagan's term in office the United States was more deeply involved in the crisis, but not primarily because of Reagan's anti-Communism. Our deepening involvement was the result of his continued commitment to two basic goals set by Carter: the prevention of a "leftist" victory and the creation of a political center.

Chapter 7

The Reagan Administration and the Salvadoran Civil War

Reagan's Salvadoran Policy

The Carter and Reagan administrations shared one basic objective in their policies toward Central America in general and toward El Salvador in particular, namely, to prevent a victory by the Left. This was, after all, the principal motive behind United States support for—some would say active participation in—the coup that overthrew the Romero government in October 1979. During his brief tenure as United States ambassador to El Salvador, Robert White repeated this dogma on several occasions and promoted a line which tended to minimize popular support for the guerrillas and the political significance of the FDR. Containment of the Left in Central America was a goal shared by relatively broad sectors of opinion within the foreign policy apparatus, irrespective of their support for currently existing policies. For example, a position paper drafted by junior analysts and circulated through dissent channels during the final stages of the Carter administration criticized United States policy toward Central America, but did not question the assumption that the Left had to be contained.[1]

The difference between Carter and Reagan, in practical terms, would have to be sought in the particular blend of reformist measures and military muscle that each man felt was necessary to resolve the crisis. This difference became apparent in the approach of the Reagan administration to three issues: first, the question of human rights abuses and indiscriminate killings by the Salvadoran armed forces; second, the question of the relationship between the Duarte government and the Salvadoran private sector; and third, the question of a political settlement to the crisis, which was closely related to the way the administration perceived the whole situation and the more effective potential remedies.

The Issue of Human Rights

The area where critics of the Reagan administration's policies toward El Salvador had most cause for concern was human rights. The administration's views on a number of issues related to human rights seemed to confirm worst-case expectations. One such issue was the role of religious activists in the conflict. The administration's reaction to the assassination of the four missionary women was a litmus test for this issue.

Emotions ran very deep. On 29 April 1980, Ambassador Robert White had sent a letter to Fr. Simon Smith, executive director of the Jesuit liaison office on missions in Latin America, expressing his concern that "a great number of people in El Salvador, specifically including the Jesuits, are so justifiably angry at the absence of human rights over the last half century that they have a psychological need for a bloody revolution."[2] Ambassador White's letter concerned the events surrounding the shooting incident at the funeral procession for Archbishop Romero in San Salvador. Official preoccupation with the church's unwitting contribution to violence, therefore, could also be found in the language of American officials before Reagan came into office. Yet it was Ambassador White's rage at the murders of the four American missionary women in El Salvador that had, after all, led to his early confrontation with and departure from the Reagan administration.

By contrast, Secretary Haig dismayed and angered critics with his careless, tactless, and offensive comments on the circumstances of the murders. Haig told the House Foreign Affairs Committee that perhaps the vehicle in which the nuns were riding tried to run a roadblock, or may have accidentally been perceived to do so, and there may have been "an exchange of gunfire" in the process. The secretary, a master of the nonresponse and the obscure reply, may have dug himself in a deeper hole when he was asked by Senator Claiborne Pell, during a hearing of the Senate Foreign Relations Committee, to explain what he meant by "exchange of gunfire." Haig said that he did not mean that the nuns were firing at people. Then he chuckled and added, "I haven't met any pistol-packing nuns in my day, Senator."[3] One outraged editorialist related the exchange a few days later and asked the secretary, "Have you no decency, Sir?"[4]

The sarcasm of the secretary's remarks was taken by many as a true measure of the administration's feelings on the issue, overlooking more sober appraisals by other key figures, like that of Ambassador Kirkpatrick. Responding to a letter addressed to her by senators Charles E. Percy and Claiborne Pell, the chairman and ranking minority member, respectively, of the Foreign Relations Committee, Dr. Kirkpatrick replied that statements that she had made during an interview on "Meet the Press" reflected her attempt, as a

political analyst, "to describe dispassionately a tragic violent scene," and
were not at all intended as a smear on the reputation of the victims. Kirkpatrick added that although the commitment of many priests and religious to
political and economic justice in Central America led their adversaries to
perceive them as political activists on behalf of the Frente (FDR), she did not
believe "that anyone's commitment to any cause or anyone's help to any
individual in any sense justifies their murder."[5]

To bolster the credibility of its approach to the human rights question and to
respond to criticism of the administration's handling of the murder of the four
American missionaries, the Reagan administration made public protestations
of its concern with violence in El Salvador. On 9 April, Department of State
spokesman William J. Dyess protested the killing of twenty-four slum-dwellers
in San Salvador by the security forces, saying that actions like this "threatened all hopes of reform and democratic progress" and disclosing that the
Salvadoran government had been asked to provide the U.S. government with
the facts of the tragedy.[6]

The administration also pressured the Salvadoran government to put more
muscle behind its apparently feeble efforts to apprehend those responsible for
the murders of American citizens in El Salvador and to stop the reckless
killing of civilians. On 5 April, Ricardo Sol Meza, a wealthy Salvadoran and
one of the owners of the Sheraton Hotel in San Salvador, was arrested in connection with the investigation into the murders of Hammer, Pearlman, and
Viera. According to Salvadoran sources, on the night before his arrest by
Salvadoran police, Sol Meza had been overheard advocating a coup against
Duarte.[7] On 9 April the commander of the infamous Treasury Police, Colonel
Francisco Morán, announced that fifty-nine members of his force had been
dismissed because of their involvement in the assassination of the twenty-four
slum dwellers.[8] Colonel Augusto Coto, spokesman for the Defense Ministry's
Press Committee, had maintained that the victims had been killed in a firefight
between guerrillas and the Treasury Police.[9] Subsequent investigation revealed, however, that the victims had been blindfolded with their thumbs tied
behind their backs and shot in the head. Apparently, none of the dismissed
agents was prosecuted. On 15 April, FBI agents working on the Sheraton
murders case arrested Hans Christ, a thirty-year-old Salvadoran and Sol Meza's brother-in-law, in Miami. Christ was held without bail pending a hearing
on a Salvadoran government request for his extradition.[10]

On 22 April, Under Secretary of State Walter J. Stoessel, Jr., assured
Archbishop John Roach, president of the National Conference of Catholic
Bishops, that the four slain missionaries were not involved in politics and that
the United States government would continue to press El Salvador to investigate their murders.[11] In the following weeks administration sources leaked to

the press that the Salvadoran government had been told to react to the evidence presented to it by the FBI or endanger United States economic and military aid.[12]

These moves reflected the administration's reaction to the intense pressure exerted by critics of its Salvadoran policy. On 7 May former ambassador White told a press conference in Rochester that the administration had known for weeks that six members of the national guard had been in custody for some time for the slaying of the four American women.[13] On 8 May administration sources disclosed that evidence developed by the FBI investigation and turned over to Salvadoran officials left little doubt about the identity of the assassins. The sources were skeptical that the evidence could produce a conviction in Salvadoran courts and averred that hard-line elements within the Salvadoran military had seized on the inconclusive nature of the evidence to obstruct the investigation and a possible trial.[14] White's accusation and the administration's disclosure forced Salvadoran defense minister, Colonel García, to acknowledge that six suspects had been in custody since 29 April. Colonel García refused to provide many details, or to disclose their names and referred his questioners to the guard's commander, Colonel Eugenio Vides Casanova. A document sent to the American embassy by the junta, and seen by some journalists, however, listed the names of three military men, including a sergeant.[15]

Whatever the reasons behind the timing of these disclosures, Congress remained adamant. On 11 May the Senate Foreign Relations Committee voted 11 to 1 to attach conditions to present and future aid to the Salvadoran government. Under the conditions, President Reagan would have to certify every six months that the junta was making "continued progress implementing essential political and economic reforms," that it remained committed to holding early free elections, and that it was achieving "substantial control" over all elements of its armed forces.[16] Through the rest of the year all the junta could do was reiterate its commitment to constituent assembly elections. Under the circumstances, both the junta and the Reagan administration tried to remain optimistic and to present the best face possible.

By the end of the month an official release by the Department of State seemed to reflect a more balanced approach to the Salvadoran situation. The language of the release was practically a carbon copy of the Foreign Relations Committee resolution. According to the department, it was the policy of the United States "to support President Duarte's *interim* government as it implements reforms, moves toward free and open elections, and works to end *all forms* of terrorism. . . . The U.S. provides economic and military assistance, with economic aid more than three and a half times the amount of military aid" (emphasis added).[17]

The allusion to Duarte's government as interim may have been designed to soothe Western European governments that could not accept Duarte as a genuine democrat, while the reference to all forms of terrorism may have been a begrudging acceptance that rightist terrorism was a problem as well. The release was ambiguous in one important respect, however. Following a detailed description of the amounts and types of aid to El Salvador, the department concluded that "the War Powers Resolution requires the executive branch to consult with Congress before U.S. armed forces are introduced into hostilities. . . . The administration has concluded that *present circumstances* do not indicate an imminent involvement of U.S. personnel into hostilities" (emphasis added).[18] Obviously, this left open the possibility of deeper involvement in the future.

Movement on the cases of the slain Americans was not followed by any marked improvement on the part of the junta to "substantially control" its armed forces or by a resolute effort to restore the rule of law in El Salvador. Hard-liners viewed the systematic campaign of violence and intimidation as a necessity; moderates assumed a fatalistic attitude and tried to look forward to the March 1982 constituent assembly elections. Both were paranoid and defensive about the adverse publicity that they had brought upon themselves.

In a letter to the Maryknoll order, President Duarte claimed that the disappearance of the Reverend Roy Bourgeois, a Maryknoll priest, had been a propaganda maneuver to discredit his government. Fr. Bourgeois had disappeared in San Salvador on 26 April, and there had been fears that he had been kidnapped and assassinated by rightist terrorists. But Bourgeois had reappeared ten days later, making some confused and contradictory statements on his whereabouts.[19] On 22 May the national guard claimed that it had cracked a "leftist conspiracy" to influence news coverage on El Salvador.[20]

The low-key approach preferred by Reagan administration officials toward matters related to human rights may have contributed to slow things down. While publicly the administration spoke of the need to act on the cases of the slain Americans, it removed one official familiar with the cases from the scene. On 27 May, U.S. consular officer Patricia Lasbury, a former Catholic nun and missionary to Peru and Brazil, was relieved of her assignment in San Salvador. Although the Department of State refused to discuss her reassignment and the embassy refused to comment, it was reported that there was apprehension about the "high visibility" that Lasbury had achieved as the embassy officer in charge of the disinterment and identification of the bodies of the four missionaries.[21] An embassy source said that Consul Lasbury had worked well with her Salvadoran counterparts and, since she had been friends with some of the victims, had remained close to the investigation after the case had been taken over by the political officer of the embassy.[22] Fears for Lasbury's safety may have been more important in the decision to remove her than were any fears that she might commit an indiscretion. But whatever the case, her removal could have been taken by the hard-line element in El Salvador as an indication that the Reagan administration was not serious about pursuing the cases of the slain Americans.

Embassy officials familiar with the cases remained deeply disturbed, however. On 25 May departing chargé d'affaires Frederic L. Chapin may have breached protocol when, at a foreign ministry reception given in his honor, he stated rather bluntly that the murders "demand justice, and the world will judge the government of El Salvador and its armed forces as a result of these cases. These cases have had a profound impact on the image of El Salvador abroad."[23]

Chapin's replacement, Ambassador Deane R. Hinton, tried to sound more upbeat as he entered the scene. On 2 June, at a press conference following the presentation of his credentials to President Duarte, Hinton expressed hope that the fifty-six U.S. military advisers in El Salvador could be reduced in the near future and defended United States assistance to a reform-minded government in El Salvador as nothing to be ashamed of. To his credit, the new ambassador referred to the Salvadoran conflict as a "civil war," becoming perhaps the first official of the Reagan administration to do so. Hinton concluded his remarks by saying that progress had been made in the case of the nuns and that he expected to receive "good news" from the junta about that case in the near future.[24] But little news would be forthcoming, and the ambassador would have to revise his expectations.

Shortly after Hinton's arrival in San Salvador diplomatic sources there believed that, if anything, the violence was getting worse, despite recognition by top officials that it was counterproductive. By that time, Colonel García and junta member Morales Ehrlich were convinced that the military's reputation resulted from Marxist misinformation. The defense minister viewed the situation as a "black conflict"—a war without quarter—and he claimed that 180 military men were under suspension for abuses of authority and that the army was taking more prisoners—whereas few or none had been taken before, since most were executed on the spot.[25]

On 16 June, Ambassador Hinton admitted that the human rights situation "is bad and continues to be bad but it's better than it was." He pledged that he would continue to pursue human rights cases, "particularly those cases involving American citizens," adding that he would do it quietly.[26] Others could not be so quiet. In early July, Marianella García, president of the Salvadoran Commission on Human Rights, declared that the level of official repression had increased since January, that at least 11,000 persons had been killed during the first six months of 1981, and that about 30 persons were dying every day during the third quarter of the year.[27] The Legal Aid Office of the Archbishop (Socorro Jurídico) believed that during the first semester of 1981,

9,250 Salvadorans had been assassinated by the armed forces and the para-military organizations.[28]

At home the administration was losing the battle over the credibility of its human rights policy. On 24 September the U.S. Senate voted 54-42 to support the Foreign Relations Committee and to condition aid to El Salvador on progress in human rights. The United Nations also had a hand in the report card. On 10 November its Human Rights Commission released a thirty-five-page report prepared by Spanish jurist José A. Pastor Ridruejo. The report concluded that although each side's share of the violence could not be estab-lished, even approximately, enough evidence was available to conclude that there had been "a consistent pattern of gross violations" of human rights since October 1979. The report also criticized the executive and judicial branches of the Salvadoran government for adopting "a very widespread attitude of passivity and inactivity toward these violations."[29] By this time, American officials in San Salvador were referring to their weekly report of deaths as the "Grim Gram."

On 20 August, Ambassador Hinton discussed the question of the human rights record of the government with correspondent Christopher Dickey. Asked about how much abuse of human rights the United States could toler-ate, Hinton replied, "they could go bananas and go back to the policies of gen-eral whatever-his-name-was [Martínez] who handled the 1932 situation. . . . It's utterly absurd that the United States would continue to support a govern-ment that adopted that kind of a policy."[30] Apparently, the ambassador was unaware that the death toll since October 1979 had already surpassed that of 1932. Hinton, and the administration that he represented, obviously believed that there was a vast difference between Duarte and Martínez—an assessment that was essentially correct. This was small consolation, however, to the vic-tims of violence. In addition, although the reformist element within the gov-ernment did not sanction the murders, public opinion made no distinction between moderates and hard-liners and attributed those murders to the govern-ment. Finally, the de facto policy of extermination of adversaries followed by the military was neither getting them any closer to defeating the guerrillas nor winning over the Salvadoran people to the government.

By the time of his interview with Dickey, Ambassador Hinton had become more pessimistic about the resolution of the case of the four slain mission-aries, and he expressed his personal conviction that while he believed that the six guardsmen were guilty, he doubted that they would ever be convicted by a Salvadoran court.[31] On 26 August, Colonel García disclosed that the six were in custody and that no formal legal action had been initiated against them.[32] The defense minister failed to clarify why the men were still incarcerated if the evidence against them was so inconclusive. Perhaps there were fears about their safety or apprehension that they might implicate others—possibly their superiors—if they were brought to trial.

The case of the slain agricultural experts provides an interesting contrast. On 27 August, Judge José Albino Tinetti ordered the temporary release of Ricardo Sol Meza on the grounds of "inconsistent statements" made by Teresa de Jesús Torres López, a Sheraton Hotel waitress and the only witness for the prosecution.[33] Hans Christ was freed by a U.S. court in September after Judge Tinetti recommended that the Salvadoran government drop extradition proceedings against him. Sol Meza was freed definitively on 22 October.[34] U.S. diplomats familiar with the case had believed all along that Sol Meza and Christ had not fired the shots that killed the three men, but were convinced that they had assisted others who had been with them that evening in carrying out the assassination.[35]

There was at least one competing version. Leonel Gómez, an associate of the slain José Viera, believed that the army was responsible for the assassination and that the army targeted Viera not because of opposition to the agrarian reform project but because he and Viera had accused some army officers of corruption. According to Gómez, who had to leave the country after four assassination attempts on his own life, the FBI's involvement in the investigation was only a sop to American critics, since there was no way that its agents could find anything.[36] In either case, those responsible for the deaths of Mark Pearlman, David Hammer, and Viera apparently had no reason to fear indiscretions.

During his "unofficial trip" to the United States in September 1981, President Duarte was asked repeatedly about his government's record on the question of human rights. On 21 September, Duarte reportedly told Vice-President George Bush that his government had dismissed six hundred national guardsmen and imprisoned sixty-four for crimes against civilians.[37] On 22 September, during testimony before the House Foreign Affairs Committee, Congressman Mary Rose Oakar (D.-Ohio), a classmate of Sr. Dorothy Kazel, asked Duarte why nothing had happened in the case of the slain missionaries since April. Duarte responded that it was up to the families of the victims to press charges.[38]

In April, after much prodding by Senator Edward M. Kennedy (D.-Mass.), the families of the victims had been received at the Department of State by Deputy Assistant Secretary James Cheek. Following this meeting the families had been in contact with David Simcox, director of the department's task force on El Salvador, who had advised them to retain the services of the same Salvadoran lawyer who had taken up the case of Pearlman and Hammer. The lawyer would have charged them $500 an hour and had demanded $20,000 in advance.[39]

Following Duarte's testimony before the committee in September, Oakar arranged a meeting between him and the relatives of the slain missionaries. The meeting lasted two and a half hours, and although the families of the victims were impressed by Duarte's sincerity and would contrast Duarte's praise of the victims with the relatively cold treatment that they had received from the administration, they did not find out anything new. Duarte informed them that he had asked for more FBI assistance to crack the case, but that was all. Ambassador Hinton, also present at the meeting, had a heated exchange with Bill Ford, brother of Sr. Ita Ford, when Hinton suggested that the investigation should be limited to the six guardsmen, who, he said, had acted on their own.[40] Following the meeting, Ford, who had criticized Duarte's government for systematically murdering its own people, summarized the impression that the Salvadoran president had made on the families. Ford said, "I think it was clear to everybody that Duarte did not realize until this trip how serious this issue was in the eyes of the American people. . . . It was clear that he got no sense of that from the State Department."[41]

Duarte's hapless, if sincere, performance left Congress skeptical and his critics unmoved. Others saw him in a difficult predicament. Former ambassador White repeated his conviction that Duarte "stood for reform, for negotiation, and for an end to the savagery of the armed forces." According to White the policies of the Reagan administration reduced Duarte's influence to nothing, and there was little he could now do to restore the rule of law in El Salvador.[42] For columnist McGrory the still unsolved murder of the nuns perfectly made the point that Duarte was "in the hands of thugs."[43] Apparently, all Duarte could do was pass the buck on to the military.

On 10 November, during his "official visit" to Washington, Defense Minister Guillermo García met with Oakar and gave her a copy of the ninety-six-page summary of the investigation, as well as some materials explaining Salvadoran law.[44] On the same day back in El Salvador, Judge Mario Alberto Rivera was saying that the inquiry was at a dead end and that there was nothing more he could do in the case. President Duarte had repeated two days earlier that he had requested additional assistance from the Reagan administration to try to solve the case. A spokesman for the American embassy in San Salvador had countered that the United States was "pushing the [Duarte] government to continue the investigation."[45] The matter seemed to rest there.

To be sure, one can recite a litany of technical, cultural, and situational factors to explain the shortcomings of a judicial system that has all but broken down under the pressures of an ongoing civil war. Unembalmed bodies must be buried immediately, complicating the process of identification. There is no central agency that compiles records, making it more difficult to match descriptions of missing persons with remains found in shallow common graves or garbage dumps. It is difficult to find judges who are willing to imperil their lives by trying such cases; those who do receive little protection. The motives for some of the killings are personal rather than political; this complicates the problem of deciding which side, if either, is responsible for which killings. The state prosecutor general lacks investigative powers; those who have those powers, the military and the police, are not inclined to investigate anything.[46]

After all of these are taken into consideration the obvious question is Why has the Salvadoran government not taken any action to strengthen the judicial system? One possible answer is that the restoration of the rule of law has a very low priority for the government and, more specifically, for the military, which sees itself engaged in a "black conflict." Another is that many members of the Salvadoran military cannot afford such a restoration, because they might then be held accountable for their own abuses of authority. In any case, the present state of affairs is not conducive to the establishment of democracy, since a democratic regime, much less a government that claims to be working for the inauguration of a democratic regime and must convince the population that it is serious about this purpose and capable of bringing it about, cannot neglect this responsibility.

It is possible but doubtful that the six guardsmen involved in the murders of the nuns were acting alone. Since the 1970s the Salvadoran military—and its counterpart in Guatemala—has perceived foreign missionaries and priests as guerrilla collaborators. Some of the women were returning from Nicaragua, and hard-liners may have seen this as an opportunity to obtain information that would implicate perceived adversaries and demonstrate their participation in subversive activities. Such information could then be used to silence church criticism and justify a general crackdown against religious activists. This attempt to corroborate a long-standing assumption may have turned into a multiple slaying following unsuccessful attempts to extract the information through torture—a procedure permitted under Decree No. 507, which legalizes the use of torture to obtain confessions.[47]

All this is speculation or, at best, a working hypothesis. The feeble actions taken in the case, however, suggest that the Salvadoran military is above the law. This may explain why by November 1981 Judge Mario Alberto Rivera had interrogated no military personnel about the murders, not even the six guardsmen.[48] Yet military witnesses saw the guardsmen getting into the van with the women at the airport.[49] At one point, President Duarte announced that the fingerprints of about twenty persons from the national guard and the Treasury Police were found in areas relevant to the case and in the women's burned-out van.[50] According to FBI reports the forensic evidence was inconclusive, but strong enough to narrow down the list of initial suspects from twenty to six.[51] The Reagan administration believed that the identity of the killers had been established.[52] Although this evidence was insufficient for conviction, it seemed promising enough to justify continuing the investigation. Yet Navy Commander Colonel Roberto Monterrosa and his four-man commission refused to continue the inquiry, and it was all but dead by November 1981.[53]

A key ingredient in the process of a transition to democracy is the ability of the group or coalition in favor of a democratic outcome to overcome the resistance of obstructionists. Of course the Reagan administration did not create the present Salvadoran crisis; nor did it invent violence in El Salvador. Moreover, the administration's policies in the area of human rights are a reflection of complex ideological and political motives and do not necessarily imply that its architects condone human rights abuses. But the case of the slain Americans gave the administration an opportunity to support Duarte in a necessary and inevitable confrontation with Salvadoran obstructionists.

In May 1981 one of the journalists covering the case of the four slain missionaries wrote, "Solving the murder of the missionaries has become an important test in U.S. public opinion about whether the administration can make good its promise to push the junta toward internal reform."[54] It was apparent that by December 1981 the administration had failed that test and, perhaps more importantly, was missing a key opportunity to make a major contribution to the resolution of the Salvadoran civil war. Instead, the administration remained at a loss as to how to cope with a "cycle of violence and counter-violence that could only be broken when a democratic solution thwarts those who seek a solution by killing."[55]

Democratic solutions, after all, do not come without effort. They must be forged. In El Salvador, a country faced with the prospect of a long civil war, saddled with a deteriorating economy, and governed in part by a moderate faction desperate for support on key issues, the prosecution of those responsible for these murders would mark an important change of direction. Instead, the moderate *aperturistas* in the government could only look to a forthcoming election for some kind of respite, while its nominal allies, the military, seemed bent on producing a military victory and continued to overlook the question of the restoration of rights. At a time when the reforms had slowed to a trickle, when the Right had returned to the offensive, and when the moderates could have used all the help they could have gotten, the administration continued to view the guerrillas as the main threat and to use geopolitical criteria to evaluate its policy options. Meanwhile, the military continued its campaign to crush the very groups whose support would be crucial to the resolution of the conflict through a political settlement that included open elections.

But columnist McGrory's timing was off. The perfect proof that the hands of the moderate civilians were tied had come before, when Attorney General Mario Zamora was able to do little to clarify the situation of the disappeared in late 1979, when Zamora was murdered in February 1980, when Archbishop Romero was killed in March of 1980, and when nothing, absolutely nothing, had happened to those responsible for these murders. Duarte's inability to deal with political murders meant that he was not any closer to thwarting the obstructionists in December 1981 than he had been when he assumed office in December 1980. The Reagan administration's inability or unwillingness to help Duarte find the opportunity as well as the means to cope with this problem implied that it was not any closer to understanding the Salvadoran crisis in December 1981 than the Carter administration had been in December 1980, or in October 1979.

The man perceived to be in the hands of thugs and the administration that kept him in power had made little progress in a key area of the Salvadoran process of transition. Despite their protestations to the contrary, neither seemed willing or able to restrain the Salvadoran armed forces. To make matters worse, the Reagan administration's preoccupation with the military aspect of the crisis and its ramifications for U.S. security made the Salvadoran military confident that it was indispensable to the ending of a civil war which they had helped start.

A Salvadoran Horror Story

The sensational details of the killings of the six North Americans may distract attention from two important facts. The first is that the overwhelming majority of the victims of the political violence have been Salvadoran citizens. The second is that most of them have been killed by the armed forces.

Regardless of which set of figures one chooses, the official figures used by American embassy staff to compile their weekly death toll report or those released on monthly and quarterly bases by the Legal Aid Office of the Archbishop (Socorro Jurídico), one can see that the human cost of the Salvadoran civil war has been mounting rapidly. Table 7-1 offers an abridged summary of the periodic data provided by Socorro Jurídico, with some indication of the largest categories of persons affected by government violence. The breakdowns presented in the table show that the principal targets of government violence are those sectors of the population suspected of sympathizing or collaborating with the guerrillas: students, teachers, clerical workers, and residents of rural areas where the fighting was concentrated during 1980–81. In addition, it seems safe to assume that many of those listed as of "unknown" occupation are part of the vast army of unemployed and underemployed which was already large in the 1970s but has now swollen considerably as a consequence of the civil war and its attendant economic crisis.

The data presented in Table 7-1 suggest that although murders committed in urban areas have attracted more attention, a large proportion of the victims have been country dwellers. After all, El Salvador is still a predominantly rural society, and the level of violence has been higher in the countryside.

Table 7-1 does not include figures on killings attributed to the guerrillas, who obviously have done some of the killing.[56] Archbishop Arturo Rivera y Damas chided the staff of the Socorro Jurídico, his own agency, for not including victims of leftist violence in their release "The Statistical Balance of the Repression." The archbishop and most knowledgeable observers, however, support the accuracy of the figures published in the report.

In a war with few prisoners each side's ability to inflict casualties on the other depends not so much on weaponry but on the frequency of engagements with the enemy, the size of the territory under one's control, and each side's definition of "enemy" itself. The guerrillas confront the army only sporadically, they control small chunks of isolated areas, and they are relatively few; yet the number of casualties in the countryside remains high. One reason for this is that guerrilla columns have become more numerous and widespread in the last year. A more important reason, however, is that the army pursues anything resembling a guerrilla, and government forces and paramilitary elements treat guerrilla sympathizers as combatants. By contrast, the guerrillas attack anyone in uniform, government officials, trade union leaders, members of ORDEN—which, although "illegal," continues to operate freely—the wealthy, and the prominent.[57]

Although estimates are hard to come by and somewhat unreliable, most impartial observers agree that in those cases in which it is possible to impute responsibility, 80 to 90 percent of the victims were killed by the armed forces or paramilitary groups. In late 1981, Colonel García estimated that 30,000 had been killed since the October coup, 24,700 of whom—according to García—had nothing to do with the conflict.

Before the Salvadoran civil war erupted in full, every small town and village in El Salvador had been activated politically, especially in the departments of Chalatenango, Morazán, and Cabañas. This was a tense situation in which the local *comandantes* or the *jefes civiles* remained close to the landowning element, the national guard garrison, and the paramilitary groups. Christian Democrats and their allies remained in contact with their leaders in San Salvador, reporting to Duarte and Morales Ehrlich if trouble erupted. Opposition elements remained visible, supported by the local chapters of the popular organizations which, in some instances, could depend on the guerrillas operating in the area to retaliate against any attack. The tension was compounded by competition between different unions trying to enlist peasants and agricultural workers. A precarious equilibrium reigned in which murders and violence were limited because the conflict, although intense, was not polarized between just two sides and no one group could dominate the rest. This schema is fairly representative of circumstances in the countryside in early 1980, but it did not last long. After the enactment of the agrarian reform statutes, in March 1980, the situation deteriorated rapidly.

One target of violence orchestrated by factions included in the government was precisely those who were to benefit from the reform. Members of the national guard, who had always received a salary supplement from local landowners and who naturally sided with them in any dispute, began to sabotage the reforms. In a series of actions so similar as to suggest a pattern, national guard elements appeared in the cooperatives organized in the largest farms, which were included in Phase I of the Agrarian Reform, and assassinated leaders of the cooperatives, as well as any ISTA officials found on the premises.

The role played by the UCS in this conflict is illustrative of the kind of complexity that one finds in the present Salvadoran situation, a complexity that can in no way be used to hide the shortcomings of the Duarte government or to suggest that the situation is beyond comprehension and rectification. The UCS had been created under the auspices of the AIFLD, an organization supported by the AFL-CIO and distrusted by many labor federations in Latin America for its anti-Communist biases and its tame trade unionism, which did not challenge the oppressor.[58] The UCS had always been viewed as too close to the government and too cooperative with the oligarchy in El Salvador. By the time of the enactment of the agrarian statutes in 1980, however, the UCS was a more militant union, and the Christian Democrats and the military moderates like Colonel Majano wanted to use it to create political support in the countryside. The military had been able to mobilize the peasantry before, as during the abortive reforms of 1976, but the PDC had always been relatively weak in the countryside. UCS leaders like José Rodolfo Viera, who at the time of his assassination had become president of the ISTA, wanted to take advantage of this new opportunity to redress long-standing grievances.

The UCS, the ISTA, and anyone associated with them became targets of rightist violence. On 5 June 1980 representatives of eight UCS departmental executive councils protested to the government demanding an end to the violence and better protection for their affiliates.[59] By November 1980, Viera could charge that 80 percent of the murders in the countryside could be attributed to the Right and that violence against the cooperatives was increasing. For Viera the level of violence in any given area was directly related to the attitudes of local military commanders toward the reforms and whether or not farms supposed to be included in Phase I had been turned into cooperatives. At the time he was murdered, Viera was pressing for implementation of Phase 2 of the Agrarian Reform, which would have affected the medium-sized farms.[60] Viera believed that implementation of Phase 2 would bring three other peasant unions over to the government's side, thereby widening its base of popular support.

Violence against the cooperatives did not abate during 1981, however, even though Alejandro Duarte, the president's son and himself the target of several assassination attempts, was in charge of a task force monitoring the situation and reporting directly to his father. On 25 February 1981, during testimony before the Foreign Operations Subcommittee of the House Appropriations Committee, AIFLD executive director William C. Doherty, Jr., claimed that, according to ISTA reports, 133 of the 184 assassinations perpetrated against land reform beneficiaries and ISTA officials could be attributed to the security forces or to elements associated with them.[61]

Written testimony submitted by the United States section of Amnesty International to the Senate Foreign Relations Committee painted a broader picture. "Amnesty International has asserted that a campaign of murder and abduction has been launched against peasants in El Salvador. The announcement of the agrarian reform program was coupled with the arrival of troops [operating in open coordination with the paramilitary group ORDEN], ostensibly to carry out agrarian reform programs. These operations have resulted in the abduction and murder of hundreds of men, women, and children, the razing of villages and the destruction of crops in the Departments of Suchitoto, Morazán, Cuscatlán, and Chalatenango."[62]

By early August 1981 Salvadoran government officials were labeling the reform program a political success, but it was only a modest one, since only 386,010 persons had benefited from the program, which had left 85 percent of the coffee, 75 percent of the cotton, and 60 percent of the sugarcane grown in El Salvador in relatively few, private hands.[63] Deeds and, more important, credit had been slow in coming to the cooperatives,[64] and the Reagan administration had come out squarely against the implementation of any aspect of Phase 2.[65] In early August, during a ceremony conferring deeds to a series of beneficiaries, Agriculture minister and junta member José Antonio Morales Ehrlich vowed that "the process will never retreat."[66] The limited political success afforded by the reforms had come at a very high price, however.

If peasants with relatively good connections with the moderates in the government paid a high price for the limited benefits afforded to them, members of other peasant organizations felt the full rage of the Right. Identified from the outset as "subversives," sympathizers and members of the UTC, FECCAS, and similar peasant organizations had to run for their lives once the state of siege was declared. Many towns were deserted, as the population of some villages simply disappeared into the countryside.

In mid-1980, journalist Richard Alan White visited the Arcatao Valley in Chalatenango. He found that all but about a dozen of the four hundred families residing in the town of Arcatao had fled; trying to locate the guerrillas, estimated by the local national guard commander at about one thousand, White and his companions found a few adolescents with small arms and shotguns and hundreds of malnourished and ill peasants—a few heads of household, old people, and, mostly, women and children. The majority had left the town months before to escape from the national guard and ORDEN. They lived under the constant threat of attack by the Salvadoran army and, as they were close to the border with Honduras, under constant harassment by the Honduran army. Their only protection came from guerrillas—some of whom were probably their missing male relatives—who dominated the Arcatao Valley. White found a similar situation in the Torola Valley, in Morazán, where government forces had retreated into the town of Perquín.[67]

New York Times correspondent Raymond Bonner found similar conditions in the department of Suchitoto, which he visited in July 1981. Bonner observed army units moving refugees out of the camp of La Bermuda into the town of Suchitoto, where the popular organizations had been strong in previous years. The department itself was one of those in which the guerrillas of the FMLN were strong, and much of the countryside was a no-man's-land. Some of the refugees being moved reported instances of army units coming into their camp in April and May and leading people away to be shot.[68] In a follow-up story, Bonner reported that the two thousand or so refugees in La Bermuda had been scattered around several locations, including an old penitentiary at Suchitoto, with little regard for keeping families together.[69] In a foray into the countryside, Bonner found poorly armed peasant guerrillas, who claimed to be in control of the area.[70]

Whether the manner in which the Salvadoran armed forces were pursuing the guerrillas resembled methods employed, unsuccessfully, by the United States in Vietnam is a question that can be argued. But it is clear that the army's first priority was to deny potential resources to the guerrillas, including seeds, animals, crops, and likely recruits, and that it paid little if any attention to winning the support of the peasantry. To make matters worse, some Department of State officials insisted on accusing some of the relief organizations, primarily Oxfam, CEDEN (Evangelical Committee of National Defense), and Caritas, of helping the guerrillas. This had the obvious impact of making the military even more careless and cruel in its treatment of the refugees. Oxfam representative Lawrence Simon complained that accusations like these had the effect of signing someone's death warrant in El Salvador.[71]

Perhaps those in the camps were lucky, if one compares them to the hundreds of thousands who were drifting inside El Salvador. In August 1981 the regional office of the U.N. High Commission on Refugees reported that about 300,000 Salvadorans, almost the same number as that which the government claimed had received benefits under its program of agrarian reform, had fled the country, while an additional 180,000 had been uprooted from their homes but were still in the country.[72] Of this total, some 140,000 had registered with the government, but about 42,000 had not, perhaps for fear of the government itself.[73] According to a U.S. AID official with the American embassy in San

Salvador, the highest concentration of refugees was in the departments of Chalatenango, Morazán, and Cabañas,[74] precisely the areas where the popular organizations had been strong, where the guerrillas were more active, controlling a corridor along the border with Honduras, and where the army viewed most refugees with extreme suspicion.

These were also the areas where the army and the guerrillas fought pitched battles for control of strategically situated towns and armed forces sweeps through the countryside resulted in a high number of peasant casualties. During 1981 the towns of Arcatao (in January and June), Perquín (in August and November), El Rosario (April), San Francisco Gotera (January), and San Agustín (October) were occupied by guerrillas, who dug in and stood their ground against the army for several days. The army was forced to commit between 1,500 and 3,000 troops to retake each of these towns. Since, in many cases, government troops are conscripts in their teens, who have only minimal training and who shoot at anything that moves, innocent civilians were shot by accident. Others were killed in aerial attacks and by artillery fire.

Army sweeps along the border with Honduras became possible after the normalization of relations with Honduras on 10 December 1980. Several instances of Salvadoran troops crossing into Honduras have been reported, including one operation against the village of Los Filos in which the army airlifted units into Honduras.[75] These sweeps, including a major one in October 1981 in the area around San Agustín on the Lempa River, are conducted by units trained by U.S. advisers, including the elite Atlacatl Brigade, which are supposed to be more "professional."[76] Reports from peasants, however, claimed that the brigade was using search-and-destroy and scorched-earth tactics.[77] According to Robert S. Leiken, a fellow and director of the Soviet–Latin America project at the Georgetown Center for Strategic and International Studies, military atrocities continued during operations in the countryside. Leiken believed that, if anything, the behavior of army units had gotten worse; decapitations and mutilations had become more frequent. Leiken's testimony was congruent with the view expressed by diplomatic sources in San Salvador that the brutality and incompetence of the army were alienating the civilian population.[78]

Whatever excuses may be offered for the army's treatment of civilians in battle zones, no reason can be offered for the well-documented instances of cold-blooded murders of refugees.[79] The Reagan administration failed publicly to condemn these atrocities and belittled reports of continued killings of civilians. Yet, conclusive proof that these reports were no exaggeration, nor the result of Marxist misinformation, came on 16 November 1981 when a group of international observers visiting the La Virtud refugee camp inside Honduras witnessed and were able to prevent an attempt by Salvadoran troops and ORDEN elements to execute a number of refugees whom they were leading away from the camp.[80]

The analogy with Vietnam and the ultimate wisdom of counterinsurgency are still impassioned themes for Americans. One American fantasy embodies the determination to stand up to what some perceive as Communist aggression. Another doubts whether the United States can or indeed should play any constructive role in the Third World. In either case, it is unjust to sacrifice the Salvadorans—either to another reactionary dictatorship or to a revolutionary government controlled by one hegemonic faction—to prove a point about American foreign policy. Those who claim that these are the only realistic choices for the Salvadorans are making two different versions of the same racist, patronizing, and imperialist argument, even if they seek to justify actions as different as military escalation or complete withdrawal by the United States.

Not all Third World conflicts are alike, and they should not be forced into the mold of one, and only one, specific instance—in this case, Vietnam. Of course for United States citizens the Vietnam experience is the best reference point. In El Salvador, however, it would take considerably less effort from the United States to produce a catastrophic outcome. There failures of omission can be as important as failures of commission. The United States has done much to complicate things by failing to help carry out more resolute action against obstructionist actors on the Right and by failing to insist on the need to give top priority to a restoration of the rule of law.

A resolution of the Salvadoran conflict, however, ultimately depends not on United States actions but on the actions of the Salvadorans themselves. This is an inference from recent history, which demonstrates that even superpowers lack the ability to control major historical processes for long periods of time, short of extreme measures such as genocide, which, needless to say, the American public will not tolerate. Congressional opposition is another structural constraint that would prevent a major escalation, while the guerrillas have shown that they can survive even a fairly efficient use of the resources available to the Salvadoran military by late 1981. Yet complete withdrawal by the United States would not necessarily result in a victory for the Left, since the Salvadoran oligarchy and its rightist associates have shown that they are capable of mounting a determined and ruthless onslaught against democratization, and they can summon large numbers of people to their cause, including those landowners not yet affected by Phase 2.

Yet counterinsurgency and repressive reformism as a solution for El Salvador must be questioned. What is the sum of reform plus genocide? What determined whether, by December of 1981, a family of Salvadoran peasants had been incorporated into one of the new agricultural cooperatives or dismembered, disemboweled, and scattered over the landscape? Was this really the solution to one hundred years of oligarchic exploitation? Under what kind of criteria could anyone believe that a great deal had been accomplished? Was this not a perverse continuation of the schizophrenic language of Salvadoran politics? Did this mean that anyone whom the cooperatives could not accommodate or whom the strategic hamlets could not shelter was to be considered the enemy?

What the Carter administration would have done in this situation will remain a matter of speculation, but, without a doubt, this process began to unfold during the Carter period. What is not pure speculation is that the Reagan administration did not help the situation by insisting that the military aspect of the crisis be given more attention and that the government abandon Phase 2 and try to reconcile itself with the private sector. This only made the government more suspect, even in the eyes of those who had benefited from the reform, and tended to confirm the suspicions of the opposition. In March 1981, former ambassador White predicted that the only way the Left could gain strength in El Salvador was for the government to move substantially to the Right.[81] This is precisely what the Reagan administration wanted to accomplish.

The Private Sector and the Salvadoran Transition

Seldom has a United States diplomatic mission made strenuous efforts to bring together two actors as dissimilar as the Christian Democrats and the organizations of the Salvadoran private sector. The irony is that if similar efforts had been made to bring together the Christian Democrats and the Social Democrats and the Communists in the FDR, the Salvadoran process of transition would have turned out quite differently. Instead the United States sought to ridicule, discredit, and minimize the significance of the FDR.[82]

The behavior of the leaders of private sector organizations suggested that there was really only one *political* faction within the Salvadoran private sector. The different organizations representing sectoral interests of the Salvadoran bourgeoisie certainly behaved as one when political questions were raised. One element which may have contributed to their cohesiveness during this period of time was that they shared an unmitigated, undiluted hatred of José Napoleón Duarte. Small wonder that efforts to bring the PDC and the private sector together produced, in their most successful instance, a shotgun wedding and, in most other cases, open warfare. The former came during the abortive general strike of August 1980, in which representatives of the private sector, the military, and the PDC came together to coordinate a common strategy to defeat the FDR strike.

Since Mario Antonio Andino resigned from the first junta, and since a number of conservative figures associated with private sector interests were not reinstated in their positions following the massive exodus of senior officials in December 1979, the Salvadoran bourgeoisie had been chafing under what it considered a "lack of representation" in the government. The Christian Democrats' reply was that the presence of the private sector within the first government formed after the October 1979 coup was divisive and allowed the bourgeoisie to sabotage the program of reforms from within. Since the bourgeoisie's attitude toward such reforms—it considered them demagogic, unrealistic, and communistic—remained unaltered, reform-minded government officials preferred to keep it at arm's length, where it could not so easily undermine plans for reform.

These private sector organizations representing the bourgeoisie were not those of the lunatic fringe that dared publicly to throw their support behind Roberto D'Aubuisson, as did the FAN and the FARO. Nor were they dominated by the oligarchic element that financed death squads from Miami or Guatemala City. Instead, these organizations represented the interests of the business community of El Salvador, which, although not actively linked to the disloyal Right, refused to come to terms with the new reality after October 1979. Despite their protestations of support for progress, their attitude became more intransigent. They demanded that the government change its economic policies, accused the government of plunging the country into economic chaos, and then demanded that the Christian Democrats abandon the government altogether. What they hoped to accomplish all along was to persuade the military to get rid of the Christian Democrats and to roll back the "unrealistic reforms." Instead of forming a coalition with the Christian Democrats they harbored the not-so-secret hope of taking their place in a new coalition with the military. The emergence of such a coalition could restore a system of reactionary despotism to El Salvador.

The Alianza Productiva (AP) emerged during the turbulent month of May 1980. The AP included the ANEP, the Chamber of Commerce and Industry, the Salvadoran Industrialists' Association (ASI), the National Federation of Small Enterprises (FENAPES), the Society of Salvadoran Merchants and Industrialists, the Federation of Professional Associations (FEPRO), the Union of Salvadoran Entrepreneurial Leaders (UDES), and the Coordinating Council for Agricultural and Livestock Enterprises (CCEA). The emergence of the AP could have meant a rejuvenation of the ANEP and could have marked an important shift in the role and political attitudes of Salvadoran private enterprise. But this was not to be the case.

In November 1980 an AP delegation went to Washington to confer with members of the Reagan transition team in order to test the waters and gauge the kind of support that the new administration would give to the Christian Democrats.[83] By March 1981, once it was apparent that Duarte had survived the Reagan transition and would remain in power for some time, the AP had begun to criticize the economic policies of the government. On that occasion the AP opposed retroactive increases in export taxes and expressed concern about the disappearance of credit sources and business failures.[84] The AP maintained the old intransigence of the oligarchy toward labor. For example, the ASI greeted some of the labor reforms introduced by the government in May 1981 with the criticism that they would generate conflicts at the wrong time.[85] In early May former ANEP official and new Salvadoran ambassador to the United States Ernesto Rivas went further, telling a press luncheon at IMF headquarters in Washington that the elections should be postponed.[86]

To be sure, the economic situation was extremely difficult. The year 1980 saw a decline in the GDP of 9.5 percent, mainly because of disinvestment. Agricultural production went down by 7 percent, while construction and trade decreased by 17.5 percent and 12.1 percent, respectively. A total of 113 companies closed down.[87] This bleak picture was not solely owing to government incompetence; nor was it—by May 1981—only a result of the civil war. Coffee had been hit by bad weather and soft export prices; cotton had become a victim of the international credit squeeze, not the guerrillas. The 1980–81 production of 199,226 bales was harvested on the lowest acreage planted in twenty years. Sugar growers had to put up with some sabotage, but they increased production from 3.4 million quintals for 1979–80 to 3.9 million quintals in 1980–81. Their main source of irritation was that INAZUCAR, the state marketing company, would not grant credit without collateral and that it demanded the right, once a loan had been granted, to step in and appropriate the harvest if it judged that mismanagement threatened its investment.[88]

The government was trying to get international credit as best it could. The United States promised $126.5 million in economic aid for calendar year 1981, including $44.9 million earmarked for the private sector.[89] Other sources of credit, however, were hesitant because of the human rights record of the government. West Germany, Denmark, Canada, and Mexico had blocked IDB credit to El Salvador in 1980 and were questioning the government's request for the initial $120 million installment of a three-year package of $360 million.[90] By September 1981 the IMF had not made a decision on this request, which had been pending since October 1980.[91]

The military remained relatively quiet during most of these wars of words between the PDC and the AP organizations. One consequence of the reforms had been to increase the fiscal base of the state, as well as to make it less dependent on the private sector. This suited the military fine, since it evened the score for the humiliation it had received from the failure of the ISTA in 1976. On the other hand, it remained relatively unenthusiastic about Phase 2 of the Agrarian Reform and about any measure that could be viewed as an attempt to pacify labor. In June, when Economy and Foreign Trade Minister

Guillermo Salazar Díaz, a political independent, made the suggestion that the wage freeze could be lifted soon, military leaders took exception. Defense Minister Guillermo García expressed the opinion that "people cannot be offered something they won't get," while Commander in Chief Jaime Abdul Gutiérrez called the Díaz proposal "a grave threat to the nation."[92] The minister left the country immediately.

Perhaps encouraged by this turn of events, the AP increased the level and frequency of its criticisms. The ASI seconded the pronouncements made by Manuel Enrique Hinds, former minister of economics under the first junta, suggesting that the Duarte government was based on "participatory democracy, which at bottom is a socialistic, coercive, and collectivist system."[93] This contrasted with a statement made in March by outgoing ASI president Eduardo Menéndez that the ASI stood for representative democracy and individual freedom and for the diffusion of private capital through productive labor.[94] Hinds, for his part, told a gathering of six hundred cheering Salvadoran businessmen that they were faced with two choices: communitarianism or communism. Behind communitarianism, he continued, there was "a steely dictatorship only comparable to Marxist tyranny."[95] Before his return to San Salvador for this engagement and for other activities on behalf of the AP, Hinds had disclosed in Washington, D.C., his new place of residence, that the private sector had declared war on the Duarte government and that it would not cease until it fell. Opposition to economic policy had turned into a political campaign against the very existence of the government.

The methods and the language utilized by the AP did not differ very much in style and substance from those utilized by the ANEP and the FARO in 1976 against the ISTA. This suggests that even though some of the businessmen who had stayed in El Salvador no longer viewed the oligarchic group outside the country as their natural leaders—as one businessman told *New York Times* correspondent Warren Hoge, "Those people in Miami must realize that they can't return as people with any position in society"[96]—they themselves did not know any better. In other words, they were as consevative and as opposed to the reform of Salvadoran capitalism as was the more recalcitrant element of the traditional oligarchy, who had, for the most part, left the country. On the other hand, by July 1981 knowledgeable observers in San Salvador were remarking on the high number of millionaires who had returned to the country recently, encouraged because they believed that the Reagan administration was pushing the Duarte government toward a more conservative position.[97]

The ANEP's executive director, Juan Sandoval, was more explicit in his own contribution to the ongoing campaign, stating that the private sector did not support what the Christian Democrats were doing in El Salvador.[98] The CCEA also joined in the chorus, issuing a declaration which blamed "the so-called structural reforms" and "the struggle for power on the left between the

PDC and the FDR" for the chaotic economic situation of the country.[99] On the day of the CCEA declaration, 30 June, the Independent Cotton Growers Front urged repeal "of the so-called land to the tiller law," demanding that all cotton lands be exempt from the act and arguing that many growers were not planting any cotton for fear that they would lose the land before harvest.[100]

On 1 July relatively few people were surprised when President Duarte accused the private sector of being his principal enemy. With language reminiscent of that used by Colonel Majano the previous December, Duarte said, "The private sector is in its final offensive to overthrow the government. The politicians of the private sector . . . want to take away all the economic reforms."[101] Duarte announced that titles would continue to be awarded in accordance with the law, but he extended the wage freeze and the accompanying freeze on certain staples, professional fees and health care services, school tuition, and rents.[102] Apparently, Duarte decided to abandon all plans for the implementation of Phase 2. This, together with the treatment received by departed minister Salazar Díaz and Duarte's failure to come out in Salazar's defense, was said to have angered Agriculture Minister Morales Ehrlich, who had put his personal prestige and more on the line to see the reforms through, and Foreign Minister Chávez Mena, a man respected in progressive Salvadoran circles, to the point of resigning.[103]

Watching this sequence of events, former ambassador Robert White scolded the Reagan administration once again for undercutting Duarte and for contributing to a slow-motion coup unfolding in El Salvador.[104] A 16 July speech by Thomas O. Enders, assistant secretary of state for inter-American affairs, had been awaited with anticipation by Salvadoran observers, who were anxious to see which way the wind was really blowing from the Reagan administration. Enders's speech gave priority to a *political solution*, which he believed would have three essential components: "The first . . . is that promises must be kept. . . . Second, there must be demonstrable progress in controlling . . . violence from all sources. . . . Third, . . . all parties that renounce violence should be encouraged to participate in the design of new political institutions."[105]

Enders's speech, announced in advance as a clarification of administration policy in El Salvador, seemed to have messages for everyone, including, of course, rightist Salvadorans. Although it certainly projected the biases of the Reagan administration, the speech was so balanced that practically everyone except the guerrillas could find a positive signal in it. Perhaps the weakest point of the speech was the contradiction produced by couching the conviction that "only Salvadorans could resolve their divisions" within the caveat that "a political solution would not succeed unless the United States sustained its assistance to El Salvador."[106]

Never one to leave matters of interpretation to others, the Salvadoran bourgeoisie returned to the offensive. On 19 July, A P representative Juan Vicente Maldonado stated his view that the speech was proof that "the United States was no longer giving unconditional support to Duarte," adding that it appeared that the United States would not continue to aid Duarte unless he adopted a more conservative economic policy and incorporated a business-man in the junta. Maldonado claimed that the A P wanted to play a positive role in developing a free-market economy along the lines of the Milton Fried-man model.[107]

Maldonado did not bother to explain how Dr. Friedman's model could coexist with a government that called itself "revolutionary" and was trying to change the undesirable features of the capitalist system of El Salvador. He may have been aware that Ambassador Hinton was not unsympathetic to the idea of closer collaboration between the P DC and the A P. Of course Hinton was continuing an effort that had been going on for some time. How a stable and centrist coalition could result from Christian Democratic communitarian-ism and laissez-faire economics was yet to be determined. Maldonado and his associates, however, were primarily interested in getting someone from the A P into the junta.

Also on 19 July, Conrado López Abreu, president of the Salvadoran Cham-ber of Commerce, repeated a charge frequently made by the Salvadoran Left, namely, that the Duarte government stayed in power only because of the sup-port of the United States. López added that he and other representatives of the A P had discussed their drive to join the government with Hinton and that the ambassador had not rejected what they were trying to do.[108] Hinton acknowl-edged his role in the "big, delicate negotiations" that were going on, but he "refused to negotiate in the press."[109] Although Duarte denied that any nego-tiations were taking place, an unidentified cabinet minister admitted that the government was talking to businessmen, but not to those sharing the conser-vative views of Maldonado and López.[110]

On 22 July, Duarte accused business of trying to destabilize his government and of actively working to persuade the armed forces to oust him for his al-leged contribution to the economic chaos of the nation. "I want to stress," Duarte said, "that extreme rightist groups have infiltrated some groups and are bent on destabilizing the government."[111]

The expected changes in the junta did not take place. René Fortín Magaña, a member of the 1960 junta and former dean of the law school of the National University, did not join the junta as it had been rumored he would.[112] The government had hoped to incorporate F E N A P E S president Luis Mendoza, but apparently decided that there was no need to do so; or perhaps Mendoza did not want to take his organization out on a limb. Magaña's group, formed primarily by conservative professionals and businessmen, became a political party, the Acción Democrática (A D), shortly thereafter. Magaña denied that the A D was merely a front for landowners.

On 31 July, Ambassador Hinton was still trying to salvage the situation. During a speech to a lunch gathering of the American Chamber of Commerce of El Salvador, he urged the PDC and the A P to come together, since neither the Christian Democrats nor the private sector would survive a Marxist take-over. Hinton also used the opportunity to praise Duarte's record, defended the government's austere monetary and fiscal policies, and argued that the main problem with the economy was the shortfall in export earnings owing to soft demand in the world markets.[113]

The AP remained undaunted, denouncing government policies during a three-day symposium. It attacked policies that had affected the oligarchy, such as the nationalization of banks and the freeze on land titles, asked for a complete repeal of Phase 2 (still in the statute books), and demanded a revamp of coffee export taxes. On a more general level the symposium requested: (1) a one-year moratorium on debts, (2) more long-term loans at lower rates of interest, (3) cuts in public sector credit, (4) a program to channel loans directly to business, (5) suspension of prepayment for letters of credit, and (6) rapid payment of the 650 million colones (about $260 million) owed to agriculturalists affected by agrarian reform.[114]

In summary, the differences between the A P—which favored the rollback of all reforms and demanded immediate relief from the burdens imposed by a world economy in recession—and the communitarianism of the PDC could not be reconciled with ease. The A N E P wanted Duarte to adopt more conservative economic policies, but protested fiscal and monetary stringency. The A P wanted to make a "positive contribution" but with the theories of Milton Friedman. More than anything else, however, they wanted Duarte out.

It was probably during August that Duarte realized that he needed to have a talk with his supporters in Washington in order to explain his views and prevent any further erosion of his influence and the disintegration of his government. On 15 September, at a rally that drew a large and relatively enthusiastic crowd to the Flor Blanca Stadium in San Salvador, Duarte asked the Left to lay down its weapons and participate in the elections.[115] He was satisfied with the turnout, which he saw as an expression of support for his government, but others, accustomed to heaping praise on the military, saw things differently. Editorials in *El Diario de Hoy* stated:

> Our people wanted to make explicit . . . its profound appreciation for
> the heroism of the soldier and of all of those who, weapons in hand,
> reject aggression. . . . Until two years ago, our country allowed,
> no doubt to comply with the program of "human rights" imposed by

Carterism, bands of hoodlums to dedicate themselves to sowing disorder
and imposing terror on the citizens. . . . Our people has given a vote
of confidence and support to its armed forces, recognizing that the
military response is the only one that can return peace to all and
the appropriate climate to rebuild the nation.[116]

Shortly after President Duarte left for a visit to the United States, a familiar
character returned to the scene. During the weekend of 19 September, Major
Roberto D'Aubuisson visited newspapers in San Salvador to announce the formation of a new political party, the National Republican Alliance (ARENA).[117]
On 28 September, as hundreds of police and soldiers watched impassively, he
announced to a press conference in San Salvador that he planned to enter the
elections.[118] It was unclear why so many elements of the army and the police
were present, but, a few weeks later, during his official visit to Washington,
Defense Minister García explained to editors and reporters of the *Washington
Post* that D'Aubuisson had reentered the country under a preelection amnesty
and that there were no warrants for his arrest outstanding.[119] It all had a
familiar ring.

Taking a cue from the low-key reception given Duarte in Washington, the
AP continued its tough talk. On 8 October a spokesman for the Alianza
accused Duarte of preparing to open direct talks with the Left and called
Duarte a "little Caesar" intent on taking El Salvador toward totalitarianism.[120]
This was a challenge not only to the Christian Democrats but also to Com-
mander in Chief Gutiérrez and Armed Forces Chief of Staff Colonel Rafael
Flores Lima, who had expressed approval of leftist participation in the elec-
tions and had shown interest in opening up a political dialogue with the
Left.[121]

During October the Salvadoran Right changed its stance and began to talk
about participating in the constituent assembly elections, but only if all the
Christian Democrats were removed from the Central Electoral Council (CCE).
Four rightist parties made this demand, including the always pliable PCN, the
minuscule Partido Popular Salvadoreño (PPS), which missed its chance to
play a constructive role in a previous political era in El Salvador,[122] Fortín
Magaña's AD, which was wooing practically the same kinds of persons who
had earlier supported the PPS, and D'Aubuisson's ARENA. Chele Medrano's
Partido de Orientación Popular (POP), representing primarily those agricultural sectors not yet affected by agrarian reform, was the only one that did not
insist on this precondition for its participation.[123]

On 31 October the government legitimated what had been taking place for
weeks by lifting the ban on political parties, whose activities had been for-
bidden since the imposition of the state of siege in March 1980.[124] On 5
November, during a meeting of the Political Forum, a conference including

all six legal parties contesting the election, the Christian Democratic members of the CCE were ousted by a 4–2 vote.[125] Not content with this victory, spokesmen for the rightist parties said later that they would move to restructure the regime; to demand the replacement of the ministers of labor, education, and the interior and of the president of the ISTA; and to ask for the resignation of all mayors and departmental governors, many of whom were Christian Democrats.[126] The Christian Democrats reacted to these demands by calling the initiative a "paper coup."[127]

The Christian Democrats tried to put the best face on events. They hoped that the continued support of some key military figures, plus the Reagan administration's inability to move them much further to the right, would see them through the constituent assembly elections, set for 28 March 1982. Although the PDC leadership did not expect these elections to give it the ability to control the army—indeed, it could not realistically expect to capture the majority of the sixty seats up for grabs—it did hope to use the elections to build for the future "within the realm of the possible."[128]

Meanwhile, instead of warning the Salvadoran Right to behave itself—which he had failed to do a single time since coming to office—Secretary of State Haig continued to denounce Cuban interventionism, to ask the Pentagon to prepare contingency plans for any eventuality, and to threaten Nicaragua.[129] However, the other important foreign ally of the Christian Democrats—and perhaps the only true ally they had left—took exception to this and made a different pitch. On 19 November 1981, Venezuelan President Luis Herrera Campins, himself a Christian Democrat, told reporters in Washington that he had expressed his concern to the White House about the United States's neglect of the threat from the right in El Salvador.[130] Duarte received another boost on 8 December when the Organization of American States voted 22–3 to endorse a resolution approving of the Salvadoran elections.[131]

Trying to assuage his conservative critics, Duarte adopted some of the views of Secretary Haig and borrowed a page or two from the secretary's repertoire of tough anti-Communist rhetoric. In early October, Duarte recalled Salvadoran Chargé d'Affaires Joaquín Maza Martelli from Managua. On 9 October, in a speech to the American Chamber of Commerce of El Salvador, Duarte rejected a Nicaraguan offer of mediation.[132] A month later he sent a letter to the editor of the *Miami Herald* denouncing a "campaign of misinformation being orchestrated by Cuba and the Soviet Union to destabilize his government" and praised the Salvadoran armed forces for the "heroic battle" that they were waging.[133]

But the Salvadoran Right was unmoved. The Alianza Productiva boycotted the annual Miami Conference on the Caribbean, at which Duarte was a featured speaker. In an open letter to Florida Governor Robert Graham, published as a full-page advertisement in the *Miami Herald*, the Alianza claimed that Duarte "proposes to set up an economic system [that] will eliminate the private sector and free enterprise. . . . In accordance with the scheme outlined by Mr. Duarte, private ownership would practically disappear in El Salvador and be substituted by state ownership."[134] Duarte told the six hundred or so businessmen and government officials from the Caribbean area who attended the Miami Conference that he supported private enterprise, but he also treated them to a series of platitudes.[135] The AP's López Abreu, who was in Miami along with a host of Alianza representatives, claimed that his organization was seeking to elect a "centrist government" in the March elections.[136] Members of the Cuban Christian Democratic Movement in Exile chided the Alianza for "an attitude typical of the Salvadoran right wing" and blamed the latter for the country's political turmoil.[137]

On 6 December the ANEP and FENAPES issued a joint statement in El Salvador to complain about the lack of definition in the economic policies of the government: "The prospect that continues is one of total discouragement, of insecurity and foundering, with the only certainty being that, on the road on which the country is going, without much delay, our economy will be in complete bankruptcy, with the tremendous consequence that [this] holds for all Salvadorans."[138] What the statement did not mention, and what the Salvadoran bourgeoisie refused to admit, was that the political problems that accompanied the economic problems were very much the result of actions undertaken by a class that had failed to meet its historical responsibilities. Before, when they had dominated the private sector, the members of the traditional oligarchy had monopolized control of the ANEP and kept others at bay. Now, their ability to maintain their monopoly weakened, they sought, and got, the support of sectoral associations representing the interests of the bourgeoisie (AP) and the petite bourgeoisie (FENAPES). The deterioration of the economy was certainly squeezing the Salvadoran businessmen, but it appears that they had more in mind than access to government policy. What they ultimately wanted was nothing less than a preservation of authoritarian capitalism.

Perhaps the conservative Salvadoran businessmen knew something that the Carter and Reagan administrations did not want to acknowledge: historically, when the United States has been forced to choose between democracy and capitalism in Central America, it has always opted for the latter. Columnist Meg Greenfield characterized the not so difficult choice usually made in situations like that in El Salvador in the following:

> This country has developed a ritual for failing in our confrontations
> with Third World turmoil. . . . The basic formula . . . involves . . .
> a couple of competing analyses of the turmoil that are at odds over what

the cause of the trouble is, but as one in their unrealistic, oversimpli-
fied approach. . . . Still, the wishful thinking and fantasies of the
military-minded, anti-communist right strike me as being probably less
harmful to the possibility of doing things well in these turbulent places
than do the comparable fantasies of the romantic, reform-minded
left. That may be merely because I keep expecting more insight and
discrimination from this quarter—and God knows the crashed assumptions of the past ten years should have produced more of both.[139]

Inept as the two views may be, Greenfield's analysis cannot be extended to
the Salvadorans themselves. As the foregoing pages have shown, it is difficult
to imagine that Salvadoran rightists did "less harm" to the process of transition begun on 15 October 1979 than the supposed idols of "romantic reform-
minded leftists" would have done, had they been in power. Perhaps to Greenfield and other commentators all Third World conflicts look alike, but to
anyone interested in getting to the bottom of the Salvadoran conflict, facile
stereotypes do not suffice.

The fantasy in this case was not that of liberals concerned with human
rights but that of anyone who believed that a centrist coalition could be
formed in El Salvador with the participation of the oligarchy, that such a
formula could be sold as a "pluralist solution," and, most important of all,
that it would put the Salvadoran process back on course. And, in an election,
would the Salvadoran military, despite its promises of noninterference, not
revert to its customary tactics and engage in some "creative" accounting of
the vote? Finally, should an electoral fraud take place, would the United
States repeat the mistakes of 1972 and 1977 and remain aloof?

The elections could constitute a new beginning, insofar as they could
demonstrate popular support for the embattled moderates left in the government and offer an opportunity for that government, endorsed by a popular
consultation, to move forward to the inauguration of a democratic regime.
But just as a judicial restoration could not come about without a confrontation
with military hard-liners, an electoral resolution of the crisis could not come
without a confrontation with the Right and the private sector organizations.

In short, in supporting an electoral strategy for resolution of the Salvadoran
crisis the administration was joining a process in which, sooner or later, it
would have to support the moderates in one or more confrontations with the
obstructionists. Contrary to what Greenfield observed elsewhere in her column, this implied a very painful choice, especially since it meant that the
Reagan administration would have to confront Salvadoran reality with its own
American fantasies.

The Politics of Negotiation

The Frente Democrático Revolucionario (FDR) was created on 1 April 1980 by the Coordinadora Revolucionaria de Masas (CRM)—an alliance that included the FAPU, the LP-28, the UDN, and the Bloque Popular Revolucionario (BPR)[140]—plus the Movimiento Nacional Revolucionario (MNR), the Movimiento Popular Social Cristiano (MPSC), the Movimiento de Liberación Popular (MLP), and forty-nine labor unions, including the FSR, FENASTRAS, FUSS, FESTIAVTSCES, STISSS, and STIUSA.[141] Interest associations like MIPTES (professionals) and AGEUS (students), as well as the University of El Salvador, were also represented. In essence, the Frente is a broad coalition of petit bourgeois and working-class elements led by intellectuals, technocrats, and trade union activists.

In assessing the degree of support enjoyed by the Frente in El Salvador, FDR spokesmen and sympathizers naturally exaggerate its strength, while the Salvadoran government and its allies tend to underestimate it. The Frente suffered a serious setback with its unsuccessful attempt to organize a general strike in August 1980. FDR publications point out the lengths to which the government went to suppress the strike, although it is apparent that the call failed to produce the degree of support expected by the FDR.[142] Yet one can still take issue with Duarte's contention that the Frente can no longer mobilize thousands of demonstrators, for during most of 1981 El Salvador was under a state of siege, and during and after the state of siege anyone daring to march in the streets was literally taking his life in his hands. Whatever the numerical strength of the FDR, it represents a broad spectrum of opinion, as well as the legitimate interests of important sectors of Salvadoran society.

In its first public declaration, released on 18 April 1980, the FDR emphasized organizational and programmatic objectives. Furthermore, it denounced the repressive methods of the government, as well as the support of the United States and its military assistance, and defended the right of those sectors threatened with extinction by the ongoing repression to arm and defend themselves.[143] Shortly thereafter, FDR Secretary General Enrique Alvarez expressed the goals of his organization as follows: "to create and develop a national government that is both anti-oligarchic and anti-imperialist and whose policy is based on: the broadest pluralistic participation of the people in the management of the government, the strict respect of human rights, the right of self-determination, . . . a mixed economy which protects small and medium-sized businesses, [and] new regulations . . . concerning foreign investments which will take the national interest into account."[144]

The reformist tone of the declaration can be interpreted in several ways. Some would charge that it illustrates another instance of "useful fools" paving the way for Communists, disguised as "agrarian reformers," to come to power, but that is, stated simply in the Salvadoran vernacular, *una babosada* [nonsense].[145] Many of the organizations affiliated with the FDR maintained their separate programs and goals in their public pronouncements, and the differences between the more radical and the more moderate among these are there for anyone to see.[146]

The problem is, of course, Which of the programs would prevail? This would depend on how the Salvadoran civil war was resolved, whether by political or military means. In El Salvador, however, an antioligarchy orientation is not necessarily subversive, since there is ample evidence of the Salvadoran oligarchy's reluctance to operate under a democratic formula, even if the governments constituted under such a formula had purely reformist orientations. In short, the movement to democracy in El Salvador cannot incorporate the oligarchy in a transition government, although it can certainly incorporate businessmen who are willing to cooperate in a system that includes labor unions and more state regulation of the economy.

During 1980 the Carter administration practically ignored the FDR and hoped that the reforms implemented would steal the thunder from the FDR and undermine its constituency. As we have seen, however, those reforms were implemented only halfheartedly, and the disloyal Right managed to drive a wedge between the PDC and the FDR and to push the FDR further into the arms of the guerrillas. The architects of Carter's policy may have been trying to avoid further bloodshed by postponing the incorporation of the FDR into the political process, but the results were practically the same, since the Right made little distinction between the PDC and the FDR anyway. The Reagan administration's attempts to bring the Right and the PDC together did not get anywhere; if anything, they put the moderates in the government in a more exposed position.

To this writer the adoption of a moderate common platform by "subversive" organizations is not necessarily a conspiracy—as rightist or uninformed individuals may aver—but a result of the fact that the minimum common denominator among the participants in the FDR coalition is a peaceful and inclusive reformism, which appears "radical" in the Salvadoran context. In other words, the tactical alliance—others will insist it is a strategic alliance—bringing together the popular organizations, the guerrillas, and the moderate opposition forces was a matter of survival. The moderates could not afford to stand around and wait for a certain execution, while the guerrillas needed the degree of international support and legitimacy that the presence of the Social Democrats would bring to their political front. This is a fact that has been repeated on numerous occasions by FDR and guerrilla spokesmen. These statements tend to gloss over their differences, but they do confirm that their alliance is a pact for survival.[147] Whatever the nature of the relations between the FDR and the FMLN leadership, the former has maintained that it seeks a pluralist regime, unrestricted participation in the political process, respect for human rights, a nonrepressive army, a mixed economy, and nonalignment.[148] One difference between these goals and those of the moderates in Duarte's government is the ability and willingness of each to confront the obstructionists on these issues and to overcome their resistance.

The longer and bloodier the conflict, the more likely it is that the proponents of the *vía armada* will increase their strength and popularity and relegate the FDR to a secondary role. The corollary of this is that the sooner a political solution is achieved, with all the complications and increased tension that this would entail, the more likely it would be that no one group would be able to dominate. In summary, by late 1981 the alternatives remained a reincorporation of the FDR to consolidate the center or a prolongation of the civil war and a return to reactionary despotism.

The attitudes of the Carter and Reagan administrations toward the FDR have contained a perceptible element of scorn. Both had different motives for their attitudes, but they have been equally disconcerting to those who have offered themselves as mediators in the Salvadoran conflict. The Carter administration's constant reference to the FDR as an insignificant political force betrayed irritation with the Social Democrats and dissident Christian Democrats for having abandoned the first Junta Revolucionaria de Gobierno in December 1979, for successfully mobilizing opinion in Western Europe against United States intervention in El Salvador, for persuading Western European governments to adopt a more vocal and critical attitude toward United States policy in El Salvador, and for making common cause with Marxist-Leninist guerrillas.

The attitude of the Reagan administration toward the FDR seemed to be based on this last, that is, on the company that the FDR kept, as well as on the diplomatic successes that the FDR was able to score during 1981. The most important difference is that the Reagan administration identified the FDR as the enemy and tried to isolate it, discredit it, and ignore it, and, as a result, to make its position more precarious vis-à-vis the guerrillas. Apparently, senior American officials could not believe that the Social Democrats could be any more successful in controlling the guerrillas than the PDC had been in controlling the army. True as this conclusion may be, in the sense that "the guys with the guns" ultimately achieve control in revolutionary situations, the Reagan administration made a serious mistake in underestimating and trying to cut down the FDR. The administration claimed to be working to create political conditions that would reduce the level of violence in El Salvador. We have seen, however, how its approach to the conflict made the PDC very vulnerable. The same was true with respect to its approach to the FDR.

Any attempt to create a center in Salvadoran politics will have to include the FDR. This entails bringing the groups under the FDR umbrella back into the political process. This cannot come about without a restoration of the rule of law, which was, after all, the main reason for the breakdown of the first junta and the formation of the FDR, and this restoration cannot come about without a confrontation with the rightist element that has been obstructing the process of transition from its beginning. On the other hand, this restoration could be completed even if one or more of the guerrilla groups continued fighting. Under a rule of law the powers of the state could be used in a restrained and lawful manner to deal with problems requiring official action, including the neutralization of those who continue to try to destroy the regime.

Such a course runs counter to the best judgment of American officials, but failure to take this option entails grave risks as well. The continued exclusion of the Left and the creation of a "center" with a coalition that includes the organizations representing the political line of the oligarchy can only mean an escalation of the terrible human toll and, ultimately, the restoration of a regime of reactionary despotism. The United States, as an influential actor, must then accept its complicity in deepening a civil war and producing the outcome that its actions intended to prevent in the first place. Of course the United States did not invent violence in El Salvador, but its attempt to create a center out of obstructionist elements and its pretension that these elements will support "moderate reformism" is a diplomatic mistake and a misreading of Salvadoran history. Such an attempt does not serve either our interests or those of the Salvadorans; nor does it contribute to the democratic cause in Latin America and elsewhere.

When considering whether the PDC and the FDR could come to terms, it is important first of all not to underestimate the distance between these two groups. This distance was the result not only of differences in ideology and tactics between Social and Christian Democrats but also of the personal acrimony and distrust that had grown up between the two since the New Year's crisis of the first junta. Important figures had been killed, things had been said, each had taken actions to neutralize the other, and each believed that it was acting in the best interests of the country. In addition, each was outflanked by an armed associate. The Christian Democrats had to worry that the moment the army suspected them of negotiating over the future configuration of the Salvadoran armed forces, "none of them would be able to reach the border."[149] The FDR was at pains to state that their interest in negotiations could not come at the expense of their alliance with the guerrillas.[150] The proponents of violence on both sides, therefore, were increasing the distance between the PDC and the FDR: the military by not accepting a cease-fire and the guerrillas by their unwillingness or inability to lay down their weapons.

Second, let us not forget the degree to which the initial approach taken by the Reagan administration distracted attention from the real issues, and from the real obstacles to their solution. Having read the text and documents contained in the Special Report prepared by the Department of State, I have little to add to the criticisms made by Robert G. Kaiser of the *Washington Post*,[151] and Jonathan Kwitny of the *Wall Street Journal*.[152] Kwitny found at least thirteen flaws and inconsistencies in the report, while Kaiser, in an analysis that included additional documents that did not appear in the report, concluded that the picture was substantially different from that drawn by the administration. Clearly, the weapons came from many sources and dealers, including arms remaining from the Nicaraguan revolt that had been in Costa Rica, not Nicaragua. Of course the Cubans and the Nicaraguans would help in whatever way they could, but that help could not be termed decisive, as the Reagan administration had insisted. The full story of the flow of arms in Central America is much more complex than what has appeared in press reports or the administration has been willing to admit. But in the final analysis, although both Cuba and Nicaragua admitted that they had assisted the guerrillas—and where else could the guerrillas turn?—the administration failed to make a convincing case for its brief that the Salvadoran civil war was managed and sustained by outside forces.[153]

More relevant for the discussion here, Secretary of State Haig used the "Cuban connection" as a trump card during all of 1981, reacted to every success registered by the Salvadoran guerrillas with threats against Nicaragua, and seemed to favor a military solution to the crisis. Not only that but, given the extremity of some of Haig's pronouncements, others—including Duarte,[154] Colonel García, [155] the Pentagon,[156] and President Reagan[157]—had to take issue with him—and looked moderate by comparison. Perhaps, and there is some evidence to suggest that this was the case, at least during Reagan's first year in office, the secretary was playing a role assigned to or appropriated by him. This strategy did not legitimize the policy of the administration. If anything, performance of that role seemed to annoy many persons, including supporters as well as opponents of the policies of the administration toward El Salvador. These tough pronouncements gave certain encouragement to the Salvadoran rightists, confused the objectives of the administration's initiatives, and gave reason for alarm to many who were trying to move the Salvadoran process toward a peaceful resolution.

But despite the distance between the PDC and the FDR, and despite the "noise" coming from officials in the Reagan administration, there was some movement, especially toward the latter part of 1981. It appeared that third-party efforts to initiate a dialogue were beginning to pay off. The FDR acknowledged that it did not perceive all sectors of the government as incompatible with itself,[158] and the Christian Democrats and a few military officers realized the need to come to terms with the FDR. It is difficult to imagine why the PDC, supported by the United States and able to monopolize credit for reforms, would entertain negotiations with the FDR which put its delicate alliance with the military in jeopardy. The reason may be that the PDC itself was already in jeopardy.

It appeared possible that time was running out for the Christian Democrats. Their legitimacy could not be completely restored by an election held under uncertain conditions; nor was the future certain beyond that election of March 1982. Their ability to win a confrontation with the obstructionists in the armed forces and in the private sector was simply not there, assuming that it ever existed. Whatever victories they could claim against the Frente were Pyrrhic: they undercut a natural ally in the struggle against the obstructionists. Their program of reforms had become stalled and was in danger of being dismantled. The serious deterioration of the economy during 1980 and 1981 had the private sector on a war footing and made it increasingly unlikely that the state could come up with the funds to pay for and consolidate the operations of an additional number of agricultural cooperatives. Worse still, there was no quick fix for the economy.

Gains on the labor question and the whole issue of relations with labor, not to mention relations with the peasantry outside the reform program, posed a serious dilemma for the PDC. Most of the largest labor federations had not come to terms with the government by December 1981; industry was operating—when it did—at 50-percent capacity, and some of the largest employers were at war with the government.

Most important, the premise that the PDC had managed to create a center was very difficult to sustain. The party was not presiding over a popularly elected government that was simply exercising its legitimate right of self-defense against insurgency. The scope and nature of military operations suggested much more than that. A "government" party is, in the final analysis, responsible for the acts of that government, and the PDC's excuse that it was unable to control the security forces could not be offered indefinitely. The party had to stand on the entire record of the government, whether it liked it or not.

Basically, there had been two governments in El Salvador since 15 October 1979 and, despite the coincidence of their immediate objectives, they could not help but confront each other sooner or later. Even if everything went well, and the solution proffered by Duarte and endorsed by the Reagan administration was put in place, one government would eventually have to become dominant. The first government consisted of the network of civilian figures associated with Duarte. This government presided over civil society and managed the reform program, trying to do both as best it could, but its inability to return the state to a rule of law sent the reforms awry, brought its legitimacy into question, and made it an accomplice in many of the excesses perpetrated by the second government of El Salvador.

This second government monopolized the effective powers of the state, depriving the first of any claim to control over the affairs of the state, and emphasized the pacification of the country. Given the interpretation that the military managers of that government had of the transition—that it was essentially a "black conflict" requiring extreme solutions—the inevitable result has been a political regime that must be termed authoritarian. The members of that government, centered around Defense Minister Guillermo García and other military leaders, seemed most reluctant to abandon their counterinsurgency strategy against the guerrillas or to cooperate in any negotiations to redefine the role of the armed forces in Salvadoran politics.

This division of the Salvadoran state was basically unstable and could not be maintained indefinitely. The Christian Democrats were aware of that. The division had resulted from an attempt to embrace both the forces of transition and the forces of obstruction within a "pluralist" framework in order to ease tensions and avoid civil war. It did not work. Attempts to reequilibrate the process with a PDC–private sector coalition did not and cannot work. The FDR was well aware of that. The problem was whether the Reagan administration was aware of it.

If the United States is to derive a lesson from the Salvadoran experience, it should be that our best response to a process of transition is to adjust to the changing circumstances of that process and not to try to impose what appears to us to be *the one best and only imaginable solution*. If we have learned to live with dictatorship, we must learn to live with its aftermath. If we are content to let nature take its course and to allow the forces of history to work without interference under a dictatorship, why should we do otherwise when those forces bring about its downfall?

Democracy implies risks. In El Salvador the transition to democracy entails risks in the restoration of the rule of law, the neutralizing of the obstructionists, and the reincorporation of the Social Democrats, the popular organizations, and whatever extremist actors are willing to accept the norms of the democratic process and take their chances like everybody else. The United States can make a contribution if it is prepared to allow the Salvadorans to take their chances; otherwise, we should leave them alone.

The Guys with the Guns

Until early 1982 the media had failed to offer to the North American public an accurate and comprehensive description of the Salvadoran guerrillas based on direct observation. The guerrillas were scattered and isolated and did not appear to have much interest in showing their strengths and weaknesses to foreign correspondents. Estimates of their numbers varied. In February 1981, at the time that the Department of State released its Special Report, the Pentagon estimated their strength at about 3,700 full-time and 5,000 part-time combatants.[159] In March, Defense Minister García put their number at about 2,000 regulars. The conventional wisdom had it that neither side could defeat the other and that a military resolution to the conflict was not going to end the crisis in the near future.[160]

The greatest weakness of the guerrillas was their fragmentation, caused by personal rivalries among guerrilla leaders and differences over tactics and goals. The Fuerzas Populares de Liberación (FPL) emerged when Salvador Cayetano Carpio led a dissident faction out of the orthodox Communist party of El Salvador (PCS) in 1970. A split within the FPL itself—over the adequacy of Che Guevara's *foco* theory—led to another division and to the formation of the Ejército Revolucionario del Pueblo (ERP) in 1971. In turn, a dissident group left the ERP in 1975 following the assassination of its leader, poet Roque Dalton, at the hands of his own comrades, and formed the Fuerzas Armadas de Resistencia Nacional (FARN). A smaller and lesser-known group, the Partido Revolucionario de los Trabajadores Centroamericanos (PRTC), emerged in the mid-1970s, while the Fuerzas Armadas de Liberación (FAL) was created by the PCS after the collapse of the first junta and the incorporation of the party into the armed struggle against the government. In addition to periodic shortages of weapons and ammunition, the guerrillas suffered from poor communications between the different groups. Finally, there was disagreement about tactics: the FPL called for a prolonged popular insurrection, and the FARN favored an all-out insurrection.[161]

Apparently, the FPL, the FARN, and the FAL agreed on some form of collaboration in December 1979. A letter addressed to Fidel Castro and dated 16 December 1979 alludes to an agreement ratified by these three organizations.[162] The ERP remained aloof and did not join in the agreement. In May 1980, following the creation of the Frente Democrático Revolucionario (FDR), which had taken place the previous month, the ERP joined the FPL, the FARN, and the FAL to integrate a Dirección Revolucionaria Unificada (DRU).[163] The DRU helped coordinate the political initiatives of the guerrillas and ease their collaboration with the moderate leftists who controlled the FDR. Yet the DRU fell short of becoming the unified command that would provide better military coordination between the guerrillas. This did not emerge until the Frente Farabundo Martí de Liberación Nacional (FMLN) was created in late 1980, bringing together these four guerrilla groups and the PRTC.

In essence, the FDR is dominated by the Social and Christian Democrats and Marxist independents who abandoned the government in December 1979, while the FMLN is controlled by the Marxist-Leninist leadership of the guerrilla organizations. A seven-person political diplomatic commission links the two, with Mario Aguinada, second in command of the PCS, serving as liaison between the two coalitions. The MNR's Guillermo Ungo is the president of the commission and has served as its principal spokesman. Even though Ungo obviously has no control over the design and the execution of the military strategy of the DRU-FMLN, it is a mistake to consider him a mere figurehead. In addition, although the FMLN is beyond the effective control of the FDR, this does not mean that the latter is without resources of its own. Much of the prestige of the leftist opposition to the Salvadoran junta has resulted from the presence and efforts of Ungo and his closest associates. While a military victory by the guerrillas would leave the moderates of the FDR in a subordinate and dependent role, at the present time they are capable of taking a major role in a negotiated settlement. Figure 7-1 lists the leaders in this alliance between the FDR and the FMLN.

The nucleus of the DRU consists of the five commanders of the guerrilla organizations, assisted by Aguinada and "Ana María," who is Carpio's deputy in the FPL. Eight *comandantes* from the different groups make up the rest of this fifteen-member body. Some differences remain concerning the possibility of negotiations with the government. The FPL and the ERP are reported to be most distrustful of such efforts and would, therefore, tread a more careful path. The FARN was reportedly in contact with some military officers through its mass organization, the FAPU, which is the one that has acted with greatest independence vis-à-vis any guerrilla group. These contacts may have come to an end, however, with the departure of Colonel Majano. Despite the hoopla about Shafik Jorge Handal being a major figure among the guerrillas, the PCS lags behind the FPL, the ERP, and the FARN, since it joined the movement much later, and the strength of its own FAL is yet to be determined. Most observers agree that the FPL probably accounts for about 50 percent of the manpower of the guerrillas, while the FARN—as a result of a series of spectacular kidnappings—has the richest purse. By mid-1981 the guerrillas continued to have difficulty coordinating their actions, as most of the strength of the FPL was in Chalatenango Department, while that of the ERP—the second largest group—was concentrated in Morazán.

The perception of the military strength of the guerrillas changed considerably during the fall of 1981, as they were able to carry out a widespread campaign of sabotage against economic targets (this was treated as terrorism, but this writer reserves the use of that term to describe violent actions against people). The campaign culminated in the destruction of the Puente de Oro, a Pan American Highway bridge over the Lempa River, in October 1981. Apparently, field coordination was improving, and a joint FPL-ERP operation was established in Usulután Department. On 27 January 1982 the guerrillas scored a major psychological blow and an important military success with an attack on the Ilopango air base that destroyed a number of helicopters and jet

FIGURE 7-1
The Coalition between the FDR and the FMLN

Unified Revolutionary Directorate (DRU) (15 members)	Political-Diplomatic Commission (7 members)
Salvador Cayetano Carpio (FPL) Fermán Cienfuegos (FARN)[a] Joaquín Villalobos (ERP)[b] Shafik Jorge Handal (PCS/FAL) Roberto Roca (PRTC) Mario Aguinada (PCS) Ana María (FPL) Comandantes: Jonas, Leonel, Hugo, Venancio, Baltasar, Jacinto, Marko, and Alejandro.	Guillermo Manuel Ungo (MNR), president Mario Aguinada (PCS), coordinator Rubén Zamora (MPSC) Fabio Castillo (MLP) José Napoleón Rodríguez Ruiz (FAPU) Ana Guadalupe Martínez (LP-28) Salvador Samayoa (FPL)

Note: It is difficult to determine the role of the Coordinadora Revolucionaria de Masas (CRM) in this arrangement. Reagan administration sources claim that the DRU took over the functions of the CRM. If this was actually the case, then the CRM existed but for a few months and all the mass organizations are formally under the control of the commanders of the guerrilla groups with which they are affiliated. See Figures 3-2, 4-2, and 4-3 above, for more details about the membership, ideology, and organizational characteristics of most of the groups identified here.

a. Real name Eduardo Sancho.
b. Real name René Cruz.

fighters.[164] Coverage of these events and a new willingness on the part of the guerrillas to make themselves more accessible to representatives of the U.S. media resulted in a series of lengthy stories that provided a somewhat more accurate picture of the guerrilla movement.[165]

Evaluating these accounts, one can contrast the description there with that from other sources. For example, the accounts confirm that the leadership of the guerrilla groups is composed primarily of a dedicated group of Marxist-Leninists. To acknowledge this is not to justify the position of those who insist that the Salvadoran conflict is an East-West issue but simply to accept the description that these men and women have given of themselves. Journalists who have visited with the guerrillas have been able to verify this and also to observe a distinction between the "pragmatic radicalism" of the predominantly religious peasants found with the guerrillas and the more deeply ingrained and better integrated Marxist view of the predominantly urban cadre.[166] The latter were making efforts to transmit their vision to the *muchachos* (boys) and the *compas* (comrades),[167] but if precedent can offer any guidance, the most important factor in changing a person's perspective from that of fighting "to end the repression," as most peasants say, to fighting for the installation of a Marxist regime will be the very facts of the struggle, particularly the continuation of the repression that drove many peasants into the camp of the guerrillas in the first place. According to recent eyewitness accounts, that repression is still going on in the army's use of counterinsurgency tactics that affect civilians as well as guerrillas and indiscriminate bombings from the air.[168] These are more important in radicalizing the populace than any revolutionary theories; moreover, in El Salvador these theories are often confirmed by facts, and facts speak for themselves.

Apparently, the first objective of the guerrillas is to be able to negotiate from a position of military strength if they fall short of an outright military victory. By early 1982 they had established this position not only from their control of a larger chunk of territory but also from an increased ability to strike at major government and military targets and to sabotage the economy. The stronger they become, the more likely it is that they could emerge as a dominant force in any future settlement.

Guerrilla commanders have tried to suggest that one would not necessarily lead to the other. Juan Ramón Medrano, an ERP *comandante* interviewed by John Dinges at a rebel camp in Usulután, addressed this point.

> We have been maturing little by little and we have demonstrated
> sufficient awareness of the complexity of the world and international
> politics of the moment to know that we cannot impose any kind of
> radical government from one day to the next. . . . And even more we
> believe that a radical plan would be injurious to our country [and] simply

provoke or justify attitudes of belligerence toward us. . . . If someone might have said at some time that we want the destruction of the Army, we are sure that that was indeed an error. . . . The institution as such can remain as long as it adheres to the guidelines of a government of broad national participation. . . . We are not going to trust any kind of guarantee that does not contemplate the recognition of military power for our organization.[169]

Comandante Jonas, who, like Medrano, is also a member of the DRU, was more succinct and to the point in his interview with Alma Guillermoprieto. He told her that the guerrillas' program "includes the formation of a government of ample participation and a new style army, incorporating healthy elements of the government forces and our own guerrilla columns. We want to negotiate a settlement but, realistically, we know the regime will never talk to us unless it is forced to do so by our position of military strength."[170]

This disposition to talk has been there for some time. The guerrillas themselves came out with a proposal for unconditional talks with anyone—junta, military, private enterprise—in October 1981. It is significant that it was the FLP, through Commander Ana María, who disclosed this desire in a secret interview. While expressing this willingness to talk, the guerrilla leader advanced some details of their program, including: (1) a reintegrated government that would incorporate representatives of the insurgents, their political allies, and others interested in resolving El Salvador's basic problems, (2) national independence and self-determination, (3) a restructured army composed of guerrillas and soldiers who were free of complicity in genocide, (4) freedom of religion, (5) a mixed economy, (6) a nonaligned foreign policy, and (7) elections.[171] This put the guerrillas on record as asking for the same kind of settlement that the FDR had been insisting on all along.

On 15 December 1981 the FDR had its second openly acknowledged meeting with the Department of State when Rubén Zamora and Francisco Altschuld met with Deputy Assistant Secretary Ted Briggs to discuss the possibility of negotiations. After the meeting, Zamora described the FDR proposal. The Frente had proposed that talks take place between the junta and the FDR with representatives of other governments present as witnesses to the negotiations. The discussions were to be open and wide ranging, and the Salvadoran people were to be kept informed about their course. There were to be no preconditions for the talks. Zamora concluded by saying that the discussions would have to address three substantive issues sooner or later: the question of the restoration of the rule of law, the holding of elections, and the problem of two armies.[172]

The Reagan administration responded to these developments with the decision to train sixteen hundred Salvadoran troops and commissioned officers in the United States.[173] In February 1982 the administration certified that the Salvadoran government was making progress along the lines stipulated by the congressional resolution of 1981 and tacked on a request for an additional $55 million in military aid.[174] Finally, Secretary Haig pledged that the United States would do "whatever is necessary" to prevent a leftist victory in El Salvador,[175] while Assistant Secretary Thomas Enders claimed that the decisive battle for Central America was being waged in El Salvador.[176]

While their armed allies prepared for what appeared to be a new round of fighting, two former comrades paused and looked at the difficult road ahead. Slumped in a wooden rocking chair in San Salvador, José Napoleón Duarte tried to remind a visiting correspondent that the leftist subversives were not the only enemy of the Salvadoran transition.[177] In Washington, having completed a round of visits to congressional leaders, the FDR's Rubén Zamora argued that the PDC would be out if either side were to achieve a military solution.[178] Social and Christian Democrats remained divided not so much by irreconcilable ideological differences as by circumstances that neither could control. While it remained to be seen whether reason would ultimately prevail over violence, it was certain that the interests of the Salvadoran nation would not be served by a continuation of the latter.

Chapter 8

Illusion and Reality

The Salvadoran Election of 1982

The principals in the Salvadoran transition entered the constituent assembly election of 28 March 1982 with very different expectations. The Right had initially opposed the election. As the date of the election approached, however, the Salvadoran private sector began to perceive it as an opportunity to remove Duarte and the Christian Democrats from the government once and for all. The disloyal element in the Salvadoran Right wanted to go much further; for them the election represented a chance to restore the system of reactionary despotism. Major Roberto D'Aubuisson became the leader of this effort. The always malleable PCN, which many observers had discounted as a serious contender, prepared quietly, trying to bring its machinery into gear, make a good showing, and offer itself as a partner in a rightist coalition. The Christian Democrats, who had floated the idea of the election in December 1980 out of desperation, saw their fortunes decline and began to explore the possibility of a coalition. The FDR, which could not realistically participate, assumed that the election would be but another exclusionist fraud, while the guerrillas hoped and made efforts to insure that people would stay home on election day.

The more prominent foreign actors involved in the transition—the Socialist International (SI), the Venezuelan government, and the Reagan administration—had their own goals and apprehensions. The SI found itself in the uncomfortable position of having to denounce the election, since its FDR allies had been left out. Both redoubled their efforts to launch a negotiated settlement, but the drive for the election had too much momentum. The Venezuelan Christian Democrats, who had supported Duarte all along, did their best to improve and assist in the planning of the election, which employed a ballot and a system of proportional representation very similar to Venezuela's. They hoped that the election would vindicate their besieged coreligionaries and offer them a respite. Finally, the Reagan administration wanted to use the election to weaken and isolate the Left, to discredit the guerrillas, to produce a government that could be presented as legitimate and worthy of continued support, and, possibly, to force the Christian Democrats to form a coalition with one of the parties representing the private sector in order to diminish the strife between the two.

None of these actors had its expectations met fully or its hopes dashed completely. In the short run the disloyal Right profited the most from the outcome of the election, while the guerrillas were probably the biggest losers. The Christian Democrats won the election, but they lost power. The military and the Reagan administration finally had a "popularly elected government" to work with, but a government dominated by the element that could provoke Congress to rescind aid. The FDR proved that its presence was important in any overall settlement in order to prevent the Christian Democrats' being overwhelmed by the Right. In essence, the election was genuine, but it did not break the stalemate. Nor did it produce an alignment which put the obstructionists at a disadvantage. The election was an important watershed; it helped give an idea of the relative strength of the different contenders, but it did not solve the major questions of the transition.

The Integrity of the Election

Most observers of the Salvadoran election, including this writer, and most representatives of the international media covering the event agreed that the election was genuine.[1] The election offered a limited but real choice; there was some latent and some overt intimidation, but it did not come from a single source; the proceedings were reasonably orderly; and the votes were counted without manipulation.

There can be little doubt that the election presented Salvadorans with a clear-cut choice, despite the absence of the FDR. The fact that the Salvadoran electorate recognized the salience of that choice may be seen in the division of the bulk of the votes between the PDC and the ARENA. Seven out of every ten valid votes went to these two contenders. No other party or group of candidates came close to these two; nor were their campaign messages and platforms as clear and unambiguous as those of the PDC and ARENA.

Roberto D'Aubuisson was the most forceful and visible campaigner. He toured the country incessantly and visited every department twice. His message was straightforward: defeat the guerrillas by escalation and roll back the socioeconomic reforms.[2] His coffers were brimming, and he had no problem buying considerable space in the local press. ARENA retained a Salvadoran affiliate of the McCann Erickson advertising firm, adding a touch of Americana to the major's campaign. On election eve ARENA headquarters was a beehive of activity, a combination armed camp and middle-class enclave.[3] The mood was festive, even though the building had been attacked scarcely a month before.[4] Many of the campaign volunteers and poll watchers receiving their instructions for the election spoke English and were very cordial. The place could have passed for the campaign headquarters of any candidate in a U.S. election except that many persons wore sidearms and armed guards were everywhere.

Professor Thomas Anderson and this writer had the opportunity to talk at some length with Ing. Mario Emilio Redaelli, director of control for the campaign and secretary general of ARENA. Redaelli's father was tortured and killed during the peasant revolt of 1932; Radaelli was eight months old at the time. Although an amiable host, Redaelli did not hide his anti-Communism and his animosity toward the Christian Democrats. He showed us a letter, presumably written by PCS Secretary General Shafik Handal, which demonstrated that Adolfo Rey Prendes, until recently the mayor of San Salvador and the head of the PDC ticket to the constitutent assembly, and Ovidio Hernández, the PDC minister of the interior, were actually members of the PCS. Redaelli believed that the PDC's call to postpone the election was an attempt to avoid defeat, and that the Christian Democrats were embarked on a series of maneuvers to steal the elections.[5] In addition, he complained that the Ley Electoral Transitoria of January 1982 had failed to incorporate any of the proposals submitted by the five opposition parties and that it gave an unfair advantage to the PDC. Redaelli was not prepared to tell us what ARENA would do in case of a fraud, but he stated that a second-place finish for his party would not necessarily be a result of government fraud.[6]

The ideological and social distance between ARENA and the PDC was, to say the least, considerable. The campaign messages of ARENA focused on the shortcomings of the Christian Democrats, whom they blamed for the country's poor economic condition and for the placing of too many restraints on the Armed Force. These messages were reinforced by those of the PCN, which sought, among other things, to depict PDC leaders as embezzlers and common thieves.[7] The PDC's main contender was ARENA, however, and that party was receiving the support of the disloyal Right.

By contrast, the campaign of the PDC was relatively subdued. The advantage of incumbency was diluted by a provision in the Ley Transitoria barring public officials from campaigning. This limited the leadership of the PDC to a series of major addresses in which it delivered the party's message. The PDC was vulnerable in two areas: the deterioration of the economy and the still-unresolved question of uncontrolled government violence.

Duarte addressed the nation by radio and television on 20 January 1982. He defended the party's record in office, arguing that the PDC had tried to manage a process of transition from dictatorship to democracy while under continuous threat from extremists. He further stated that the party was pursuing reasonable economic policies and that the electoral solution was the only alternative to violence. Defending the PDC covenant with the Armed Force, which he said sought to improve the military institution and bring it closer to the people, he reiterated his charge that rightist extremists in the Chamber of Commerce, the ANEP, the AP, and other private sector organizations were trying to destroy the possibility of democracy and to prevent Salvadorans from achieving social justice.[8]

On 24 January, Planning Minister Atilio Viéytez delivered a rebuttal to a document prepared by the Chamber of Commerce of El Salvador. Following a discussion of the performance of the different sectors of the economy during 1981, Viéytez pointed out that the chamber had omitted two crucial points in its document: the flight of almost 3 billion colones since 1979 and the depressed export prices for cotton, sugar, and coffee.[9]

The defense of the government's economic record was coupled with an attack on the elements that were trying to restore El Salvador to pre-1979 conditions. Without mentioning D'Aubuisson or ARENA, many campaign messages of the PDC depicted the party as the best alternative to extremism, and as the most decided supporter of peace. In its final message the PDC warned the electorate that a vote for the rightist parties would be a vote for injustice, inequality, authoritarianism, oppression, fraud, and corruption. In essence, then, Salvadorans had a clear-cut choice between the anti-Communist, hard-line, and laissez-faire approach of ARENA and the reformist, incremental, and communitarian approach of the PDC.[10]

Concerning the question of intimidation, Duarte and the Christian Democrats insisted all along that the election would be fair. The Armed Force, for its part, proclaimed that it would guarantee and respect the result, as well as the safety of the voters on election day.[11] There was intimidation during the campaign, however, as well as acts of violence related to it. D'Aubuisson was shot at on 27 February and wounded slightly. Rafael Rodríguez González, a high-ranking official of the PCN, was murdered by unknown assailants. Labor Minister Julio Samayoa, who served as campaign coordinator for the PDC, was fired upon. On 17 March four Dutch journalists who were trying to make contact with a guerrilla unit were assassinated.[12] Threatening phone calls were received by journalists covering the election.[13] A series of banners appeared around San Salvador asking journalists to "tell the truth." By election day, though, the contingent of foreign journalists was so massive that no further threats were reported, and in general correspondents had free access to polling stations and no official interference in their attempts to contact the guerrillas.

The most obvious form of intimidation, of course, was the compulsory requirement to vote. Following Salvadoran custom, as well as the practice of many other Latin American countries, the Ley Electoral Transitoria of January 1982 made voting compulsory. The rate of voter turnout has always been relatively high in El Salvador, even in meaningless elections. Therefore, there is something akin to a habit of voting in El Salvador, if only to stay out of trouble with the government. In some elections public employees had their checks withheld until they established that they had voted; apparently, this was also the case in 1982. Official penalties for nonvoting were set by the election law at between 2 and 50 colones, except in cases of indigence, in which the fine could not exceed 2 colones.[14] Moreover, since the guerrillas urged a boycott of the elections, nonvoting could be interpreted as proof of guerrilla sympathies and expose one to the worst kind of retribution. In short, many voters may have gone to the polls on 28 March simply to avoid possible repercussions.

The particular method that the government used to enforce compulsory voting—and to prevent multiple voting—makes it hard to judge how much these threatened sanctions influenced voter turnout. Article 36 of the election law mandated that the right thumb of every voter be impregnated with "very visible and indelible ink."[15] This was changed by Decree No. 966 of 5 February 1982 to read "invisible and indelible ink," purportedly to assuage fears of retribution from the guerrillas. Special lamps were to be used to check for this mark. Article 100 of the law prescribed that the seal of the municipality be stamped on the *cédula* (individual identification card) of every voter.[16] In the ten days following the election government officials could request to see the cards in order to enforce the law and assess penalties.

The Consejo Central de Elecciones (CCE) printed illustrated descriptions of the eight different steps required to cast a vote in all the newspapers on the days preceding the election, asking that the *juntas receptoras de votos*, that is, the officials and party representatives posted at every voting table, display these instructions where voters could see them.[17] The one discrepancy between these printed instructions and the procedure established by article 100 was precisely the stamping of the municipal seal on the *cédula*. Whatever the reason for this omission, its effect may have been to lead some citizens to believe that their *cédulas* would not be stamped. This confusion may have affected the likelihood of voting for some, but this is difficult to assess, for it is doubtful that all of the voters fully understood the whole complicated process.

The fact remains, however, that this form of official coercion affected only the likelihood of voting and not the *preference* of the voter, since there was no way to check how the vote was cast.[18] Given the format of the ballot (see Figure 8-1), which was practically identical to that used in recent Venezuelan elections, anyone, even in the crowded and cramped conditions observed by the author at most polling stations that he visited on election day, could have simply invalidated the ballot or left it blank. According to official figures, close to 9 percent of the voters invalidated their ballots and an additional 3

FIGURE 8-1
Ballot Utilized in the Salvadoran Constituent Assembly
Election of 28 March 1982

percent left them blank. Even though one must be careful in interpreting the meaning of null and blank voting in Latin American elections, about 12 percent of the voters refused to express any preference or could not express their preference on election day.[19] Finally, an untold and difficult to measure, yet nevertheless large, number of Salvadorans simply did not vote.

The evidence available and the pattern of events preceding the elections suggest that most of the intimidation affected turnout and not preference. The massive foreign presence, the presence of party representatives in every *junta*, and the absence of major complaints of systematic fraud from any of the participants suggest that the votes were counted as cast.[20]

The FDR condemned the election as exclusionist and unrepresentative. FDR officials continued to seek negotiations, however, while the guerrillas intensified their military operations.[21] During the campaign the guerrillas managed to attract attention to themselves with a series of attacks, including the one against the Ilopango airbase in late January and numerous engagements with the army. In late February, guerrilla leader Roberto Roca vowed that the guerrillas would intensify their military effort and that this just happened to coincide with the election.[22] A series of major battles were fought in late February around the Guazapa volcano and in Santa Ana, San Miguel, and San Vicente in early March. In the days prior to the election the guerrillas attacked the CCE headquarters in San Salvador and engaged in a campaign to destroy public transportation vehicles.[23] On election day the owners of many of these vehicles kept them out of circulation, transportation came to a virtual standstill, and most people had to walk a few kilometers in order to vote. During that day small guerrilla units engaged in firefights with Salvadoran army and national guard units in the vicinity of polling stations, delaying the election in those places by several hours. This was the case in Apopa, in San Antonio Abad, where twelve guerrillas were killed, in San Francisco Gotera, and in a score of other towns.[24] In Usulután a four-day battle for control of the departmental capital prevented the election from taking place at all.[25] Although the guerrillas, to my knowledge, never fired upon would-be voters, their strategy was clearly to disrupt the elections and remind everyone that the country was still in the throes of civil war.

In an effort to manage the security problem the CCE kept the number of *puestos de votación* (polling stations) small, so that the army, the national guard, and the police would not have to spread themselves too thin. For the whole country there were 298 *puestos* housing 4,556 *juntas receptoras de votos*. In San Salvador, a city of 750,000, there were 500 *juntas*, but these were clustered in only 13 *puestos*.[26] Although this was a vast improvement over the 1977 election, when residents of the capital could vote at only *one* polling place, it practically guaranteed long lines at every polling station. While this inconvenienced the voters, it was a public relations coup for the government: by mid-afternoon the lines were still long, and the international media called the turnout "massive." The long lines may have also helped to forestall the possibility of a person voting more than once. As election day wore on, in fact, the concern was with whether everyone in line would be able to vote, especially in areas without electricity, where the polls were supposed to close down by 4:00 P.M. There is no way of estimating how many people went home without voting or how many *juntas* sought and obtained permission to extend the deadline past 6:00 P.M.[27]

Thus, under the circumstances, the election went well and many more people than anticipated did vote.[28] Given the polarization of opinion about the Salvadoran process in the United States and elsewhere, however, others may utilize the details of this description to draw different conclusions.[29] An incident witnessed by the author during a tour of parts of the country on election day may help validate my interpretation of what most Salvadorans were trying to do with their votes on that day.

Professor Thomas Anderson and this writer observed the Salvadoran campaign during 24–29 March. Not being official observers, we circulated very much on our own and followed our own agenda. On election morning we accompanied correspondent Stephen Kinzer and free-lance photographer Barry Allen in what was going to be a trip along the Troncal del Norte highway, from Apopa, a small town northeast of San Salvador, through Chalatenango. In general this area is not very sympathetic to the government or to the Right. It includes the "Indian country" around the Guazapa volcano, Suchitoto and its environs, where the popular organizations had been very strong, and the town of Aguilares, where Father Rutilio Grande was murdered. Voting in the area would serve as a good barometer of how seriously the election was being taken by the people.[30]

At 7:00 A.M. the streets around the center of Apopa were deserted, as patrols of the army and the national guard tried to drive a band of *muchachos* or *subversivos*, as the guerrillas are called by the people and by the security forces, respectively, from the area between the town square and the Vicente Acosta school, the polling station for the municipality. The guerrillas were trying to delay and obstruct the election. The military was trying to drive them out, but looked very disorganized. After we had been in the area for about a half hour, a sergeant came into the plaza and shouted that the way was clear. This is when we saw the Salvadoran election come alive, as people began to appear from everywhere and to walk toward the school. Many were in their Sunday best. Most were in good spirits. Our presence intrigued them, and their questions enabled us to ask some of our own during the hour that it took us to negotiate the three blocks between the town square and the school.

We were especially intrigued by the number of young males in the crowd. One tends to think of the members of this group as guerrillas, army conscripts, or disappeared persons. Yet they were very much in evidence and provided most of the entertainment during lulls in the shooting.

It was difficult to believe that these people were braving a firefight because they feared a greater evil. Most of the people that we talked to in Apopa went to vote not for the *políticos* but for themselves.[31] They were quite realistic about the limited efficacy of the election, but they saw it as the only way they could endorse a peaceful solution to *their* crises: missing relatives, violent incidents, uncertainty, harsh economic conditions, and death. Most Salvadorans interviewed during that day said that they hoped that, somehow, the election would help to stop the killing.[32]

Regardless of one's fantasies about El Salvador, to dismiss the hardships that hundreds of thousands of Salvadorans endured in order to cast their votes is to deprive them of their own meaning. Perhaps it is possible to argue that to "violent Central Americans," elections do not mean anything or that many of them have been deprived of their basic human rights for so long that they could not possibly take elections seriously. But to use these arguments to ignore what the Salvadorans themselves tried to say on 28 March 1982 is no longer an attempt to understand but, instead, a dogmatic and self-serving exercise. To be sure, their statement may have been diluted by subsequent events, but the power grab of the Right and the exclusion of the Left should not obscure the fact that, first and foremost, Salvadorans voted for an end to *their* conflict. They came out to vote in a much larger number than anticipated primarily because they wanted to make use of this massive action to urge an end to violence and civil war. This transcended the real choice between Duarte and D'Aubuisson and constitutes the most important message delivered that day.

The Results of the Election

The rightist power grab following the election and the presence of the disloyal Right in the new Salvadoran government, has created the impression that the Right won the latest Salvadoran election, but this was not the case. First, in their head-to-head competition the Christian Democrats beat ARENA. Second, despite the opposition's invective and its vitriolic attacks on the PDC, only ARENA emerged from this election as a party that can represent the disloyal Right in El Salvador. The others are too minuscule, like the PPS and the POP; are loyal to the democratic system, like the AD; or are simply parties that do not really follow ideologies, but instead, leaders and orders, like the PCN.

The election established the PDC as the foremost political force among the parties that participated in the election. This fact has been forgotten in the confusion that followed the election, when it became evident that the PDC could not form a coalition, but it is a vitally important piece of information. Despite having to campaign on a less than favorable record on the economic and human rights questions, the party won a plurality of the vote nationally, and in ten of the fourteen departments. Nationally, the PDC got 35 percent of the total vote and 40 percent of the valid vote, while ARENA got about 26 and 29 percent, respectively. (A summary of the election's results is presented in Table 8-1.)

It is difficult to estimate how much the PDC benefited from votes that would have gone to the parties included in the FDR. Given the current level of animosity between *frentistas* and *democristianos*, however, it is doubtful that many potential FDR votes wound up on the PDC column.

It is also difficult to estimate the causal factors behind the PDC plurality, at least on a departmental basis. Looking at the compilation of returns by department in Table 8-2, it becomes apparent that guerrilla activity does not provide a good explanation of the vote. The PDC did both very well—Chalatenango and Morazán—and very poorly—Cabañas—in the areas of the most intense guerrilla activity during the last two years. But it did very well, coming in first, in departments with very recent intense guerrilla activity—Santa Ana, San Miguel, and San Vicente.

Another possible influence on the strength of the PDC vote is the facts of socioeconomic reforms. How well did the PDC do in areas where the Agrarian Reform has been a reality, primarily the western region of the country?[33] Comparing the data presented in Table 8-3, which documents the extent of phase I of the reform shortly before the election, with the departmental voting returns presented in Table 8-2, it becomes evident that this does not provide a much better explanation of the PDC vote. Essentially, we find that, once again, the PDC vote fluctuates wildly in relation to the explanatory factor under scrutiny.[34] For example, if we look at the returns and order the departments by percentage of the vote for the PDC—as done in a descending order in Figure 8-2, we find that Morazán and Chalatenango, departments where the PDC obtained its largest pluralities, there were, respectively, only two and nine cooperatives. In addition, 30 percent of the area under Phase I in Chalatenango had been abandoned by the time of the election. By contrast, the number of cooperatives was also low in the departments where the PDC did worst, Cuscatlán and Cabañas, with two cooperatives each. Of course this does not deny the significance of the agrarian question in the present Salvadoran crisis. As a matter of fact, this theme provided one of the issues which fueled the campaign. But it does indicate that one single aspect of this question cannot explain the fortunes of a party that has tried to address it during the last two years in the middle of a civil war. Such factors as landowner resistance, level of violence related to the reform, degree of cooperation from local military and government officials, and guerrilla presence must also be considered, and, unfortunately, not all of those data are available, on a systematic basis, at the departmental level.

Perhaps the neatest explanation of PDC and ARENA strength at the departmental level is given by a geographic cleavage of sorts, which reflects a geographical specialization of agricultural labor, dividing the country into the "old coffee" departments of the west and the rest. ARENA did well in the "old coffee" departments of Ahuachapán, Chalatenango, Sonsonate, and Cuscatlán. This differentiation had considerable political significance at the time of the election of 1982, since one of the issues of the election was precisely whether or not Decree No. 207, "Land to the Tiller," was going to affect lands dedicated to other agricultural crops. Opposition to this was the centerpiece of the campaign of the agrarian front and, incidentally, the first issue that the majority coalition in the assembly took up in its bid to reverse the reforms of the Christian Democratic juntas.[35]

The election also established ARENA as the vehicle of the reactionary coalition and as the most important element in the Salvadoran Right. ARENA ran well, much better than expected, but it captured only four departments: Usulután, Cuscatlán, Ahuachapán, and Cabañas. Despite its intense competition with the PDC, the fortunes of ARENA were not influenced solely by the strength of the PDC in the different departments. As Figure 8-2 shows, the ARENA vote at the departmental level does not increase gradually with the decline of the PDC vote but fluctuates on its own. This reflects not only the presence of the PCN as a third force, influencing the overall distribution of the vote, but also the local blend of the factors mentioned above that relate to the land question and to the level of violence. However, the ARENA strength should not be interpreted as a direct result of intimidation. One should not ignore the impact of fifty years of anti-Communist propaganda, the low educational level of the population, and the fact that the guerrillas have also killed people. ARENA may or may not be able to preserve this level of support, but its showing in 1982 suggests that there is a sizable segment of the population that identifies with the hard-line stance of Roberto D'Aubuisson and with the intransigence displayed by ARENA ever since its inception.

It is difficult to gauge what lies behind the results involving the other parties. For example, it is likely that the PCN lost its most reactionary element to ARENA. Similar splits have affected the PCN in the past and, this time, those who left had much greater intensity about the issues and a more specific focus. What was left of the PCN was probably its traditional rural constituency and a political machine dating back to its "official" days which includes some labor, middle-class, and bureaucratic elements. The PCN continues to look to the military for guidance, and since the distance between the military *institution* and the reactionary coalition has increased, not only since 15 Oc-

FIGURE 8-2
Approximate Distribution of the Vote for the PDC and ARENA, by Department

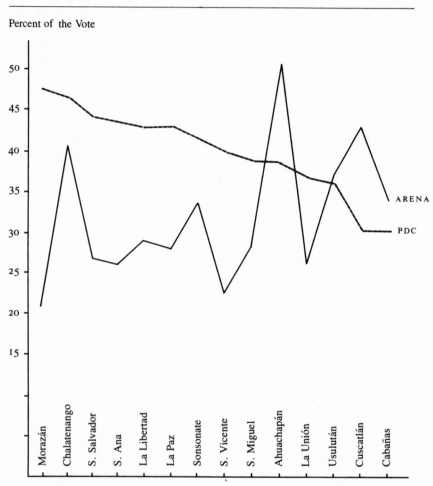

Percent of the Vote

Source: Computed from U.S. Department of State, *Foreign Broadcast Information Service,*
VI, Central America, 1 Apr. 1982, pp. 1–2.

tober 1979 but, more important, since the ISTA crisis of 1976, ARENA and the PCN may have trouble working together. The military brass is also distrustful of D'Aubuisson and very concerned about how the actions of the former major and his party may affect United States military aid. The 1982 constituency of the PCN and its relation with the military may make the ARENA-PCN coalition unstable, and they may not have much in common beyond their anti-Communism and a common hatred for the PDC.[36] Finally, the PCN retains a somewhat more pragmatic outlook than does ARENA, and although basically a conservative party, it is not as ideological or as impassioned as ARENA.

The Acción Democrática has democratic roots, since its principal leader, René Fortín Magaña, was a member of the junta of 1960. Despite its liberal economic outlook the AD does not appear to be reactionary, at least certainly not disloyal. The AD made its best showing in San Salvador (see Table 8-2) and managed to capture two seats in the assembly. This was somewhat less than had been anticipated. Apparently, the AD could have formed a government with the PDC had they captured a sufficient number of seats. At one point, it was reported that the party was prepared to join the PDC in the opposition if the Christian Democrats were excluded from the government after the election. The AD seems to be competing for the support of a constituency very similar to that of the PPS, which got only one seat in the assembly. As a result of this and of the good showing by ARENA, it is difficult to figure out how much of the industrial and commercial bourgeoisie supported the AD and the PPS and did not run after ARENA. The PPS, however, is definitely more conservative than the AD, at least at the level of the leadership. Chele Medrano's Party of Popular Orientation (POP), which is basically the FUDI of the 1970s, was no longer so attractive to the agrarian front, which now had ARENA, and as a result the POP got not even one seat in the assembly.

A final reflection on the results of the election concerns those who were not represented in it: the MNR, the MPSC, and the other Social Democratic parties included in the FDR. The MNR ran in coalition with the PDC in 1972 and 1977, and the MPSC is a splinter of the latter. Thus it had been unclear how much of its original constituency the PDC had been able to retain. The 1982 election clarified this, suggesting that the PDC had held its constituency in the urban middle and lower classes and had attracted peasant support through the UCS. This does not mean, however, that the FDR has no support.

One may engage in speculation about how large that support actually is. Since the PDC does not have majority support, the FDR parties have a tremendously significant role to play not only as the representative of the Left in possible future elections but also as the most compatible partner for the PDC in any future attempts to set up a center-left government. The PDC needs the support of the parties included in the FDR to counterbalance the Right. Had these parties been able to participate in the 1982 election, the outcome would have been very different. As a matter of fact, that participation would have been the acid test of whether the United States and the Salvadoran military were really interested in neutralizing the rightist obstructionists. As it was, the election was an important watershed, but it did not result in a neutralization of the obstructionists; nor did it strengthen the position of the *aperturistas*. Instead, the exclusion of the democratic Left indicates that the rightist obstructionists are still very much in command.

The Salvadoran Transition after the Election

The aftermath of the constituent assembly election of 28 March 1982 demonstrates that, during this first stage of the Salvadoran transition, the strongest actors have had what amounts to a veto power over the actions of their antagonists. Many other events of the transition could be mentioned to support this contention, but the outcome of the election illustrates the point well.

The outcome has been labeled "half a win," "a bare cupboard," "a return to the point of departure," and a "Pyrrhic U.S. victory."[37] Yet none of the major actors has left the scene, even though the Reagan administration exaggerated the setback suffered by the guerrillas.[38] The outcome of the election remained inconclusive in early June 1982. The process remained stalemated, and the key ingredient of a democratic resolution, the neutralization of antidemocratic obstructionists, remained but a distant possibility.

The Christian Democrats won the election, only to lose power. They finally showed off their leftist opposition in an election, only to discover that they will need the support of the Social Democrats if they want to form an effective government in the future. The disloyal Right put itself in office through the election, after two years of failed coup attempts, but its rising influence was held in check by the United States and the Salvadoran military. The United States finally had a government "elected by the people" in El Salvador but one controlled by a man described as a "pathological killer." The military brass got the safe and uncomplicated election that it could tolerate at this time, but it also got an unwieldy arrangement and a militant faction in the new government whose proposed actions put it on a collision course with the U.S. Congress. In addition, the military institution must once again worry about the disruptive effects of middle-rank officers being courted by the disloyal Right, now in government. The guerrillas grabbed their share of headlines but their morale and prestige suffered considerably. The FDR did not participate in the election, and its absence contributed to an electoral outcome that makes a democratic resolution all the more difficult. In summary, each antagonist— and it is exceedingly important to emphasize that there are quite a number of these in El Salvador at the present time, and not just the "government" and the guerrillas—took and delivered some blows.

But there is a clue to this kaleidoscope. First, the present Salvadoran government has no better chance of moving toward democracy than did any of the juntas constituted since the October 1979 coup. The ideological heterogeneity of the government is tremendous, for it includes truly antagonistic actors. This government cannot move anywhere unless it sheds its pluralist pretense, and the more likely outcome will be the departure of the Christian Democrats who, sooner or later, will have to move to the opposition.

Second, the dominance of the disloyal Right in the assembly means that the increased domestic and international legitimacy that an elected government could have derived from the election will probably be wasted. It is clear that the disloyal Right intends to sabotage and reverse the modest achievements of the transition.[39] In addition, its rise to power has served as a signal for a renewal of rightist violence. Forty-eight villagers were massacred by men dressed in army uniforms scarcely one month after the election, and three Christian Democratic mayors and nine other party activists have been killed since the election.[40] Corpses of persons executed by death squads have reappeared in traditional drop-off areas around San Salvador.

Third, given the lack of acceptable alternatives, the Reagan administration will try to make this arrangement work. It has conditioned the continuation of aid on the existence of a coalition government.[41] Despite the good intentions of Provisional President Alvaro Magaña, however, the new arrangement is not a government but a contraption, and all the power and prestige of the United States cannot make this contraption work for long in a manner acceptable to the American public and the Congress. In recognition of his official position the administration lifted the ban imposed in June 1980 on D'Aubuisson which had prevented him from traveling to the United States.[42] Attempts to improve the image of the ineffable major, however, will not work either. The administration is forced to work with the rightists but, judging by what has happened in similar situations in other countries, it is unlikely that D'Aubuisson and ARENA will become useful instruments for a democratic transition in El Salvador.

Contrary to what some conservatives in the United States are trying to pretend, neither the major nor ARENA, the umbrella organization that the reactionary coalition has entrusted to him, can be described as "democratic capitalists."[43] They have come to power to give another try to the 1977–79 attempt by General Carlos Humberto Romero to stabilize the Salvadoran crisis through a restoration of reactionary despotism. This is their real intention, one which they stated publicly throughout the campaign. This is what they promised to their constituency. This is what people in El Salvador expect them to do.

In summary, the new alignment has made the restoration of reactionary despotism a distinct possibility. This does not mean that the chances for democracy are lost, since the outcome of a process of transition does not depend upon the actions of only one actor. In the short run, however, the outcome of the election has compromised the chances for a democratic resolution to the crisis.

Conclusion

In this century, El Salvador has experienced a series of crises that could have culminated in the inauguration of a democratic regime. The coup of 15 October 1979 initiated the most recent of these. Like several previous opportunities for a democratic transition, this one began with a military coup. A *junta de gobierno* was organized, which soon gave way to a more moderate one. The more extremist element of the Right maintained a relentless pressure against the enactment of any reforms and, once some were enacted, launched a violent campaign to stall the process and insert a new and decidedly conservative government that would reverse it. The military remained the key participant during the entire process, acting as the final arbiter in the most important decisions, retaining veto power, and staying above the law. The *aperturistas* were finally overwhelmed because they could not overcome the combined strength of the oligarchy and the military.

The process initiated in October 1979, however, differed from the previous ones in several respects. The reforms brought about by this transition undermined the basis of oligarchic domination. A real political party established direct links to the independent organizations of the popular sector and the working class. Peasants were given some modest yet real benefits. The reformist government stayed in office for over two years, thanks in large part to the support of the United States, and was able to hold a relatively free and fair election. Radical sectors of the petite bourgeoisie, the working and popular classes, and the peasantry organized a guerrilla army that battled the Armed Force to a standstill. Finally, the international linkages of the crisis became more pronounced, threatening to turn a civil war into a regional military conflict.

The Salvadoran military did not fill the power vacuum created by the oligarchy crisis of 1932, and during the last forty years it has prevented others from attempting their own solution. Throughout, though, a very broad and strong coalition has been necessary to conduct one of these crises to a democratic outcome.

The historical roots of the present crisis are Salvadoran. The United States' involvement in it has been deepening, however, and its attempt to exclude the

Left from the process in order to forestall a Communist takeover has contributed to the present protracted conflict. In addition, two American administrations have tried to stabilize the situation around a "center" comprising historical enemies that could and would not reconcile their differences.

Democracy and capitalism are not incompatible. As a matter of fact, most
democratic regimes exist within capitalist states. Those states have implemented some kind of redistributive scheme, however, in order to buy
social peace. Once this basic question is settled the political process deals
with other questions in an incremental fashion, centering on the interaction
between a government bound by the law and responsible and autonomous
intermediary institutions of interest representation that restrain the exercise of
public authority.

The plan to join democracy and capitalism in El Salvador is fraught with
difficulties, not the least of which is the necessity for a thorough reform of the
capitalist state. Given the characteristics of contemporary Salvadoran society,
the oligarchic capitalism of El Salvador cannot be maintained without a great
degree of coercion. The process that started in October 1979 began to address
this fundamental problem and made some notable gains, but it had at the same
time to bring the Salvadoran state under the rule of law.

On the economic question the managers of the Salvadoran transition received some cooperation from the Armed Force. In their attempt to enforce a
lawful state, however, they had to confront the military and the oligarchy. The
civil war complicated this. Basically, little has been accomplished thus far.

No adequate settlement of the Salvadoran crisis is possible without the
resolution of these two issues: the socioeconomic question, centering on the
issue of tenure and utilization of land, and the human rights question, centering on the issue of the supremacy of the law. For the moment, the situation is
polarized between the vision of D'Aubuisson and the Salvadoran Right and
that of José Napoleón Duarte and the Christian Democrats. The former,
conscious of the historical precedent, are confident in their ability to survive
these crises and in the logic that requires the subordination of democracy to
economic expediency. At bottom, what they are defending is neither democratic nor truly capitalist. The Christian Democratic vision is that things can
be different, but history and precedent are against it.

It has been argued here that a democratic outcome to the present crisis is
not possible without the reincorporation of the democratic Left. The collapse
of the first junta, the precarious situation of the Christian Democrats during
1980–82, and the outcome of the 1982 election support this argument.

The United States can still play an important role in the present crisis, a
crisis which it did not create but which it has helped complicate. Unfortunately, the ideological make-up of the Reagan administration makes it unlikely
that the administration will perceive an alliance between the Social and Chris-

tian Democrats as a viable and legitimate option. This is the greatest but not the only mistake that the U.S. could make. The attempt to solve the crisis through an outright military victory may be enhanced by the return of Salvadoran troops trained in the United States, and by the guerrillas' slow recovery from their setback at the election. The temptation to link the Salvadoran crisis to other conflicts is still there.

The true colors of the disloyal Right are hard to hide. The U.S. Congress is not likely to accept that the disloyal Right is embarked on a reformist path and spearheading the defense of human rights in El Salvador. With the change in hemispheric relations brought about by the war between Britain and Argentina, the United States can no longer count on much outside help to do the dirty work in Central America. The fall of the Christian Democrats from power has led to a reevaluation of the situation by Venezuela, which had been a crucial partner in United States policy toward El Salvador. Finally, the level of violence may escalate again, not so much between the military and the guerrillas in the countryside, as between ARENA and PDC operatives in the cities. The whole fragile arrangement could unravel very quickly.

The yearning for peace expressed by Salvadorans on 28 March 1982 should not go for nothing; the lofty rhetoric that it generated has already been spent. Ordinary Salvadorans are waiting for an amelioration that cannot come the way they anticipated it. They cannot simply sit and wait until the Christian Democrats or some other *aperturista* faction finally wins a majority and manages to control the Armed Force. They have been waiting since 1972; the country has been waiting since 1932.

If precedent prevails the disloyal Right will have its way, and the election of 1982 will have marked the end of another attempt at a democratic transition—a cruel irony. If democracy is to emerge, the *aperturistas* need help. Those now in the government who want to restore reactionary despotism may, by their intemperate use of power, finally force a reluctant Reagan administration to link future aid to the maintenance of the reforms and, equally important, to the defense of human rights.

In this sense the United States could be the difference between history and hope, but it must be willing to run some risks. The greatest of these is not that El Salvador may become another Nicaragua or another Vietnam. Instead, the greatest risk is that we may have to accept that we are just the difference and not the essential ingredient.

Appendix: Tables

TABLE I-I

The Growth of National Government in El Salvador
as Measured by Average Tenure
of Presidential Incumbents,
1824–1979

Period	Years	Number of Different Incumbents	Average Tenure in Office (years)[a]
Federation	1824–1838	17	.82
Transition	1838–1841	8	.38
Informal republic	1841–1859	42	.43
Liberal republic	1859–1898	22	1.77
Oligarchic republic	1898–1931	11	3.00
Military Dominance:			
Personalist rule	1931–1948	8	2.13
Institutional rule	1948–1979	9	3.44

Source: Adapted from El Salvador, Casa Presidencial, *El Salvador,
1974–1975* (San Salvador: Departamento de Relaciones Públicas,
1974).
a. Average number of years in power for each incumbent during the
period.

Appendix

TABLE I-2
The Growth of Government and Successful Military Coups

Period Considered	Successful Coups	Frequency (years)[a]
1841–1866	42	.62
1890–1915	3	8.67
1916–1941	1	26.00
1944–1961	5	3.60
1962–1979	1	18.00
1841–1979	52	2.67

Source: Adapted from Flores Pinel, "Golpe de Estado," p. 892.
a. Number of years lapsed between successful coups during the period.

TABLE 2-1
Use of Private Credit in El Salvador,
1961–1975 (percentages)

Economic Sector	1961[a]	1965[a]	1971[a]	1975[a,b]
Agriculture	26.0	28.2	30.3	35.0
Coffee	(14.9)	(11.7)	(16.3)	(17.8)
Cotton	(6.3)	(7.5)	(8.3)	(10.4)
Sugar	(.7)	(2.5)	(1.7)	(1.2)
Cereals	(.4)	(.6)	(1.0)	(2.6)
Livestock	(.8)	(1.3)	(1.0)	(.7)
Other agricultural	(3.9)	(4.6)	(2.0)	(2.3)
Other[c]	74.0	71.7	69.7	65.0
Total credit[d]	312.0	417.0	673.0	903.0

Source: Computed from Burke, "Sistema de Plantación," p. 485, statistical appendix, chart 2 (from Banco Central de Reserva de El Salvador).

a. Includes credit by the Banco Hipotecario de El Salvador. Current prices, end-of-year balances.
b. Jan.–July only.
c. Includes industry, transportation, finance, retail and wholesale commerce, utilities, and services.
d. In millions of colones.

TABLE 2-2

Salaries of Coffee Workers in El Salvador
for Selected Years, 1952–1980

Crop Years	Colones per Day[a]
1979–80	14.25
1978–79	9.75
1970–71	3.57
1965–66	2.55
1964[b]	1.61
1952[b]	1.57

Source: *Latin America Commodities Report*, CR-79-03a, 7 December 1979, p. 4; and Daniel and Ester Slutzky, "Estructura de la Explotación," p. 105.

a. Colones in current prices.
b. One colón = US$ 0.40.

TABLE 2-3

Sources of Income of the Majority of Families in
the Agricultural Sector in El Salvador, 1975

				Sources of Income (percent)			
			Average	From	From cultivation		
Categories	Number of Families	Percent of Total	Net Weekly Income	Salaries	Grains	Fruit	Other
Landless	166,922	40.9	15.23	51.6	—	19.9	28.5
Under 1 ha.	138,838	34.1	19.28	31.4	24.9	26.3	17.4
Between 1 and 2 has.	62,385	15.3	26.67	18.7	33.8	27.6	19.9
Between 2 and 5 has.	24,400	6.0	49.55	5.9	63.6	17.9	12.6

Source: Computed from Burke, "Sistema de Plantación," pp. 476, 479 (from United Nations, UNDP/OTC, 1976, charts 5, 12, and 18).
Note: Salary figures in colones, at current prices. One hectare is equal to 2.471 acres.

TABLE 3-1
Contemporary Presidential Races in El Salvador

Year	Government	Opposition
1950	PRUD: Oscar Osorio (57%)	PAR: José A. Menéndez (43%)
1956	PRUD: José M. Lemus (94%)	PAR: Enrique Magaña (3%)
		PAC: Rafael Carranza (3%)
		PAN: Roberto E. Canessa (dq.)
		PDN: José A. Díaz (dq.)
1962	PCN: Julio A. Rivera (92%)	blank ballots (8%)
1967	PCN: Fidel Sánchez (54%)	PDC: Abraham Rodríguez (22%)
		PAR: Fabio Castillo (14%)
		PPS: Alvaro Martínez (10%)
1972[a]	PCN: Arturo Molina 334,600	UNO: José N. Duarte 324,756
		FUDI: José A. Medrano 94,367
		PPS: José A. Rodríguez
		Porth 16,871
1977	PCN: Carlos H. Romero	UNO: Ernesto Claramount
	812,281	394,661

Source: 1950–67: Mario Monteforte Toledo, *Centroamérica*, 2:78–80; 1972–77: Stephen Webre, *José Napoleón Duarte*, pp. 171–72.

Note: The UNO was a coalition composed of the PDC, the MNR, and the UDN.

a. Official results. According to the UNO the results were PCN: 317,535; UNO: 326,968.

TABLE 4-1
Political Violence in El Salvador, 1972–1979

Categories	Administration	
	Molina	Romero
Initiated by government:		
Political assassinations	37	461
Wounded by security forces	78	88
Prosecuted for political offenses	113	477
"Disappeared"	69	131
Other terrorist acts	9	15
Priests killed	2	4
Initiated by the guerrillas:		
Attacks	31	60
Killings of security personnel	24	58
Killings of paramilitary personnel	18	74
Wounded in guerrilla attacks	11	14
Kidnappings	8	16

Source: López Vallecillos, "Rasgos Sociales," p. 871.

TABLE 7-1

Estimates of the Number of Victims of Government and
Rightist Violence from January through September 1981

Cumulative Total through	Total Killed	Principal Occupational Categories of Victims				
		Peasants	Employees	Students	Teachers	Unknown
30 September[a]	10,714	4,239	467	321	51	5,128
30 June[b]	9,250	3,868	368	281	44	4,334
31 March[c]	5,335	—	—	—	—	—

Source: SALPRESS weekly news summaries as follows:

a. with data from Socorro Jurídico release of 3 November 1981.

b. with data from *Solidaridad*, issue of 12 July 1981.

c. *Miami Herald*, 26 April 1981, p. 18C; no breakdown reported.

Note: Other categories omitted because of low frequency or unsystematic reporting.

TABLE 8-1
Final Results of the Constituent Assembly
Election of 28 March 1982

	Votes	Percentage of Valid Votes	Percentage of Total Votes	Seats
ARENA	383,632	29.32	25.83	19
AD	98,364	7.52	6.62	2
PCN	248,964	19.03	16.76	14
PDC	526,890	40.27	35.48	24
POP	12,151	.92	.82	—
PPS	38,504	2.94	2.59	I
Total valid votes	1,308,505	100.00	88.10	—
Null votes	127,442	—	8.58	—
Blank votes	49,238	—	3.32	—
Total votes	1,485,185	—	100.00	—

Source: Computed from U.S. Department of State, *Foreign Broadcast Information Service, VI, Central America*, 2 Apr. 1982, 1.

TABLE 8-2

Approximate Distribution of the Vote in the Constituent
Assembly Election of 28 March 1982, by Department

Department	Voting Percentage for:						Total Valid Votes
	PDC	ARENA	PCN	AD	PPS	POP	
S. Salvador	44.36	26.65	10.67	12.55	4.42	1.36	289,650
S. Ana	44.07	26.62	15.68	8.69	3.61	1.33	124,505
S. Miguel	37.75	28.17	26.31	5.67	2.10	—	102,356
La Libertad	42.90	29.02	15.45	7.71	3.46	1.46	136,825
Usulután	34.55	35.94	18.12	6.19	3.62	1.58	43,538
Sonsonate	40.14	32.80	17.71	6.33	3.02	—	95,983
La Unión	35.03	25.50	32.89	3.25	1.81	1.52	61,432
La Paz	42.90	27.46	21.51	5.46	2.67	—	48,153
Chalatenango	46.22	41.37	4.85	4.05	2.24	1.28	33,941
Cuscatlán	28.47	42.25	21.62	4.68	1.90	1.09	55,384
Ahuachapán	37.37	52.97	4.36	4.24	—	1.07	39,648
Morazán	47.29	21.20	24.78	5.04	1.69	—	20,634
S. Vicente	39.38	22.02	30.63	6.03	1.93	—	34,302
Cabañas	28.12	34.84	34.29	2.76	—	—	23,033
National	40.79	30.04	17.38	7.78	3.05	.96	1,109,384

Source: Computed from U.S. Department of State, *Foreign Broadcast Information Service,
VI, Central America*, 1 Apr. 1982, pp. 1–2.

TABLE 8-3

Cooperatives Organized under Phase I of the Agrarian Reform,
December 1981

Department	Number of Cooperatives	Total Area	Number Abandoned
Ahuachapán	27	21,174	—
Santa Ana	28	27,669	3
Sonsonate	34	42,424	—
La Libertad	54	56,167	4
Chalatenango	9	10,846	I
San Salvador	14	19,399	2
Cuscatlán	3	4,923	I
La Paz	43	37,426	3
Cabañas	2	1,042	—
San Vicente	27	24,486	9
Usulután	46	40,280	7
San Miguel	20	28,864	I
Morazán	2	1,856	—
La Unión	17	23,120	I
Unknown location	—	—	35

Source: *Proceso*, 2, 55 (1–7 March 1982), p. 8, from Pecchi and Company, Agrarian Reform in El Salvador. Study presented to the Agency for International Development, Washington, D.C., December 1981.

Note: All areas are in *manzanas*. One *manzana* is equal to approximately 17 acres. *Land area abandoned* refers to the land affected by the Reform, turned over to cooperatives and then abandoned by the cooperativists for lack of credit or other difficulties. *Percent abandoned* refers to the cooperatives abandoned as a percent of all cooperatives. *Percent, area abandoned* is the proportion of the land affected by the Reform which has now been abandoned.

Land Area Abandoned	Percent Abandoned	Percent, Area Abandoned
—	—	—
1,243	10.7	4.5
—	—	—
3,320	7.4	5.9
3,288	11.1	30.3
2,863	14.1	14.7
439	33.3	8.9
2,165	6.9	5.8
—	—	—
5,036	33.0	20.6
5,530	15.2	13.7
831	5.0	3.0
—	—	—
2,056	5.9	8.9
27,897	—	—

Notes

CHAPTER I

1. Walter, "Trade and Development," pp. 23–28.
2. Computed from data presented by Walter, ibid., p. 35.
3. Computed from data presented by Walter, ibid., pp. 21, 80.
4. For an example see Anderson, *Matanza*, p. 10.
5. Aubey "Entrepreneurial Formation," p. 281.
6. Torres Rivas, *Interpretación*, p. 86.
7. Anderson, *Matanza*, pp. 40–42.
8. Ibid., pp. 51–55.
9. Abel Cuenca, a Salvadoran rebel leader, survived the revolt of 1932; cited by Anderson in ibid., p. 85.
10. Ibid., p. 136.
11. Marroquín, "Estudio sobre la Crisis," p. 117.
12. Ibid., pp. 118 and 158 (n. 3).
13. "Active state" is a term coined by historian James W. Wilkie to describe how the Mexican state reacted to the crisis of the Depression. Although lacking the resources necessary to become a "welfare state," the state nevertheless proceeded to become very active in the regulation of the economic system. See Wilkie, *Mexican Revolution*, pp. 66–81, for definition and discussion.
14. "Positive state" follows the usage of Lowi, *End of Liberalism*, pp. 57–58.
15. Marroquín, "Estudio sobre la Crisis," pp. 137–38.
16. Minister Suay in Memoria de Hacienda, 1929, p. 4, cited by Marroquín in ibid., p. 123.
17. Anderson, *Matanza*, p. 148.
18. Marroquín, "Estudio sobre la Crisis," pp. 139–40.
19. Anderson, *Matanza*, p. 149.
20. Diario Oficial, 8 Jan. 1935, cited by Marroquín in "Estudio sobre la Crisis," p. 140.
21. Anderson, *Matanza*.
22. Marroquín, "Estudio sobre la Crisis."
23. Anderson, *Matanza*.
24. Webre, *José Napoleón Duarte*, p. 10.

CHAPTER 2

1. For more details on this important episode of contemporary Salvadoran politics see Krehm, *Democracia y Tiranías*, pp. 107–25.
2. The term "Nasserism" is used as suggested by Wiarda, "Latin American Development Process," pp. 464–68.
3. "Reactionary despotism" follows the definition proposed by Giner, "Political Economy and Cultural Legitimation," pp. 19–21.
4. Monteforte Toledo, *Centroamérica*, 2:27, 28, 45. See also Webre, *José Napoleón Duarte*, pp. 20, 49–50, and 90 (n. 34).

5. López Vallecillos, "Rasgos Sociales," p. 872, and Webre, *José Napoleón Duarte*, p. 196.

6. Leal, "Mexican State," pp. 50–52.

7. Purcell and Purcell, "Nature of the Mexican State," p. 39.

8. Aubey, "Entrepreneurial Formation," pp. 270–71, 275–76.

9. I am indebted to José Simán for his worthwhile comments and criticisms of the first draft of this study and, in particular, for sharing with the author his intimate knowledge of this important aspect of Salvadoran life.

10. Colindres, "La Tenencia de la Tierra," p. 471.

11. Colindres's *Fundamentos Económicos de la Burguesía Salvadoreña* (San Salvador: UCA Editions, 1977) is an indispensable source for anyone concerned with how land tenure patterns and agricultural exploitation schemes allowed the Salvadoran oligarchy to make the dollars that paved the road to diversification and control of the banking sector.

12. Colindres, "La Tenencia de la Tierra," p. 471.

13. The Third Census actually underestimates the true extent of land concentration, since it uses units of production, and not individual producers, as its basic unit of analysis. This masks the incidence of multiple ownership and, as a result, underestimates the actual concentration of units of production in the hands of what are basically the same family groups.

14. One hectare equals 2.471 acres.

15. Colindres, "La Tenencia de la Tierra," pp. 466–67.

16. *Latin America Commodities Report* 3, no. 42 (26 Oct. 1979): 154.

17. Sebastián, "Camino Económico," p. 950.

18. One quintal equals 100 pounds.

19. According to Zamora, "¿Seguro de Vida o Despojo?" pp. 513 (n. 6), 533–34.

20. Sebastián, "Camino Económico," pp. 950–51.

21. Guidos Véjar, "Crisis Política," pp. 512–13.

22. López Vallecillos, "Fuerzas Sociales y Cambio Social," p. 558.

23. Guidos Véjar, "Crisis Política," pp. 512–13.

24. Sebastián, "Camino Económico," p. 951.

25. Browning, *El Salvador*, and Walter, "Trade and Development."

26. Wickizer, *Coffee, Tea, and Cocoa*, pp. 463–64.

27. Slutzky and Slutzky, "Estructura de la Explotación," pp. 111–12.

28. Zamora, "¿Seguro de Vida o Despojo?," pp. 513–14.

29. Mooney, "Gross Domestic Product," p. 505, table 8.

30. Ibid., pp. 504–5.

31. Sebastián, "Camino Económico," p. 950.

32. Burke, "Sistema de Plantación," p. 478.

33. El Salvador, *Anuario Estadístico, 1966*, vol. 3, chart 1, p. 1.

34. Raynolds, *Rapid Development*, pp. 95–96.

35. For an authoritative account of that war see Anderson, *War of the Dispossessed*.

36. Burke, "Sistema de Plantación," pp. 476 and 481.

CHAPTER 3

1. López Vallecillos, "Fuerzas Sociales y Cambio Social," pp. 560–61.

2. Ibid., p. 560.

3. Monteforte Toledo, *Centroamérica*, 2:26–30.

4. López Vallecillos, "Fuerzas Sociales y Cambio Social," p. 561.

5. Webre, *José Napoleón Duarte*, p. 37.

6. Parker, *Central American Republics*, p. 158.

7. Ibid., p. 159.
8. Webre, *José Napoleón Duarte*, p. 41.
9. Ibid., p. 40.
10. Aubey, "Entrepreneurial Formation," p. 270.
11. Inter-American Development Bank, *1979 Report*, p. 20, table I–10.
12. Monteforte Toledo, *Centroamérica*, 1:304.
13. Wynia, *Politics and Planners*, pp. 92–93.
14. See above, pp. 00–00.
15. See Mayorga, "Crítica de las Ideologías."
16. Monteforte Toledo, *Centroamérica*, 2:43.
17. Webre, *José Napoleón Duarte*, p. 126.
18. Ibid., pp. 91–92.
19. Ibid., p. 160.
20. Ibid., pp. 170–76.
21. Ibid., pp. 176–80, for more details on this revolt.
22. Simán, "La Esperanza," p. 1043.

CHAPTER 4

1. See Baloyra, "Theoretical Aspects of the Transition," for an extended discussion of this matter.
2. Andino Martínez, "Estamento Militar," pp. 624–28, and charts 3 and 4, provides a detailed list of high-ranking officers appointed to the directorships of autonomous institutes and other state enterprises by Molina and by Romero.
3. For a discussion of the characteristics of these BA regimes see Cardoso, "Characterization"; Garretón, "Seguridad Nacional"; Riz, "Formas de Estado"; and Zermeño, "Estado y Sociedad."
4. See Sebastián, "Camino Económico," pp. 428–29, 431.
5. Campos, "Seguridad Nacional," pp. 477–78.
6. Ibid., pp. 478–80.
7. Mariscal, "Militares y Reformismo," pp. 16, 22–27, and Menjívar and Ruiz, pp. 489–90, follow this line of analysis which has considerable merit. However, it is difficult to see how something that was not consolidated, the national security state, could be in crisis.
8. López Vallecillos, "Rasgos Sociales," p. 869.
9. Guidos Véjar, "Crisis Política," pp. 514–16.
10. Ibid., p. 514.
11. López Vallecillos, "Rasgos Sociales," pp. 869–70.
12. See Anderson, *Matanza*, chaps. 6–9, for more details.
13. Ungo, "Consideraciones," pp. 452–53.
14. Ibid., pp. 453–56.
15. Zamora, "¿Seguro de Vida o Despojo?" pp. 519, 521.
16. Sebastián, "Criterios," pp. 580, 584.
17. Ungo, "Consideraciones," p. 453.
18. Ibid., p. 455.
19. Menjívar and Ruiz, "Transformación Agraria," p. 490.
20. *Estudios Centro Americanos*, 335/336 (Sept.–Oct. 1976), p. 612.
21. Ibid., p. 611.
22. Ibid.
23. Ibid., p. 615.

24. Ibid., p. 613.

25. Ibid., pp. 617–18.

26. Ibid., p. 618.

27. Ibid., pp. 614–15.

28. Ibid., pp. 619–20.

29. Valero Iglesias, "Nueva Legislación," p. 569 (nn. 2, 5, 6, and 7).

30. Zamora, "¿Seguro de Vida o Despojo?" pp. 525 (note 28) and 534.

31. Ibid., p. 525.

32. See the list in *Estudios Centro Americanos*, 335/336 (Sept.–Oct. 1976), p. 612.

33. Zamora, "¿Seguro de Vida o Despojo?" p. 529.

34. See *Estudios Centro Americanos*, 335/336 (Sept.–Oct. 1976), pp. 626–32, for the reasons why some outside actors opposed the ISTA Project, and pp. 622–33, for the rationale utilized by the UCS and the PCS to support it.

35. Menjívar and Ruiz, "Transformación Agraria," p. 496.

36. Zamora, "¿Seguro de Vida o Despojo?" pp. 526–27.

37. See the editorial "¡A Sus Ordenes, Mi Capital!" in *Estudios Centro Americanos*, 337 (Nov. 1976), pp. 637–43.

38. In the opinion of Guidos Véjar, "Crisis Política," p. 514, among others.

39. López Vallecillos, "Fuerzas Sociales," p. 560.

40. Ibid.

41. Guidos Véjar, "Crisis Política," p. 514.

42. Zamora, "¿Seguro de Vida o Despojo," p. 527.

43. For a discussion of the pastoral and theological underpinnings of the attitude of the Catholic church see Paredes, "Situación de la Iglesia," and Sobrino, "La Iglesia."

44. For a brief account of the work of Fr. Grande and other Catholic priests by outside lay observers see Allman, "Rising to Rebellion," pp. 32–35, and Buckley, "Letter," pp. 61, 64, and 66–67.

45. See Ungo, "Derechos Humanos," for commentary, description, and discussion of the domestic impact in El Salvador of the reports on human rights violations prepared by the Department of State (pp. 490–92), the British parliamentary commission (pp. 492–96), and the Inter-American Commission on Human Rights of the Organization of American States (pp. 496–502). Ungo's own conclusion stressed the failure of the military governments to legitimize their systematic violations of human rights during the 1970s (p. 506).

46. *Latin America Political Report* 12, no. 40 (13 Oct. 1978): 315.

47. Guidos Véjar, "Crisis Política," p. 517.

48. Ibid., p. 518.

49. Samayoa and Galván, "Movimiento Obrero," pp. 595–97.

50. *Estudios Centro Americanos*, 369/370 (July–Aug. 1979), pp. 729–32, presents a list of the principal labor organizations of El Salvador. For description and commentary on the role of labor during the critical months leading to the coup of 15 October 1979 see Samayoa and Galván, "Cierre Patronal," pp. 793–800.

51. Anderson, *Politics and Economic Change*, pp. 97–106.

52. Martín Baró, "Fantasmas," pp. 285–86.

53. Campos, "Seguridad Nacional," pp. 934–40.

54. *Endurecimiento* means "hardening." I did not include a detailed discussion of the electoral fraud of 1977 in order to avoid burdening an already long and detailed chapter. A brief account of this important episode may be found in Webre, *José Napoleón Duarte*, pp. 196–201.

55. See Flores Pinel, "Golpe de Estado," pp. 888–90, for further elaboration.

CHAPTER 5

1. Samayoa and Galván, "Cierre Patronal," p. 794.

2. See "Al Borde de la Guerra Civil," *Estudios Centro Americanos*, 371 (Sept. 1979), pp. 735–40, for the opinion of those intellectuals.

3. See "Plataforma del Foro Popular," *Estudios Centro Americanos*, 371 (Sept. 1979), pp. 843–45, for more details.

4. Flores Pinel, "Golpe de Estado," p. 895.

5. The opinion of López Vallecillos, "Rasgos Sociales," p. 878. See also Flores Pinel, "Golpe de Estado."

6. As cited by López Vallecillos, "Rasgos Sociales," pp. 879–80.

7. "Proclama de la Fuerza Armada de El Salvador," *Estudios Centro Americanos*, 372/373 (Oct.–Nov. 1979), pp. 1017–18.

8. López Vallecillos, "Rasgos Sociales," p. 880.

9. Ibid., 879.

10. The government was formally constituted by Resolution No. 4, issued by the junta on 22 October 1979. For the composition of the first cabinet of the government see *Estudios Centro Americanos*, 374 (Dec. 1979), p. 1109.

11. Ibid., pp. 1110–11.

12. Ibid., pp. 1109–10.

13. The final report of the Special Commission on the disappeared may be found in *Estudios Centro Americanos*, 375/376 (Jan.–Feb. 1980), pp. 136–39.

14. *Estudios Centro Americanos*, 374 (Dec. 1979), p. 1113.

15. Ibid., pp. 1114–15.

16. *Estudios Centro Americanos*, 377/378 (Mar.–Apr. 1980), pp. 370–72, reproduces a 3 March 1980 declaration by ABECAFE protesting Decree No. 75. The decree was published in the 2 January 1980 issue of the Diario Oficial.

17. *Estudios Centro Americanos*, 374 (Dec. 1979), p. 1117.

18. The letter was sent on 26 October 1979 and was reprinted in *Estudios Centro Americanos*, 372/373 (Oct.–Nov. 1979), pp. 1032–33.

19. An American correspondent who visited El Salvador in early summer 1981 reported having seen a squad of eight national guardsmen delivering the payroll of one of the *fincas* that had escaped nationalization. "By then," this correspondent wrote, "I knew of the close relationship between the National Guard and the landowners, but I couldn't help asking him if he didn't find such a system unusual." The landowner responded, "I suppose you're right, . . . but that's the way it has always been here" (Buckley, "Letter," p. 61).

20. See *Estudios Centro Americanos*, 372/373 (Oct.–Nov. 1979), pp. 1025–26.

21. Ibid., pp. 1027–29.

22. Ibid., p. 1030.

23. Campos, "El Papel," p. 944.

24. Ibid.

25. See *Estudios Centro Americanos*, 375/376 (Jan.–Feb. 1980), pp. 117–118.

26. Ibid., p. 117.

27. Ibid.

28. Ibid., p. 118.

29. See Gil et al., "Peaceful Transition," pp. 40–46, 101–7, and 134–35.

30. "El COPEFA Responde," *Estudios Centro Americanos*, 375/376 (Jan.–Feb. 1980), pp. 119–20.

31. Ibid., emphasis added.

32. Jiménez Cabrera viewed them as "neopopulist reformists." See "Alternativa Reformista," pp. 967–69.

33. "La Fuerza Armada al Pueblo Salvadoreño," *Estudios Centro Americanos*, 375/376 (Jan. 1980), pp. 132–33.

34. Ibid., p. 125.

35. Ibid., p. 126.

36. Ibid., pp. 127–28.

37. For the text of some of these communiqués see *Estudios Centro Americanos*, 377/378 (Mar.–Apr. 1980), pp. 359–70.

38. *Estudios Centro Americanos*, 375/376 (Jan. 1980), pp. 128–30.

39. The text of this platform was reproduced in *Estudios Centro Americanos*, 377/378 (Mar.–Apr. 1980), pp. 343–45.

40. *Estudios Centro Americanos*, 375/376 (Jan. 1980), pp. 133–36.

41. Ibid., p. 130.

42. *Estudios Centro Americanos*, 377/378 (Mar.–Apr. 1980), pp. 372–74.

43. For more details see Escobar, "Línea de la Muerte."

44. See *Estudios Centro Americanos*, 377/378 (Mar.–Apr. 1980), for the message addressed by the Popular Tendency of the PDC to the national convention of the party (pp. 374–76); for a joint letter signed by Roberto Lara, Francisco Díaz, Héctor Dada, Rubén Zamora, Alberto Arene, and Francisco Paniagua stating their reasons for resigning from the PDC (pp. 378–79).

45. Ibid., pp. 379–80.

46. Ibid., pp. 380–81.

47. Ibid., pp. 383–84.

48. Ibid., pp. 396–97.

49. Ibid.

50. *Latin America Weekly Report*, WR-80-15, 18 Apr. 1980, p. 4.

51. *Estudios Centro Americanos*, 377/378 (Mar.–Apr. 1980), pp. 402–403.

52. See text of Decree No. 153 in ibid., pp. 386–89.

53. Ibid., pp. 391–92.

54. Ibid., pp. 390–91. The state of siege was still in effect at the time of the second anniversary of the coup, 15 October 1981.

55. See a transcript of his presentation in *Estudios Centro Americanos*, 381/382 (July–Aug. 1980), pp. 780–84.

56. See the editorial "Estado de Sitio," in ibid., pp. 663–66.

57. For the sake of clarity I have added some elements to Giner's original formulation. See Giner, "Cultural Legitimation," pp. 19–25.

58. For more details see Baloyra, "Deterioration," p. 41.

59. For a critical evaluation of the reform see Wheaton, *Agrarian Reform*, pp. 10–14.

60. See notes 52 and 53, above.

61. Wheaton, *Agrarian Reform*, p. 11.

62. Text in *Estudios Centro Americanos*, 377/378 (Mar.–Apr. 1980), pp. 391–93.

63. Ibid., p. 371.

CHAPTER 6

1. Technically, prosecutor Méndez had fifteen days during which to file charges of treason and sedition against the conspirators, but none was forthcoming.

2. *Miami Herald*, 17 May 1980, p. 22A.

3. Jack Anderson's syndicated column echoed Ambassador White's charge that conservatives

in the United States were undermining the policies of the Carter administration toward El Salvador. The column quoted a Defense Intelligence Agency (DIA) report which concluded that "the threat of anarchy and of a total collapse of the economy are as great a danger as that posed by the growing strength of the guerrillas" (*Miami Herald*, 2 July 1980, p. 7A).

4. *Miami Herald*, 9 July 1980, p. 4A.

5. *Washington Post*, 5 Sept. 1980, p. A21.

6. *Christian Science Monitor*, 21 Nov. 1980, p. 4.

7. *Washington Post*, 29 Nov. 1980, p. A14.

8. *Estudios Centro Americanos*, 377/378 (Mar.–Apr. 1980), pp. 376–79.

9. Ibid., pp. 396–98.

10. Ibid., p. 377.

11. Ibid., p. 375.

12. *El País* (Madrid), 7 Sept. 1980, as quoted in the feature article "Falsa partida entre dos coroneles," by Carlos María Gutiérrez.

13. This description is taken from "Report to the President."

14. Rogers and Bowdler were accompanied by Dr. Luigi Einaudi of the Department of State's Bureau of American Republics. They flew into Honduras by commercial carrier and from there to El Salvador by military aircraft. During the mission's stay in El Salvador several anonymous threats were delivered against its members by individuals believed to be associated with the Right.

15. "Report to the President."

16. *New York Times*, 16 Jan. 1981, p. 6.

17. *New York Times*, 19 Jan. 1981, p. 11.

18. Ibid.

19. *New York Times*, 22 Jan. 1981, p. 14.

20. *New York Times*, 11 Jan. 1981, p. 27.

21. The former provided by Salvadoran right-winger Roberto D'Aubuisson during a trip to Washington in June 1980. The latter was the characterization provided by Senator Jesse Helms (R.-N.C.) in his testimony against White's confirmation as ambassador to El Salvador. See U.S., Congress, Senate Committee on Foreign Relations, "Nomination of Robert E. White," p. 10.

22. For a glimpse of Helms's activities see Elizabeth Drew, "Jesse Helms," *New Yorker*, 20 July 1981, especially pp. 86 and 90–93. One of the stormiest episodes involved the nomination of Ernest W. Lefever to head the department's Office of Human Rights. Lefever had to withdraw his nomination.

23. To keep this discussion succinct I will omit a number of references to developments within the Reagan administration which seem to have contributed to this. Perhaps more relevant during the early days of the administration were the frequent clashes between Secretary Haig and National Security Advisor Richard Allen, Secretary of Defense Casper Weinberger, Presidential Advisor Edwin Meese, and United Nations Ambassador Professor Jeane J. Kirkpatrick. I can only speculate on the degree to which fights about bureaucratic turf may have impinged on the formulation of policy toward El Salvador. On the other hand, the struggle between Haig and Helms over the question of appointments to senior positions at the Department of State became more visible and, as far as the Salvadoran crisis is concerned, may have been one more signal to the Salvadoran Right that a more sympathetic group of policy makers would soon be in office.

24. As quoted in a *New York Times* story on 10 June 1981, p. 8.

25. Respectively, U.S., Department of State, Bureau of Public Affairs, *Communist Interference*, and U.S., Department of State, *Documents Demonstrating*.

26. *Communist Interference*, p. 1.

27. Ibid.

28. *New York Times*, 27 Feb. 1981, p. 4.

29. *Newsweek*, overseas edition, 9 Mar. 1981, p. 12.

30. *Washington Post*, 27 Feb. 1981, p. A27.

31. Ibid.

32. *Miami Herald*, 21 Feb. 1981, p. 12A.

33. According to the analysis of the Special Report conducted by reporter Jonathan Kwitny of the *Wall Street Journal*, the tonnage of the weapons delivered to the guerrillas was extrapolated from the cargo-hauling potential of several trucks listed in Document N—in the book of documents—of the captured lot (*Wall Street Journal*, 8 June 1981, pp. 1, 10). The published reproductions of the document in question consist of three pages of what must be a magnified copy of the original. One of the pages includes a map; all are full of figures attributing different quantities—of weapons or personnel, it is not clear—to the different guerrilla groups, perhaps in connection with actions mentioned in the document. Only on one page is there specific reference to tonnage, and this is nowhere near two hundred tons. As far as this writer can tell from the evidence disclosed in the book of documents, the guerrillas had a supply operation going, but it was rather modest.

34. *New York Times*, 25 Mar. 1981, pp. 1, 3.

35. This attracted front-page coverage the next day, 26 February. See *Miami Herald*, pp. 1A, 18A; *New York Times*, pp. 1, 6; and *Washington Post*, pp. A1, A24.

36. For samples of editorial opinion see *Miami Herald*, 27 Feb. 1981, p. 6A, and *New York Times*, 27 Feb. 1981, p. 26. Also John Armitage, "Dubious U.S. Course in El Salvador," *Christian Science Monitor*, 3 March 1981, p. 23; and the irrepressible satire of Russell Baker "Indians Did It in Smoke," *New York Times*, 4 Mar. 1981, p. A27.

37. Juan de Onís, "Now Hear This," *New York Times*, 1 Mar. 1981, sect. 4, p. 1; William LeoGrande, "El Salvador, Vietnam, Take Two," and John McMullan, "Robert White vs. the Dogs of War," *Miami Herald*, 1 Mar. 1981, pp. 1E and 4E, and 2E, respectively.

38. For example, two long articles by Karen de Young, "El Salvador: A Symbol of World Crisis," *Washington Post*, 8 March 1981, and "Reagan Sends a Message to Moscow via El Salvador," *Washington Post*, 9 March 1981.

39. See excerpts of a debate between former ambassador Robert White and Dr. Jeane Kirkpatrick, ambassador to the United Nations, in *New York Times*, 8 Mar. 1981, sect. 4, p. 1.

40. *Miami Herald*, 5 Mar. 1981, p. 29A. At this time, Graham had not become a member of the Reagan administration, but Fontaine was serving as an expert on Latin America in the National Security Council.

41. *New York Times*, 7 Mar. 1981, pp. 1, 4.

CHAPTER 7

1. See "Dissent Paper," ESCATF-D no. 80-3.

2. Shirley Christian, "Salvador Policy Galvanizes U.S. Churches," *Miami Herald*, 26 Apr. 1981, p. 30A.

3. As related by Anthony Lewis in "Showing His Colors," *New York Times*, 29 Mar. 1981, p. E21.

4. Ibid.

5. U.S., Congress, Senate, Committee on Foreign Relations, *The Situation in El Salvador*, p. 235.

6. *New York Times*, 10 Apr. 1981, p. 3. On the evening of 7 April units of the Treasury Police dragged twenty-three men from their homes in the small village of Soyapango and executed them. Seven more who refused to leave their homes were shot in front of their families (*Miami Herald*, 16 Apr. 1981, p. 22C).

7. *Miami Herald*, 16 Apr. 1981, pp. 1A, 26A.

8. *New York Times*, 10 Apr. 1981, p. 3.

9. *Miami Herald*, 8 Apr. 1981, p. 8A.

10. *New York Times*, 16 Apr. 1981, pp. 1, 4.

11. *Miami Herald*, 23 Apr. 1981, p. 32A.

12. See *Christian Science Monitor*, 30 Apr. 1981, pp. 1, 9, and *Washington Post*, 2 May 1981, pp. A1, A14.

13. John M. Goshko, "U.S. Knows Who Killed Nuns, but Evidence Is Shaky," *Miami Herald*, 9 May 1981, p. 22A.

14. Ibid.

15. *Miami Herald*, 10 May 1981, pp. 1A, 15A.

16. *Miami Herald*, 12 May 1981, p. 6B.

17. U.S., Department of State, Bureau of Public Affairs, *Gist* (May 1981).

18. Ibid.

19. *Miami Herald*, 20 May 1981, p. 11D.

20. *Miami Herald*, 23 May 1981, p. 22A.

21. *Miami Herald*, 28 May 1981, p. 30A.

22. Ibid.

23. Ibid.

24. *Miami Herald*, 3 June 1981, p. 18A.

25. *New York Times*, 6 June 1981, p. 9.

26. *Miami Herald*, 18 June 1981, p. 10C.

27. *Latin America Regional Reports, Mexico and Central America*, RM-81-06, 10 July 1981, p. 2.

28. *Solidaridad*, 12 July 1981.

29. *New York Times*, 11 November 1981, p. 6.

30. Christopher Dickey, "Army, Right Seen Boosting Power; Left Expected to Ignore Salvador Vote," *Washington Post*, 31 Aug. 1981, pp. A1, A11.

31. Christopher Dickey, "U.S. Could Raise Aid to El Salvador," *Washington Post*, 21 Aug. 1981, p. A16.

32. *Miami Herald*, 28 Aug. 1981, p. 17A.

33. Ibid. For a review of the evidence available and of the depositions of Torres and Sol Meza see Shirley Christian, "Slayings Are Test for Salvador Court," *Miami Herald*, 19 May 1981, p. 7C.

34. *Miami Herald*, 23 Oct. 1981, p. 10D.

35. Shirley Christian, "G.I. Asks Reward Share in Salvador Murder Case," *Miami Herald*, 2 Oct. 1981, p. 17A.

36. Tom Fiedler, "FBI Investigating Murders in El Salvador," *Miami Herald*, 14 Apr. 1981, p. 16A. The linkages between the two cases are myriad. For example, Judge Héctor Enrique Jiménez was called to the capital to take on the Sheraton murders case; he had been handling the nuns' murder-rape case until then. I have not been able to ascertain why and when Judge Tinetti substituted for Judge Jiménez in the Sheraton case, how Judge Mario Alberto Rivera took over the nuns' case, or if he was the only judge active in the case after Jiménez was transferred. On 4 February 1982, Judge Bernardo Rauda Murcia was assigned to the nuns' case after Rivera's unexplained resignation. Judge Rauda Murcia is the Salvadoran magistrate who, after fourteen months of uncertainty and ambiguity, finally initiated formal proceedings against the guardsmen. For the early developments in those proceedings see Christopher Dickey, "One of Suspects Is Said to Confess in El Salvador," *Washington Post*, 9 Feb. 1982, pp. A1, A13; Christopher Dickey, "Salvadorans Arraigned in Nuns' Death," *Washington Post*, 11 Feb. 1982, pp. A1, A25, A26; and Christopher Dickey, "Salvadoran President Calls Six Detained in Nuns' Case 'Guilty,'"

Washington Post, 12 Feb. 1982, p. A46. In early January 1982 the Fifth Criminal Court of El Salvador finally, and quietly, dropped all charges against Sol Meza and Christ, the two suspects in the Sheraton case, on the grounds of insufficient evidence. See *Miami Herald*, 5 Jan. 1982, p. 7A.

37. Barbara Crossette, "Salvador's President, in U.S., Tells of Crackdown on Army," *New York Times*, 22 Sept. 1981, p. 4.

38. According to Mary McGrory, "Our Recent Past Is Haunting Duarte's Efforts to Win Friends," *Washington Post*, 24 Sept. 1981, p. A3.

39. Ibid.

40. Mary McGrory, "Pressure Over Missionaries' Death Is Only Card," *Washington Post*, 1 Oct. 1981, p. A3.

41. Ibid.

42. Robert E. White, "The U.S. and El Salvador," *New York Times*, 2 Oct. 1981, p. 27.

43. McGrory, "Pressure."

44. According to Mary McGrory, "The Pentagon, Praise Be, Is Showing Restraint on El Salvador," *Washington Post*, 12 Nov. 1981, p. A3.

45. Raymond Bonner, "Salvador Inquiry Stalled in Slaying of U.S. Nuns," *New York Times*, 13 Nov. 1981, p. 8.

46. Loren Jenkins, "Salvadoran Justice Cowed by Violence," *Washington Post*, 2 May 1981, pp. A1, A14; Warren Hoge, "Soldiers Are the Villains in Salvador Horror Tales," *New York Times*, 5 June 1981, p. 4; and Bonner, "Salvador Inquiry," provide valuable information on the breakdown and near total paralysis of the judicial system of El Salvador.

47. Dr. Fernando Méndez, vice-president of the Salvadoran Human Rights Commission, asked the government to rescind the decree, which also authorizes the prosecution of minors and violates articles 175 and 177 of the Salvadoran constitution (*SALPRESS*, 8 Sept. 1981, p. 1).

48. Bonner, "Salvador Inquiry."

49. Father Paul Schindler, the first North American to reach the women's shallow grave and one of the few witnesses to give a deposition in the case, claimed that embassy sources communicated this to him in early January 1981. Fr. Schindler told correspondent Bonner that the questions that government investigators asked of him were absolutely worthless and centered primarily on why he had begun to disinter the bodies without permission from the local justice of the peace (Bonner, "Salvador Inquiry").

50. Duarte announced this at a press conference in which he also said that the investigation into the murder of Archbishop Romero had been completed (*New York Times*, 14 Mar. 1981, p. 6). At the press conference, Duarte also disclosed that investigators had found the site where the women were raped and shot (*Miami Herald*, 14 Mar. 1981, p. 30A). See also James Nelson Goodsell, "U.S. Stiffens Salvador Policy, Tells Junta to Clean Up Its Act," *Christian Science Monitor*, 30 Apr. 1981, pp. 1, 9.

51. Goshko, "U.S. Knows."

52. Ibid.

53. Bonner, "Salvador Inquiry." On 4 February 1982, Judge Bernardo Rauda Murcia was assigned to the case. On 10 February, Judge Rauda presided over the arraignment of six men charged with the murder. Four of the accused had been in custody since April 1981, including former national guard sergeant Luis Antonio Colindres Alemán, who was in charge of the patrol that apprehended the women. The two other suspects were arrested in late January 1982. All had been dismissed from the national guard on 9 February, since Salvadoran military personnel cannot be tried for murder by civilian courts. See Christopher Dickey, "Salvadorans Arraigned in Nuns' Deaths," *Washington Post*, 11 Feb. 1982, pp. A1, A25, A26.

54. Goshko, "U.S. Knows."

55. U.S., Department of State, Bureau of Public Affairs, *El Salvador*, p. 6.

56. Officials at the American embassy in San Salvador compiled the number of deaths for which the FARN assumed responsibility in fourteen war bulletins issued by this guerrilla group between January 1980 and February 1981. This compilation resulted in a total of 1,100 deaths caused by the FARN. For more discussion and contrast among estimates offered by different sources—including the American embassy in San Salvador, the Ministry of Defense, the Socorro Jurídico, and the Documentation and Information Center of the Central American University (UCA)—see John Dinges, "Compiling the Body Count," *Washington Post*, 27 Jan. 1982, pp. A1, A16.

57. See Christopher Wenner, "Kidnapping Is Old Weapon and Perhaps the Cruelest," *Miami Herald*, 14 June 1981, p. 5D. See also Christopher Dickey, "Kidnapping Becoming a Fact of Life for Latin America," *Washington Post*, 4 Oct. 1981, p. 1H.

58. For a critique of AIFLD activities in El Salvador see Wheaton, *Agrarian Reform*, pp. 2–4, 7, 10, 16–17, and 19. Apparently, someone forgot to tell the assassins of Hammer, Pearlman, Viera, and the countless ISTA officials who had been killed since 15 Oct. 1979 that their victims were really "white revolutionaries" who did not intend to change anything in El Salvador.

59. Ibid., p. 19.

60. Juan de Onís, "2 Salvadoreans Held in U.S. Aides' Deaths," *New York Times*, 16 Apr. 1981, pp. 1, 4.

61. Daniel Southerland, "New Allegations against Rightists in El Salvador," *Christian Science Monitor*, 4 Mar. 1981, pp. 1, 9.

62. U.S., Congress, Senate, Committee on Foreign Relations, *The Situation in El Salvador*, p. 240. This statement by Amnesty International is congruent with the evidence presented in Table 7 concerning the targets of government violence. The statement described violence against academicians, journalists, internal refugees, human rights monitors, and the church (ibid., pp. 240–41).

63. Raymond Bonner, "Salvador Land Program Aids Few," *New York Times*, 3 Aug. 1981, pp. 1, 4.

64. Ibid.

65. Raymond Bonner, "In Salvador's Many-Sided Conflict, the U.S. Presence Is Potent," *New York Times*, 8 July 1981, p. 4.

66. Shirley Christian, "Reforms Bring Peasants Land and a Mortgage," *Miami Herald*, 14 Aug. 1981, p. 26A.

67. Richard Alan White, "El Salvador between Two Fires."

68. Raymond Bonner, "Refugees in Salvadoran Camp Are Forced to Move by Army," *New York Times*, 6 July 1981, pp. 1, 4.

69. Raymond Bonner, "For War's Castaways, Prison Is Home in Salvador," *New York Times*, 10 July 1981, p. 2.

70. Ibid.

71. *Latin America Weekly Report*, WR-81-25, 26 June 1981, p. 9.

72. Shirley Christian and Guy Gugliotta, "2 Years of Civil War Have Left one Salvadoran in 10 Homeless," *Miami Herald*, 25 Aug. 1981, p. 20A.

73. Shirley Christian, "Refugees Real Losers in Salvador War," *Miami Herald*, 25 Aug. 1981, pp. 1A, 22A.

74. Ibid.

75. Raymond Bonner, "Salvador Troops Fly to Honduras," *New York Times*, 22 July 1981, p. 3.

76. *Miami Herald*, 29 Oct. 1981, p. 13C.

77. Alma Guillermoprieto, "Salvadoran Rebels Said to Gain Territory," *Washington Post*, 10 Nov. 1981, pp. A1, A21, A22.

78. Ibid., p. A21.

79. Some of these are related in Confederación Universitaria Centroamericana, *Los Refugiados Salvadoreños*.

80. See Alma Guillermoprieto, "Foreign Visitors Avert Kidnapping of Salvadorans," *Washington Post*, 19 Nov. 1981, p. A20. Also *Newsweek*, 30 Nov. 1981, p. 63.

81. *New York Times*,8 Mar. 1981, sect. 4, p. 2

82. See below, pp. 155–58.

83. See above, chap. 6.

84. *Latin America Weekly Report*, WR-81-13, 27 Mar. 1981, pp. 6–7.

85. *Miami Herald*, 3 May 1981, p. 25A.

86. *Latin America Weekly Report*, WR-81-19, 15 May 1981, p. 4.

87. Alma Guillermoprieto, "Business Wars on Government in El Salvador," *Washington Post*, 27 June 1981, pp. A1, A12.

88. *Latin America Regional Reports, Mexico and Central America*, RM-81-08, 18 Sept. 1981, p. 5.

89. Guillermoprieto, "Business Wars," p. A12.

90. *Latin America Regional Reports, Mexico and Central America*, RM-81-08, 18 Sept. 1981, p. 5.

91. *Latin America Weekly Report*, WR-81-36, 11 Sept. 1981, pp. 3–4.

92. Guillermoprieto, "Business Wars," p. A12.

93. Ibid.

94. *La Prensa Gráfica*, 30 Mar. 1981, p. 26.

95. Guillermoprieto, "Business Wars," p. A12.

96. Warren Hoge, "Salvadoran Business Is Not for the Timid," *New York Times*, 25 May 1981, pp. 1, 18. Another businessman told Hoge, "Small businessmen like me always left politics to the big men . . . and what happened? They got up and split" (ibid.).

97. An impression confirmed by Raymond Bonner at a Fourth of July party given by Ambassador Hinton and attended by some of these millionaires among the three hundred or so guests (Bonner, "In Salvador's Many-Sided," p. 4).

98. Guillermoprieto, "Business Wars," p. A12.

99. Raymond Bonner, "Salvador Leader Says Biggest Threat Is from Rightist Businessmen," *New York Times*, 2 July 1981, p. 6.

100. Ibid.

101. Ibid. In February 1982 a weary Duarte reiterated these views to an American correspondent. Describing the behavior of parties vying for private sector support in the constituent assembly elections of March 1982, Duarte said that they "have joined the democratic process but they don't believe in democracy. . . . They want to go back to being a privileged class—they want the oligarchy back" (Beth Nissen, "Unexpected Enemies," *Newsweek*, 15 Feb. 1982, p. 34).

102. Bonner, "Salvador Leader."

103. *Latin America Regional Reports, Mexico and Central America*, RM-81-06, 10 July 1981, pp. 1, 2. Morales Ehrlich had two guerrilla sons, José Antonio, 22, incarcerated at Santa Tecla prison, and Carlos Ernesto, 21, rumored dead. See Warren Hoge, "Salvador's Agony Tears a Family Apart: 2 Sons of a Junta Member Are Rebels," *New York Times*, 4 June 1981, p. 2.

104. *Miami Herald*, 13 July 1981, p. 14A.

105. U.S., Department of State, Bureau of Public Affairs, "El Salvador: The Search for Peace," *Current Policy*, no. 296, pp. 2–3.

106. Ibid.

107. Raymond Bonner, "Salvadoran Right Seeks More Power," *New York Times*, 20 July 1981, p. 1.

108. Ibid.

109. Ibid.

110. Ibid.

111. *Miami Herald*, 23 July 1981, p. 9D.

112. *Miami Herald*, 24 July 1981, p. 2D.

113. *Latin America Regional Reports, Mexico and Central America*, RM-81-07, 14 Aug. 1981, pp. 4–5.

114. Ibid.

115. *New York Times*, 17 Sept. 1981, p. 4.

116. From two editorials in *El Diario de Hoy*, 18 Sept. 1981.

117. Crossette, "Salvador President," p. 4.

118. *Miami Herald*, 29 Sept. 1981, p. 14A.

119. Alma Guillermoprieto, "Parties Support Ouster of Junta in El Salvador," *Washington Post*, 11 Nov. 1981, p. A35.

120. *Miami Herald*, 9 Oct. 1981, p. 16F.

121. *Miami Herald*, 29 Sept. 1981, p. 14A. See also *Latin America Regional Reports, Mexico and Central America*, RM-81-09, 23 Oct. 1981, pp. 1, 2.

122. See above, pp. 44, 46–47.

123. *Latin America Regional Reports, Mexico and Central America*, RM-81-09, 23 Oct. 1981, p. 1.

124. *Miami Herald*, 1 Nov. 1981, p. 18F.

125. *Miami Herald*, 6 Nov. 1981, p. 24A. Medrano's POP was the only opposition party that did not join in this power grab and voted with the Christian Democrats against the motion.

126. Ibid.

127. Guillermoprieto, "Parties Support," p. A35.

128. A candid observation made by the astute Christian Democratic mayor of San Salvador Adolfo Rey Prendes, cited by Dickey, "Army, Right Seen," p. A11.

129. More on this below, p. 158.

130. Jackson Diehl, "U.S. Told to Stand Firm against Salvadoran Right," *Washington Post*, 20 Nov. 1981, p. A32.

131. *Washington Post*, 9 Dec. 1981, p. A18.

132. *Miami Herald*, 10 Oct. 1981, p. 18A.

133. The letter was printed simultaneously with an editorial reply in which Duarte was asked to stop seeing ghosts and to refrain from obscuring the truth with the conventional mythology. See both in *Miami Herald*, 9 Nov. 1981, p. 6A.

134. The letter of the Alianza appeared in the *Herald*'s edition of 30 Nov. 1981, p. 12A. See also Guy Gugliotta, "Support for Free Enterprise Pledged by Salvadoran Chief," *Miami Herald*, 1 Dec. 1981, p. 15A.

135. Ibid.

136. Ibid.

137. Ibid.

138. *Miami Herald*, 6 Dec. 1981, p. 16C.

139. "An American Disease," *Newsweek*, 2 Nov. 1981, p. 120.

140. See Figure 7, above.

141. *New York Times*, 2 Apr. 1980, p. 10. See also *Estudios Centro Americanos*, 377/378 (Mar.–Apr. 1980), p. 346.

142. See CIDES—Centroamérica, "Notas, El Salvador," no. 1, 19 Aug. 1980.

143. *Estudios Centro Americanos*, ibid.

144. From a facsimile, n.d.

145. Anyone with even a casual acquaintance with Dada, Mayorga, Ungo, and Zamora—to name a few who were in the first junta and in the first cabinet of the Gobierno Provisional

Revolucionario—knows different. However, this does not deny the difficult predicament in which they found themselves.

146. The reader may consult the following sources and draw his own conclusions: LP-28, "Programa de Gobierno," and FAPU, "Este es el programa," in *Estudios Centro Americanos*, 377/378 (Mar.–Apr. 1980), pp. 347–56; and MPSC, "Carta de denuncia," and MNR, "Posición del MNR," in *Estudios Centro Americanos*, 381/382 (July–Aug. 1980), pp. 773–79.

147. For example, the statement made by Guillermo Manuel Ungo, who replaced Enrique Alvarez as secretary general of the FDR after the latter was assassinated, at a press conference in Mexico City. See Alan Riding, "Salvadoran Spreads Word Abroad: Back the Rebels," *New York Times*, 29 Jan. 1981.

148. Expressed by Rubén Zamora in a telephone interview with *Newsweek*. See "The Cubans Do Not Arm Us," *Newsweek International*, 9 Mar. 1981, p. 12.

149. The private confidence of a Salvadoran cabinet minister to Raymond Bonner; see "U.S. Stand Is Countered by Many in El Salvador," *New York Times*, 8 July 1981, p. 2.

150. In September 1981, Ungo complained that Duarte was trying to divide the FDR-FMLN coalition by inviting only the MNR and the UDN to participate in the March election (*Miami Herald*, 22 Sept. 1981, p. 22A). In October, Zamora argued that "to ask our forces to give up their weapons and to place ourselves at the mercy of the army and the police would be political and physical suicide" (*Miami Herald*, 2 Oct. 1981, p. 17A). Given the reasons that drove these men out of the first junta and the Christian Democrats' inability to guarantee anyone's safety, one cannot call their position unreasonable.

151. "White Paper on El Salvador Is Faulty," *Washington Post*, 9 June 1981, pp. A1, A14.

152. "Apparent Errors Cloud U.S. 'White Paper' on Reds in El Salvador," *Wall Street Journal*, 8 June 1981, pp. 1, 10.

153. On 18 June the department released a twelve-page rebuttal, insisting that the inescapable conclusion was that Cuba and other Communist and radical states have interfered in El Salvador. See *Miami Herald*, 19 June 1981, p. 28A.

154. On 9 November 1981, disputing Secretary Haig's assessment of the military situation in El Salvador. See Raymond Bonner, "Salvador Chief Rebuts Haig, Says War Is Not Stalemated," *New York Times*, 10 Nov. 1981, p. 1.

155. Also on 9 November, responding to the Haig assessment. See Al Kamen, "Salvadoran Insists Government Troops Control All of Country," *Washington Post*, 10 Nov. 1981, p. A23.

156. Leslie H. Gelb, "Haig Is Said to Press for Military Options in Salvador Dispute," *New York Times*, 5 Nov. 1981, pp. 1, 4.

157. On 10 November, assuring a press conference that he did not believe that the situation required in any way, nor had his administration considered, actual military intervention. John Goshko, "Salvadoran Favors Blockade of Nicaragua," *Washington Post*, 11 Nov. 1981, p. A1.

158. Mayorga, "Tragedy and Hope," p. 8.

159. *Latin America Weekly Report*, WR-81-09, 27 Feb. 1981, p. 10.

160. Juan Vásquez, "Salvador Fighting Could Go On for Years," *Miami Herald*, 16 Mar. 1981, p. 18A. Also Daniel Southerland, "Victory Eludes Both Sides in El Salvador War," *Christian Science Monitor*, 16 Mar. 1981, p. 7; and Guy Gugliotta and Shirley Christian, "Salvadoran War: Both Sides Are All Punched Out," *Miami Herald*, 16 Oct. 1981, pp. 1A, 26A.

161. For a controversial yet basically accurate discussion of the rivalries among guerrilla groups see Zaid, "Enemy Colleagues," pp. 17–27.

162. A facsimile of the letter appears as Document A in U.S., Department of State, *Documents Demonstrating*.

163. *Latin America Regional Reports, Mexico and Central America*, RM-80-07, 15 Aug. 1980, pp. 6–7.

164. See Raymond Bonner, "Salvador Bridge: Its Loss Is Serious," *New York Times*, 9 Nov.

1981; Guillermoprieto, "Rebels Said to Gain"; John Brecher et al., "Not Winning Is Losing," *Newsweek*, 23 Nov. 1981, pp. 63–64; and Christopher Dickey, "Rebels Damage Jets, 'Copters in El Salvador," *Washington Post*, 28 Jan. 1982, pp. A1, A16.

165. See, for example, John Dinges, "Salvadoran Rebels Hold Base," *Washington Post*, 22 Jan. 1982, pp. A1, A20, A21; Alma Guillermoprieto, "Salvadoran Peasants Describe Mass Killings," *Washington Post*, 27 Jan. 1982, pp. A1, A16; Alma Guillermoprieto, "Peasant Rebels Farm and Fight," *Washington Post*, 31 Jan. 1982, pp. A1, A16; Alma Guillermoprieto, "Rebels Struggle with Backwardness," *Washington Post*, 2 Feb. 1982, pp. A1, A10; Christopher Dickey, "Salvadoran Guerrillas Sustain Attack on City," *Washington Post*, 3 Feb. 1982, pp. A1, A16; Raymond Bonner, "On the Attack with Salvador Rebels," *New York Times*, 3 Feb. 1982, p. 6; and Steven Strasser et al., "Escalation in El Salvador," *Newsweek*, 15 Feb. 1982, pp. 32–35.

166. The observation of Guillermoprieto in "Rebels Farm," p. A16, and in "Rebels Struggle," p. A1. Also the view of White, "El Salvador between Two Fires," and of Allman, "Rising to Rebellion," who derived this impression from earlier contacts with irregular peasant guerrillas.

167. Guillermoprieto, "Rebels Struggle," p. A10, where she recounts a conversation with an ideological worker at one of the FMLN camps in Morazán and she reports that Javier, a column commander, told her that every guerrilla squad includes a political director.

168. Guillermoprieto, "Peasants Describe," and Philippe Bourgeois, "Running for My Life in El Salvador," *Washington Post*, 14 Feb. 1982, pp. C1, C5.

169. Dinges, "Rebels Hold Base," p. A21.

170. Guillermoprieto, "Rebels Farm," p. A16.

171. Christopher Dickey, "Salvadoran Left Widens Talks Offer for Widened, Unconditional Talks," *Washington Post*, 3 Dec. 1981, pp. A1, A39.

172. *Miami Herald*, 19 Dec. 1981, p. 28A.

173. The decision was announced by Fred Ikle, undersecretary of defense, during his 15 December testimony before a subcommittee of the Senate Foreign Relations Committee (*Miami Herald*, 23 Dec. 1981, p. 8B). The first group arrived at Fort Bragg, N.C., on 9 January 1982 (*Miami Herald*, 12 Jan. 1982, p. 6C). On 24 January a second group arrived at Fort Benning, Ga. (*New York Times*, 25 Jan. 1982, p. 8). The third and final contingent arrived at Pope Air Force Base, near Fort Bragg, on 12 February (*Durham Morning Herald*, 13 Feb. 1982, p. 6A).

174. For the polemics involved in this renewal of aid to El Salvador see Steven V. Roberts, "Rift on El Salvador Grows in Congress," *New York Times*, 4 Feb. 1982, pp. 1, 8. See also John M. Goshko, "ACLU Accuses El Salvador of Repression," *Washington Post*, 27 Jan. 1982, p. A17, and Christopher Dickey, "Record on Rights Entitles Salvador to Aid, U.S. Says," *Washington Post*, 29 Jan. 1982, pp. A1, A29. The president certified the aid on 28 January. See John Goshko, "More Assistance Eyed after Leftist Attack," *Washington Post*, 29 Jan. 1982, pp. A1, A28.

175. Bernard Gwertzman, "Haig Pledges U.S. Will Act to Block Salvador Rebels," *New York Times*, 3 Feb. 1982, pp. 1, 6.

176. See two articles by William Chapman, "U.S. to Send More Aid to El Salvador," *Washington Post*, 2 Feb. 1982, and "Doubling of Military Aid to El Salvador Is Sought," *Washington Post*, 9 Feb. 1982, p. A13. Also Strasser et al., "Escalation," p. 32.

177. Nissen, "Unexpected Enemies," p. 34.

178. Jane Whitmore, "A Publicity Offensive," *Newsweek*, 15 Feb. 1982, p. 35.

CHAPTER 8

1. See *Washington Post*, 29 Mar. 1982, p. A17; and Sam Dillon, "Voter Fervor Draws Praise of Observers," *Miami Herald*, 29 Mar. 1982, p. 10A. For the reaction of American corre-

spondents see James Brooke, "War-wise Peasants Dodge, Then Vote," *Miami Herald*, 29 Mar. 1982, pp. 1A, 11A; Christopher Dickey, "Turnout Heavy in El Salvador, Thousands Vote despite Rebel Threats," *Washington Post*, 29 Mar. 1982, pp. A1, A13, A14; Guy Gugliotta, "Salvador Turnout Massive," *Miami Herald*, 29 Mar. 1982, pp. 1A, 10A; and Stephen Kinzer, "Long Lines Slow Tally; Results Today," *Boston Globe*, 29 Mar. 1982, pp. 1, 4.

2. For details on the substance of D'Aubuisson's remarks in public appearances see Warren Hoge, "Salvador Candidate Called a 'Killer' Running Well in Election Campaign," *New York Times*, 19 Feb. 1982, p. 4; Shirley Christian, "Guns and Votes: Campaigning, El Salvador-style, Is Risky," *Miami Herald*, 22 Feb. 1982, pp. 1A, 16A; and Don Bohning, "U.S. Policy Facing Defeat if Salvador Rightists Win," *Miami Herald*, 14 Mar. 1982, p. 23A. D'Aubuisson's campaign also sought to improve the image of the major by insisting that his crime was his anti-Communism, and his support for democracy and free enterprise, values now abandoned by liberal democrats in the United States bent on glorifying the Salvadoran guerrillas (*El Mundo*, 24 Mar. 1982, p. 15).

3. An observation derived in a visit by the author to the campaign headquarters of ARENA on 27 Mar. 1982.

4. Five persons were wounded in the attack, including Dr. Ricardo Avila Moreira, a member of ARENA's directorate.

5. *El País*, 10 Mar. 1982, p. 2. Two of the charges made by ARENA at the time were that the CCE had printed two million ballots and that the PDC hoped to invalidate many ARENA votes by telling people to tear the coupon off the ballot before casting their vote.

6. Interview with Ing. Mario Emilio Redaelli, 27 Mar. 1982.

7. See *El Mundo*, 24 Mar. 1982, p. 17.

8. Secretaría de Información, "Mensaje del Ing. José Napoleón Duarte," pp. 3, 5.

9. Secretaría de Información, "Mensaje del Ministro de Planificación," p. 7.

10. "Balance de la campaña electoral," *El Mundo*, 24 Mar. 1982, p. 19.

11. For Duarte, see Shirley Christian, "Duarte on Stump for 'Clean' Election amid Dust of War and Political Fraud," *Miami Herald*, 8 Mar. 1982, pp. 1A, 6A; and from his remarks at a press conference on 24 March summarized in *La Prensa Gráfica*, 25 Mar. 1982, pp. 3, 36. For the Armed Force see Secretaría de Información, "Mensaje del General e Ingeniero Jaime Abdul Gutiérrez;" also the remarks to that effect by General Guillermo García, minister of defense, during a press conference on 27 March attended by the author; and in a series of proclamations of the Armed Force; see for example *El Diario de Hoy*, 25 Mar. 1982, p. 19.

12. For the attack on D'Aubuisson see Shirley Christian, "Salvador Candidate Wounded by Gunman," *Miami Herald*, 28 Feb. 1982, pp. 1A, 26A. Redaelli blamed the Christian Democrats for the attack. See Shirley Christian, "Wounded Candidate Enters Clinic," *Miami Herald*, 1 Mar. 1982, p. 8A. On 20 March, D'Aubuisson charged that a Venezuelan assassination squad had entered the country to liquidate him. See Christopher Dickey, "Archbishop Expresses Doubt about Salvadoran Election," *Washington Post*, 22 Mar. 1982, pp. A1, A23.

For stories of other attacks see Christian, "Guns and Votes," p. 6A; Christian, "Wounded Candidate;" Loren Jenkins, "4 Dutch Newsmen Slain in El Salvador en Route to Meeting with *Rebels*," *Washington Post*, 19 Mar. 1982, pp. A1, A17. On March 19 a group of Brazilian journalists reported that soldiers had fired on their press van carrying a white flag (Sam Dillon, "Journalists Say Soldiers Fired on Them," *Miami Herald*, 20 Mar. 1982, p. 13A). President Duarte accused the disloyal Right of masterminding the violence against journalists (Paul Taylor, "Duarte Blames Far Right in Attacks on Journalists," *Washington Post*, 22 Mar. 1982, p. A22).

13. Primarily by some staying at the Hotel Alameda.

14. Consejo Central de Elecciones, Ley Electoral Transitoria, art. 145, p. 60.

15. Ibid. art. 36, sect. e, p. 19.

16. The change to invisible ink was mandated in amended language inserted in ibid. Decree

966 also changed section d of article 36 to allow people to vote in any municipality, and not only in the municipality where their *cédulas* had been issued (ibid., p. 18). By mid-afternoon on election day the batteries on many of the lamps had run down. For the prescription concerning *cédulas* see Ley Electoral Transitoria, p. 43.

17. A copy of these instructions, now in the author's possession, was taken from *El Diario de Hoy*, 27 Mar. 1982, pp. 22–23.

18. Unless the protests of the ARENA had prevailed and the coupons of the ballots, bearing a number which identified the voter in the roll kept by the *junta receptora*, had not been torn off. See Figure 8-1 and note 5, above.

19. This has been a minor point of debate among the little band of Latin Americanists interested in elections. The argument is over whether blank and null votes reflect voter apathy, ignorance, or protest. In survey work conducted in Venezuela in 1973 the author had the opportunity to probe briefly into this matter and found that the reasons for blank and null voting are more varied than protest. In the 1982 Salvadoran election, however, protest was probably the predominant motive.

20. See the sources cited in notes 1 and 2, above.

21. See Terri Shaw, "New Aid to Salvador Called Wasted Effort," *Washington Post*, 1 Mar. 1982, p. A19; and *Miami Herald*, 1 Mar. 1982, p. 8A, for the remarks of FDR secretary general Dr. Guillermo Manuel Ungo concerning the election. See also Rubén Zamora's statement in Guy Gugliotta, "Salvadoran Leftists Planning Offensive but Still Seek Talks, Rebel Official Says," *Miami Herald*, 20 Feb. 1982, p. 10A.

22. Guy Gugliotta, "Guerrilla Chief: We Won't Let Up," *Miami Herald*, 24 Feb. 1982, pp. 1A, 14A. See also Sam Dillon, , "Guerrillas Ready to 'Go for the Enemy in the Cities,' " *Miami Herald*, 21 Feb. 1982, p. 22A. The guerrillas managed to attract considerable attention and, to a degree, steal the thunder from the campaign, at least in the international media. See Shirley Christian, "As Interest Peaks in El Salvador World Journalists Battle for News," *Miami Herald*, 12 Mar. 1982, pp. 1A, 12A; and Joanne Omang, "War Story: Journalists in El Salvador Seek Elusive 'Bang-Bang,' " *Washington Post*, 28 Feb. 1982, pp. A1, A18.

23. Shirley Christian, "Salvadoran Army Ends 9th Try to Rout Rebels near Volcano," *Miami Herald*, 3 Mar. 1982, pp. 1A, 18A. Jesús Ceberio, "La guerrilla salvadoreña ataca simultáneamente en tres ciudades," *El País*, 10 Mar. 1982, p. 2; and *El País*, 11 Mar. 1982, p. 2. *Washington Post*, 26 Mar. 1982, p. A26. On 22 March alone, eighteen buses were destoyed in San Salvador (*Washington Post*, 24 Mar. 1982, p. A17; also *El Diario de Hoy*, 26 Mar. 1982, p. 6).

24. For Apopa see Kinzer, "Long Lines," and Brooke, "War-wise Peasants." The action in San Antonio Abad was particulary vicious. The fact that all the attackers were killed suggests that the Salvadoran Armed Force does not yet believe in taking prisoners. On the other hand, the guerrilla commander who ordered the attack had to know that his men had very little chance to retreat in broad daylight if they needed to. For events in San Francisco Gotera see June Erlick, "In Guerrilla Land, Vote Came with a Bang," *Miami Herald*, 29 Mar. 1982, p. 11A. See also Loren Jenkins, "Bitter Past: Villagers Hope Killing Will End," *Washington Post*, 29 Mar. 1982, pp. A1, A15; Joanne Omang, "Mechanical Problems Slow Polling,," *Washington Post*, 29 Mar. 1982, pp. A1, A16; and Loren Jenkins, "Rebels Preempt Vote in Rural Town," *Washington Post*, 5 Apr. 1982, pp. A1, A26.

25. James Brooke, "Salvadoran Troops Reclaim City from Guerrillas," *Miami Herald*, 31 Mar. 1982, p. 18A.

26. The number of *puestos de votación* and *juntas receptoras* was computed from a CCE list published in *El Diario de Hoy*, 26 Mar. 1982, pp. 24–25.

27. There were reports that some stayed open past the deadline.

28. Even the CCE itself expected a low turnout. CCE president Dr. Jorge Bustamante was

quoted at one point as saying that if the turnout exceeded 900,000 he would get drunk (Loren Jenkins, "Optimistic U.S.-Trained Doctor Runs Election Board," *Washington Post*, 23 Mar. 1982, p. A12).

As this chapter goes to press, the current issue of *Estudios Centro Americanos* includes a twenty-two-page feature article, which this author has not read, alleging that the CCE exaggerated the turnout figure (*Washington Post*, 7 June 1982, p. A23). In addition, *New York Times* correspondent Raymond Bonner has published a series of articles in early June also questioning the accuracy of the figures. I am mindful of discrepancies in the final results of the elections. Note for example the discrepancy in the total valid vote in tables 8-1 and 8-2. Final unofficial figures gave the following distribution of the vote: PDC, 429, 247 votes; ARENA, 306,662; PCN, 193,582; AD, 82, 093; PPS, 32,242; and POP, 10,465 votes. (*Washington Post*, 1 Apr. 1982, p. A19; and *La Nación Internacional*, 2–8 Apr. 1982, p. 6).

I have no way of judging the validity of these allegations, although they certainly deserve attention. However, two observations are pertinent regarding the possibility of any hitherto undetected manipulation of the election figures. First, it is difficult to believe that ARENA and the PDC would collaborate with each other in an election fraud. Sworn enemies that they are, they would not trust each other in such a delicate matter. Second, it is unlikely that any of the major parties—the only ones with the capabilities and connections to attempt it—could engage in manipulation on a major scale without being detected and denounced by the others.

29. Concerning the election see, for example, Nancy Landon Kassenbaum, "A Test for a Nation's Aspiring Democracy," and Kenneth E. Sharpe and Morris Blachman, "Making a Mockery of Electoral Democracy," in "Salvador Balloting: Two Assessments," *Miami Herald*, 28 Mar. 1982, pp. 1E, 6E.

For the reaction to the heavy turnout by the Socialist International see *La Nacion Internacional*, 2–8 Apr. 1982, p. 4. For the reaction of the FDR leadership see Víctor Hugo Murillo, "Dirigente del FDR dice que votó menos del 50 por ciento," ibid. pp. 4–5.

30. "Indian country" means a guerrilla area; for more details on this particular area see note 23, above. A report of our observation of the Salvadoran election is to appear in the newsletter of the Latin American Studies Association. The incident described here is treated with more detail in the report.

31. From conversations with local people, 28 Mar. 1982.

32. See Kinzer, "Long Lines," and by the same correspondent, "The Vote for Peace or Politicians," *Boston Globe*, 30 Mar. 1982, pp. 1, 10; and Jenkins, "Bitter Past."

33. See source for Table 8-3.

34. Such data must be considered incomplete inasmuch as they do not reflect the number of ISTA officials, UCS peasants, and other residents of the area or participants in the cooperatives assassinated by paramilitary units and guerrilla elements. For more details see "A Salvadoran Horror Story" in chapter 7, above.

35. See *Washington Post*, 20 May 1982, p. A27; John Goshko and William Chapman, "Bid to Curb Land Reform in Salvador Stirs Critics," *Washington Post*, 21 May 1982, p. A4; John M. Goshko, "U.S. Denies New Salvadoran Law Will End Land Reform," *Washington Post*, 26 May 1982; and William Chapman "Aid Request for El Salvador Slashed," *Washington Post*, 27 May 1982, pp. A1, A9.

36. ARENA officials were extremely annoyed at the PCN for having yielded to military and United States pressures on the questions of the selection of a provisional president and of the format of the new government. ARENA proved very stubborn, and it required a visit by Vernon Walters and John Carbaugh, an aide to Senator Jesse Helms, to make them budge. The military finally took matters into its own hands and asked party leaders to select as president one of three names submitted to them. ARENA wanted José Antonio Rodríguez Porth from the PPS or Roberto Escobar García of the PCN. In addition to Alvaro Magaña, the military offered the names

René Fortín Magaña, the AD leader, and Reynaldo Galindo Pohl. Once the election of Magaña could not be resisted, ARENA elected three vice-presidents and took the decree power away from the provisional president. The month-long tussle is narrated in a series of articles by Joanne Omang including: "Gen. Walters to Hold Talks with Warring Politicians," *Washington Post*, 21 Apr. 1982; "Salvadorans Said to Pick New Leader," *Washington Post*, 23 Apr. 1982, pp. A1, A18; "Vote on Salvadoran President Put Off," *Washington Post*, 28 Apr. 1982, p. A17; "Salvadoran Right Still Holding Out for the Presidency," 29 Apr. 1982, p. A30; and "Candidate Backed by Army Wins Salvadoran Presidency," *Washington Post, 30 Apr. 1982, pp. A1, A14*. *See also René Contreras, "Derecha salvadoreña denuncia 'presiones,'" La Nación Internacional*, 23–29 Apr. 1982, p. 3; Víctor Hugo Murillo, "Ejército salvadoreño: Clave en las decisiones," *La Nación Internacional*, 30 Apr.–6 May 1982, p. 7; and René Contreras, "Alvaro Magaña presidirá el gobierno de El Salvador, *La Nación Internacional*, 30 Apr.–6 May 1982, p. 6.

37. Joseph Kraft, "El Salvador Election: Half a Win," *Miami Herald*, 2 Apr. 1982, p. 29A; Guy Gugliotta, "After Salvador's Election Feast: A Bare Cupboard,," *Miami Herald*, 4 Apr. 1982, pp. 1E, 4E; Enrique Benavides, "El Salvador: Un regreso al punto de partida," *La Nación Internacional*, 2–8 Apr. 1982, p. 11; John Judls, "U.S. Wins Pyrrhic Victory in Salvador," *In These Times*, 7–13 Apr. 1982, p. 3.

38. John M. Goshko, "High Turnout Rebel Defeat, U.S. Says," *Boston Globe*, 30 Mar. 1982, pp. 1, 10.

39. Such as the question of agrarian reform. See note 35 above.

40. Joanne Omang, "Salvadoran Villagers Describe 48 Killings," *Washington Post*, 23 Apr. 1982, p. A19; Christopher Dickey, "Wave of Killings Unsettles Salvadoran Party," *Washington Post*, 1 June 1982, p. A13.

41. Joanne Omang, "Coalition Rule, U.S. Aid Linked in El Salvador," *Washington Post*, 10 Apr. 1982, p. A16.

42. John M. Goshko, "U.S. Lifts Ban on Visit Here By Salvadoran," *Washington Post*, 2 Apr. 1982, pp. A1, A20.

43. As was the contention of Rowland Evans and Robert Novak in "Salvador's 'Democratic Capitalist,'" *Washington Post*, 24 Mar. 1982, p. A15.

Bibliography

The documentary sources identify decrees, editorials, letters, and proclamations issued by the more relevant actors in the Salvadoran process of transition. Periodical sources are listed separately, and full credit has been given to the correspondents and feature writers of the different publications in the endnotes. All references to the *Estudios Centro Americanos* employ the acronym, *ECA*. Salvadoran documents are listed in chronological order; all other entries are listed alphabetically.

Decrees, Editorials, Letters, Pamphlets, and Proclamations
(in chronological order)

"Pronunciamiento del Consejo Superior Universitario de la Universidad Centroamericana José Simeón Cañas, sobre el Primer Proyecto de Transformación Agraria." *ECA* 31, 335/336 (Sept.–Oct. 1976): 419–24.

"Ley de Creación del Instituto de Transformación Agraria." *ECA* 31, 335/336 (Sept.–Oct. 1976): 591–606.

"Decreto No. 31 del Primer Proyecto de Transformación Agraria." *ECA* 31, 335/336 (Sept.–Oct. 1976): 606–10.

"Primer Pronunciamiento de ANEP." *ECA* 31, 335/336 (Sept.–Oct. 1976): 611–12.

"Segundo Pronunciamiento de ANEP." *ECA* 31, 335/336 (Sept.–Oct. 1976): 613–14.

"Tercer Pronunciamiento de ANEP." *ECA* 31, 335/336 (Sept.–Oct. 1976): 614–15.

"Respuesta del Gobierno de la República a la Asociación Nacional de la Empresa Privada, ANEP." *ECA* 31, 335/336 (Sept.–Oct. 1976): 615–17.

"Segunda Respuesta del Gobierno: Ante la Posición de la ANEP el Gobierno Responde." *ECA* 31, 335/336 (Sept.–Oct. 1976): 617–18.

"Tercera Respuesta del Gobierno: El Gobierno Reafirma Su Posición Frente a la ANEP." *ECA* 31, 335/336 (Sept.–Oct. 1976): 618–20.

"El Gobierno de la República al Pueblo Salvadoreño." *ECA* 31, 335/336 (Sept.–Oct. 1976): 620–22.

"La Unión Comunal Salvadoreña y la Transformación Agraria." *ECA* 31, 335/336 (Sept.–Oct. 1976): 622–23.

"Pronunciamiento del Partido Comunista Salvadoreño." *ECA* 31, 335/336 (Sept.–Oct. 1976): 623–26.

"Pronunciamiento del Partido Demócrata Cristiano, Frente a la Transformación Agraria." *ECA* 31, 335/336 (Sept.–Oct. 1976): 626–28.

"Pronunciamiento del Bloque Popular Revolucionario." *ECA* 31, 335/336 (Sept.–Oct. 1976): 628–30.

"Pronunciamiento del Frente de Acción Popular Unificada." *ECA* 31, 335/336 (Sept.–Oct. 1976): 630–32.

"¡A Sus Ordenes, Mi Capital!" *ECA* 31, 337 (Nov. 1976): 637–43.

"Al Borde de la Guerra Civil." *ECA* 34, 371 (Sept. 1979): 735–40.

"La Insurrección Militar del Quince de Octubre." *ECA* 34, 371 (Sept. 1979): 741–44.

"Plataforma del Foro Popular." *ECA* 34, 371 (Sept. 1979): 843–45.

"Pronunciamiento del Consejo Superior Universitario de la Universidad Centroamericana José Simeón Cañas sobre la Nueva Situación del País Tras el Quince de Octubre." *ECA* 34, 372/373 (Oct.–Nov. 1979): 849–62.

"Mensaje Dirigido a la Asamblea General de la Asociación Nacional de la Empresa Privada (ANEP) por el Presidente de la Entidad, Don Francisco Calleja Malaina, el 28 de Setiembre de 1979." *ECA* 34, 372/373 (Oct.–Nov. 1979): 1013–14.

"Proclama de la Fuerza Armada de El Salvador." *ECA* 34, 372/373 (Oct.–Nov. 1979): 1017–18.

"Llamamiento Pastoral ante la Nueva Situación del País." *ECA* 34, 372/373 (Oct.–Nov. 1979): 1019–20.

"Guerra a la Represión y Respeto a las Demandas del Pueblo." *ECA* 34, 372/373 (Oct.–Nov. 1979): 1021.

"El Ejército Revolucionario del Pueblo (ERP) ante la Situación Nacional." *ECA* 34, 372/373 (Oct.–Nov. 1979): 1022–24.

"Posición del Bloque Popular Revolucionario Frente al Autogolpe de la Tiranía Militar." *ECA* 34, 372/373 (Oct.–Nov. 1979): 1025–26.

"Las Ligas Populares 28 de Febrero no Apoyamos la Junta de Gobierno." *ECA* 34, 372/373 (Oct.–Nov. 1979): 1027.

"Porqué el Pueblo no Cree en la Junta Militar." *ECA* 34, 372/373 (Oct.–Nov. 1979): 1028–29.

"Porqué Continúa la Lucha Popular." *ECA* 34, 372/373 (Oct.–Nov. 1979): 1030.

"Porqué las Ligas Populares 28 de Febrero Nos Retiramos del Foro." *ECA* 34, 372/373 (Oct.–Nov. 1979): 1031.

"Carta de Enrique Alvarez Córdoba y Jorge Alberto Villacorta a los Empleados del Ministerio de Agricultura y Ganadería." *ECA* 34, 372/373 (Oct.–Nov. 1979): 1032–33.

"El Fracaso de Dos Modelos." *ECA* 34, 374 (Dec. 1979): 1037–42.

"La Disolución de Orden." *ECA* 34, 374 (Dec. 1979): 1075–76.

"Texto del Decreto por medio del cual Se Disuelve la Organización Democrática Nacionalista." *ECA* 34, 374 (Dec. 1979): 1110–11.

"Pronunciamiento de la UCA ante la Nueva Situación de el País (Febrero/80)." *ECA* 35, 375/376 (Jan.–Feb. 1980): 5–18.

"El Gabinete de Gobierno, Magistrados de la Corte Suprema de Justicia y Funcionarios de Instituciones Autónomas Se Dirigen a las Fuerzas Armadas por intermedio del COPEFA." *ECA* 34, 375/376 (Jan.–Feb. 1980): 117–19.

"El COPEFA Responde al Gabinete, Magistrados, y Otros Funcionarios del Gobierno." *ECA* 35, 375/376 (Jan.–Feb. 1980): 119–20.

"Renuncia de Algunos Ministros y Subsecretarios del Estado." *ECA* 35, 375/376 (Jan.–Feb. 1980): 120–21.

"Renuncia Irrevocable del Gabinete, Magistrados de la Corte Suprema de Justicia, y Funcionarios de Instituciones Autónomas, ante la Posición del COPEFA." *ECA* 35, 375/376 (Jan.–Feb. 1980): 121–22.

"Román Mayorga Quirós y Guillermo Manuel Ungo Se Solidarizan con Altos Funcionarios del Estado y Renuncian como Miembros de la Junta Revolucionaria de Gobierno." *ECA* 35, 375/376 (Jan.–Feb. 1980): 122–23.

"Renuncia del Ing. Mario Andino, de la Junta Revolucionaria de Gobierno." *ECA* 35, 375/376 (Jan.–Feb. 1980): 123.

"Carta Abierta de Ministros al COPEFA." *ECA* 35, 375/376 (Jan.–Feb. 1980): 124–25.

"La Asociación Salvadoreña de Industriales ante las Declaraciones del Ing. José Napoleón Duarte de la Democracia Cristiana." *ECA* 35, 375/376 (Jan.–Feb. 1980): 125.

"Posición de la ANEP ante el Nuevo Esquema de Gobierno Encabezado por la Democracia Cristiana." *ECA* 35, 375/376 (Jan.–Feb. 1980): 126.

"El Bochornoso Espectáculo Político Actual, Pronunciamiento del PCN." *ECA* 35, 375/376 (Jan.–Feb. 1980): 127–28.

"Nuestras Organizaciones Populares en Marcha hacia la Unidad: Posición del FAPU, LP-28, BPR, UDN." *ECA* 35, 375/376 (Jan.–Feb. 1980): 128–30.

"Manifiesto del MNR ante la Situación Nacional." *ECA* 35, 375/376 (Jan.–Feb. 1980): 130.

"El Foro Popular ante la Crisis Política Nacional." *ECA* 35, 375/376 (Jan.–Feb. 1980): 131.

"Alternativa del Partido Demócrata Cristiano para Formar el Nuevo Gobierno." *ECA* 35, 375/376 (Jan.–Feb. 1980): 131–32.

"La Fuerza Armada al Pueblo Salvadoreño." *ECA* 35, 375/376 (Jan.–Feb. 1980): 132–33.

"Manifiesto del Partido Comunista de El Salvador, de las FPL y de las FARN." *ECA* 35, 375/376 (Jan.–Feb. 1980): 133–36.

"Informe de la Comisión Especial Investigadora de Reos y Desaparecidos Políticos." *ECA* 35, 375/376 (Jan.–Feb. 1980): 136–39.

"En Busca de un Nuevo Proyecto Nacional." *ECA* 35, 377/378 (Mar.–Apr. 1980): 155–80.

"Plataforma Programática para un Gobierno Democrático Revolucionario de la Coordinadora Revolucionaria de Masas." *ECA* 35, 377/378 (Mar.–Apr. 1980): 343–45.

"Primera Declaración del Frente Democrático Revolucionario (FDR)." *ECA* 35, 377/378 (Mar.–Apr. 1980): 346.

"Este es el Programa del Gobierno que el Pueblo Necesita: Gobierno de Salvación Nacional del FAPU." *ECA* 35, 377/378 (Mar.–Apr. 1980): 353–56.

"Posición del MNR ante el Proceso de Unidad de las Organizaciones Políticas Democráticas y Populares." *ECA* 35, 377/378 (Mar.–Apr. 1980): 356–57.

"Plataforma del Movimiento Independiente de Profesionales y Técnicos de El Salvador (MIPTES)." *ECA* 35, 377/378 (Mar.–Apr. 1980): 357–58.

"Compromiso de los Profesionales y Técnicos Progresistas ante el Momento que Vive El Salvador." *ECA* 35, 377/378 (Mar.–Apr. 1980): 358–59.

"Del Partido de Conciliación Nacional a la Cuidadanía, No. 1." *ECA* 35, 377/378 (Mar.–Apr. 1980): 359–60.

"La Realidad Política Actual según el Partido de Conciliación Nacional." *ECA* 35, 377/378 (Mar.–Apr. 1980): 361–63.

"Porqué Debe Promulgarse una Nueva Constitución Política: Comité Político del Partido de Conciliación Nacional." *ECA* 35, 377/378 (Mar.–Apr. 1980): 363–65.

"La Asociación Salvadoreña de Industriales Define Su Posición ante la Situación Nacional." *ECA* 35, 377/378 (Mar.–Apr. 1980): 366.

"ANEP sobre la Posición del PDC: Un Partido sin Proyección Gubernamental y sin Apoyo Popular." *ECA* 35, 377/378 (Mar.–Apr. 1980): 366–67.

"Mensaje del Presidente de la ANEP al Pueblo Salvadoreño en un Programa de Televisión Transmitido la Noche del Viernes 29 de Febrero de 1980." *ECA* 35, 377/378 (Mar.–Apr. 1980): 367–70.

"Ante la Nacionalización del Comercio Exterior: Asociación Salvadoreña de Beneficiadores y Exportadores (ABECAFE)." *ECA* 35, 377/378 (Mar.–Apr. 1980): 370–72.

"Consideraciones del Gral. José Alberto Medrano." *ECA* 35, 377/378 (Mar.–Apr. 1980): 372–74.

"Mensaje de la Tendencia Popular Demócrata Cristiana a la Convención Nacional del Partido y al Pueblo Salvadoreño." *ECA* 35, 377/378 (Mar.–Apr. 1980): 374–76.

"Carta de Héctor Dada Hirezi al Señor Encargado Interino de la Secretaría General del Partido

Demócrata Cristiano." *ECA* 35, 377/378 (Mar.–Apr. 1980): 376–77.

"Carta de Renuncia de Héctor Dada Hirezi a la Junta Revolucionaria de Gobierno." *ECA* 35, 377/378 (Mar.–Apr. 1980): 377–78.

"Carta de Renuncia de Miembros de la Dirigencia del Partido Demócrata Cristiano." *ECA* 35, 377/378 (Mar.–Apr. 1980): 378–79.

"Carta de Monseñor Romero al Presidente Carter." *ECA* 35, 377/378 (Mar.–Apr. 1980): 379–80.

"Respuesta del Presidente Carter a Monseñor Romero, a través del Secretario de Estado, Cyrus Vance." *ECA* 35, 377/378 (Mar.–Apr. 1980): 379–80.

"Conferencia Sobre Democratización en América Latina. El caso de El Salvador: Declaración." *ECA* 35, 377/378 (Mar.–Apr. 1980): 381–83.

"Los Prelados Asistentes a la Exhumación de Monseñor Romero, ante las Declaraciones de la Junta Revolucionaria de Gobierno." *ECA* 35, 377/378 (Mar.–Apr. 1980): 383–84.

"Decreto No. 128: Reformas a la Ley de Control de Transferencias Internacionales." *ECA* 35, 377/378 (Mar.–Apr. 1980): 384–85.

"Decreto No. 153: Ley Básica de la Reforma Agraria." *ECA* 35, 377/378 (Mar.–Apr. 1980): 386–89.

"Decreto No. 154: Decreto para la toma de Posesión e Intervención de Tierras, Previas a la Vigencia de la Ley Básica de Reforma Agraria." *ECA* 35, 377/378 (Mar.–Apr. 1980): 389–90.

"Decreto No. 155: Decreto de Estado de Sitio." *ECA* 35, 377/378 (Mar.–Apr. 1980): 390–91.

"Decreto No. 158: Ley de Nacionalización de las Instituciones de Crédito y de las Asociaciones de Ahorro y Préstamo." *ECA* 35, 377/378 (Mar.–Apr. 1980): 391–92.

"Decreto No. 159: Ley Transitoria de Intervención de las Instituciones de Crédito y de las Asociaciones de Ahorro y Préstamo." *ECA* 35, 377/378 (Mar.–Apr. 1980): 393.

"Mensaje de la Junta Revolucionaria de Gobierno Dirigido por el Dr. José Antonio Morales Ehrlich al Anunciar la Ley Mediante la Cual Se Otorga la Propiedad de la Tierra a Campesinos, Aparceros y Arrendatarios." *ECA* 35, 377/378 (Mar.–Apr. 1980): 393–94.

"Decreto No. 207: Ley para la Afectación y Traspaso de Tierras Agrícolas a Favor de sus Cultivadores Directos." *ECA* 35, 377/378 (Mar.–Apr. 1980): 395–96.

"La Represión de la Derecha: De Sostén de Regímenes Pasados a Subversión de un Gobierno Revolucionario Democrático. Posición del Partido Demócrata Cristiano." *ECA* 35, 377/378 (Mar.–Apr. 1980): 396–97.

"Posición del Partido Demócrata Cristiano Frente a la Masacre del 22 de Enero de 1980." *ECA* 35, 377/378 (Mar.–Apr. 1980): 397–98.

"Manifiesto Conjunto del MIPTES, la Universidad de El Salvador y la UCA: Alto a la Represion." *ECA* 35, 377/378 (Mar.–Apr. 1980): 399–402.

"Estadísticas de la Represión." *ECA* 35, 377/378 (Mar.–Apr. 1980): 402–3.

"Segundo Manifiesto al Pueblo Salvadoreño, a los Pueblos Centroamericanos, y del Mundo, de la RN, las FPI, y el PCS." *ECA* 35, 377/378 (Mar.–Apr. 1980): 404–6.

"En Estado de Sitio Permanente." *ECA* 35, 381/382 (July–Aug. 1980): 663–66.

"Carta de Denuncia a los Demócratos Cristianos de Todo el Mundo." *ECA* 35, 381/382 (July–Aug. 1980): 773–75.

"Posición del Movimiento Nacional Revolucionario ante la Crisis Política Nacional." *ECA* 35, 381/382 (July–Aug. 1980): 775–79.

"Informe de la Junta Revolucionaria de Gobierno, al Cumplir Seis Meses de Su Administración, Rendido por el Dr. José Antonio Morales Ehrlich, ante el Pueblo Salvadoreño, el Jueves 10 de Julio de 1980." *ECA* 35, 381/382 (July–Aug. 1980): 780–84.

"Alianza Productiva: 'No al Paro de los Extremistas,' dice el Pueblo Productivo." *ECA* 35, 381/382 (July–Aug. 1980): 785–86.

"Cámara de Comercio e Industria de El Salvador: El Comercio y la Industria Defensores del Derecho a Vivir y Trabajar en Paz." *ECA* 35, 381/382 (July–Aug. 1980): 786.
"Asociación Salvadoreña de Industriales: '¡Sólo el Trabajo nos Hará Libres!' " *ECA* 35, 381/382 (July–Aug. 1980): 786–87.
"Decreto No. 43: Se Declara el Estado de El Salvador en Emergencia Nacional." *ECA* 35, 381/382 (July–Aug. 1980): 787.
Consejo Central de Elecciones. Ley Electoral Transitoria, Decreto No. 994. San Salvador, January 1982.
Secretaría de Información de la Presidencia de la República. "Mensaje del Ing. José Napoleón Duarte, Presidente de la Junta Revolucionaria de Gobierno." San Salvador, 20 January 1982.
———. "Mensaje del Señor Ministro de Planificación, Lic. Atilio Viéytez." San Salvador, 24 January 1982.
———. "Mensaje del General e Ingeniero Jaime Abdul Gutiérrez, Vicepresidente de la Junta Revolucionaria de Gobierno y Comandante en Jefe de la Fuerza Armada." San Salvador, 15 March 1982.

Other Documents

Confederación Universitaria Centroamericana (CSUCA). *Los refugiados salvadoreños en Honduras.* San José, Costa Rica: Artes Gráficas de Centroamérica, 1981.
"Dissent Paper on El Salvador and Central America." *DOS* (November 1980), ESCATF-D, no. 80-3.
Interamerican Development Bank. "Economic and Social Progress in Latin America," 1979 report. Washington, D.C.: IDB, 1980.
"Report to the President of the Special Mission to El Salvador." Abridged version, 12 December 1980.
U.S., Congress, Senate, Committee on Foreign Relations. *Nomination of Robert E. White.* Executive Report 96-31. 96th Congress, 2d session. Washington, D.C., 27 February 1980.
U.S., Congress, Senate, Committee on Foreign Relations. *The Situation in El Salvador, Hearings.* 97th Congress, 1st session. Washington, D.C.: U.S. Government Printing Office, 1981.
U.S., Department of State, Bureau of Public Affairs. *Communist Interference in El Salvador.* Special Report no. 80. Washington, D.C., 23 February 1981.
U.S., Department of State. *Communist Interference in El Salvador: Documents Demonstrating Communist Support of the Salvadoran Insurgency.* Washington, D.C., 23 February 1981.
U.S., Department of State, Bureau of Public Affairs. "El Salvador: The Search for Peace." *Current Policy,* no. 296 (16 July 1981).
U.S., Department of State, Bureau of Public Affairs. *El Salvador: The Search for Peace.* Washington, D.C., September 1981.

Magazines and Periodicals

Boston Globe
Christian Science Monitor
Durham Morning Herald
El Diario de Hoy (San Salvador)
El Mundo (San Salvador)

El País (Madrid)
Gist (U.S. Department of State)
In These Times
La Nación Internacional (San José)
La Prensa Gráfica (San Salvador)

Latin America Commodities Report
Latin America Economic Report
Latin America Political Report
Latin America Regional Report, Mexico and
    Central America
Latin America Weekly Report
Miami Herald
Newsweek

Newsweek International
New York Times
Proceso (San Salvador)
SALPRESS (Washington)
Solidaridad (San Salvador)
UnoMásUno (Mexico City)
Wall Street Journal
Washington Post

Select Publication List on El Salvador

BOOKS AND PAMPHLETS

Anderson, Thomas P. *Matanza: El Salvador's Communist Revolt of 1932*. Lincoln: University of Nebraska Press, 1971.
――――. *The War of the Dispossessed: Honduras and El Salvador, 1969*. Lincoln: University of Nebraska Press, 1981.
Browning, David. *El Salvador: Landscape and Society*. Oxford: Clarendon Press, 1971.
Krehm, William. *Democracia y Tiranías en el Caribe*. Buenos Aires: Parnaso, 1957.
Mayorga, Román. "El Salvador: Tragedy and Hope." Paper delivered at the Central American Colloquium, University of North Carolina at Chapel Hill, 13 April 1981.
Menjívar, Rafael. *Crisis del Desarrollismo: Caso El Salvador*. San José: Editorial Universitaria Centroamericana, 1977.
Parker, Franklin D. *The Central American Republics*. London: Royal Institute of International Affairs, 1964.
Raynolds, David R. *Rapid Development in Small Economies*. New York: Praeger, 1967.
Sol, Ricardo. *Para Entender El Salvador*. San José: Departamento Ecuménico de Investigaciones, 1980.
Walter, Knut. "Trade and Development in an Export Economy: The Case of El Salvador, 1870–1914." M.A. thesis, University of North Carolina, 1977.
Webre, Stephen. *José Napoleón Duarte and the Christian Democratic Party in Salvadoran Politics, 1960–1972*. Baton Rouge and London: Louisiana State University Press, 1979.
Wheaton, Philip. *Agrarian Reform in El Salvador: A Program of Rural Pacification*. Washington, D.C.: EPICA Task Force, 1980.

ARTICLES

Allman, T. D. "Rising to Rebellion." *Harper's*, July 1981, 31–50.
Andino Martínez, Carlos. "El Estamento Militar en El Salvador." *ECA* 34, 369/370 (July–Aug. 1979): 615–30.
Aubey, Robert T. "Entrepreneurial Formation in El Salvador." *Explorations in Entrepreneurial History*, 2nd ser., 6 (1968–69): 268–85.
Buckley, Tom. "Letter from El Salvador." *New Yorker*, 22 June 1981, 41–83.
Burke, Melvin. "El Sistema de Plantación y la Proletarización del Trabajo Agrícola en El Salvador." *ECA* 31, 335/336 (Sept.–Oct. 1976): 473–86.
Campos, Tomás R. "El Papel de las Organizaciones Populares en la Actual Situación del País." *ECA* 34, 372/373 (Oct.–Nov. 1979): 923–46.
――――. "La Seguridad Nacional y la Constitución Salvadoreña," *ECA* 34, 369–370 (July–Aug. 1979): 477–88.

Colindres, Eduardo. "La Tenencia de la Tierra en El Salvador." *ECA* 31, 335/336 (Sept.–Oct. 1976): 463–72.

Ellacuría, Ignacio. "La Historización del Concepto de Propiedad como Principio de Desideologización." *ECA* 31, 335/336 (Sept.–Oct. 1978): 425–50.

Escobar, Francisco Andrés. "En la Línea de la Muerte (La Manifestación del 22 de Enero de 1980)." *ECA* 35, 375/376 (Jan.–Feb. 1980): 21–35.

Flores Pinel, Fernando. "El Golpe de Estado en El Salvdor, ¿Un Camino hacia la Democratización?" *ECA* 34, 372/373 (Oct.–Nov. 1979): 885–904.

Guidos Véjar, Rafael. "La Crisis Política en El Salvador, 1976–1979." *ECA* 34, 369/370 (July–Aug. 1979): 507–26.

Handal, Shafik Jorge. "El Salvador: A Precarious Balance." *World Marxist Review* 16 (June 1973): 46–50.

Ibisate, Francisco Javier. "¿Es Capitalista el 'Capitalismo Salvadoreño?' " *ECA* 34, 369/370 (July–Aug. 1979): 535–44.

———. "La Nacionalización de la Banca: ¿Para Qué y Para Quienes?" *ECA* 35, 375/376 (Jan.–Feb. 1980): 91–94.

———. "Propiedad, Productividad, Planificación ¿Para Quién?" *ECA* 31, 335/336 (Sept.–Oct. 1976): 497–510.

Jiménez Cabrera, Edgar. "La Alternativa Reformista Frente a la Crisis Democrática." *ECA* 34, 372/373 (Oct.–Nov. 1979): 961–70.

López Vallecillos, Italo. "Fuerzas Sociales y Cambio Social en El Salvador." *ECA* 34, 369/370 (July–Aug. 1979): 557–90.

———. "Rasgos Sociales y Tendencias Políticas en El Salvador (1969–1979)." *ECA* 34, 372/373 (Oct.–Nov. 1979): 863–84.

López Vallecillos, Italo, and Víctor Antonio Orellana. "La Unidad Popular y el Surgimiento del Frente Democrático Revolucionario." *ECA* 35, 377/378 (Mar.–Apr. 1980): 183–207.

Mariscal, Nicolás. "Militares y Reformismo en El Salvador." *ECA* 33, 351/352 (Jan.–Feb. 1978): 9–29.

Marroquín, Alejandro D. "Estudio sobre la Crisis de los Años Treinta en El Salvador." *Anuario de Estudios Centroamericanos* 3 (1977): 115–60.

Martín Baró, Ignacio. "Fantasmas sobre un Gobierno Popular en El Salvador." *ECA* 35, 377/378 (Mar.–Apr. 1980): 277–90.

Mayorga, Román. "Crítica de las Ideologías Económico-Sociales en la Campaña Presidencial de El Salvador." *ECA* 27 (1972): 71–100.

Menjívar, Oscar, and Santiago Ruiz. "La Transformación Agraria en el Marco de la Transformación Nacional." *ECA* 31, 335/336 (Sept.–Oct. 1976): 487–96.

Montgomery, Tommy Sue. "Política Estadounidense y Proceso Revolucionario: El Caso de El Salvador." *ECA* 35, 377/378 (Mar.–Apr. 1980): 241–52.

Paredes, Iván D. "La Situación de la Iglesia Católica en El Salvador y su Influjo Social." *ECA* 34, 369/370 (July–Aug. 1979): 601–14.

Pons, Gabriel. "Necesidad de Revisar la Política de Vivienda." *ECA* 29, 308/309 (June–July 1974): 415–23.

Samayoa, Salvador, and Guillermo Galván. "El Cierre Patronal de las Empresas: Prueba de Fuego para el Sindicalismo Revolucionario en El Salvador." *ECA* 34, 371 (Sept. 1979): 793–800.

———. "El Movimiento Obrero en El Salvador ¿Resurgimiento o Agitación?" *ECA* 34, 369/370 (July–Aug. 1979): 591–600.

Sebastián, Luis de. "Criterios para Evaluar los Objetivos de una Reforma Agraria." *ECA* 31, 335/336 (Sept.–Oct. 1976): 571–90.

———. "El Camino Económico hacia la Democracia." *ECA* 35, 372/373 (Oct.–Nov. 1979): 947–60.

———. "Las Crisis Económicas Mundiales y Su Repercusión en El Salvador." *ECA* 29, 303/304 (Jan.–Feb. 1974): 235–51.

———. "Los Marginados de San Salvador." *ECA* 29, 308/309 (June–July 1974): 401–13.

Selva, Mauricio de la. "El Salvador: Tres Décadas de Lucha." *Cuadernos Americanos* 21 (Jan.–Feb. 1962): 196–220.

Simán, José Jorge. "La Esperanza y el Hogar del Hombre: La Esperanza, Motor de la Transformación." *ECA* 34, 374 (Dec. 1979): 1043–50.

Slutzky, Daniel and Ester. "El Salvador: Estructura de la Explotación Cafetalera." *Estudios Sociales Centroamericanos* 1 (May–Aug. 1972): 101–25.

Sobrino, Jon. "La Iglesia en el Actual Proceso del País." *ECA* 34, 372/373 (Oct.–Nov. 1979): 905–22.

Stein, Eduardo. "Comunicación Colectiva y Transformación Agraria." *ECA* 31, 335/336 (Sept.–Oct. 1976): 535–56.

UCA, Departamento de Economía. "Análisis Crítico e Interpretativo de la Plataforma Programática del Gobierno Democrático Revolucionario, en Sus Aspectos Económicos y Sociales." *ECA* 35, 377/378 (Mar.–Apr. 1980): 292–328.

Ungo, Guillermo Manuel. "Consideraciones Jurídico-Políticas sobre la Transformación Agraria." *ECA* 31, 335/336 (Sept.–Oct. 1976): 451–62.

———. "Los Derechos Humanos: Condición Necesaria para la Paz y Convivencia Social en El Salvador." *ECA* 34, 369/370 (July–Aug. 1979): 489–506

Valero Iglesias, Luis Fernando. "La Nueva Legislación Agraria y los Requisitos para una Efectiva Liberación del Campesinado." *ECA* 31, 335/336 (Sept.–Oct. 1976): 557–71.

White, Richard Alan. "El Salvador between Two Fires." *America*, November 1980, 262–66.

Zaid, Gabriel. "Enemy Colleagues: A Reading of the Salvadoran Tragedy." *Dissent* (Winter, 1982): 13–40.

Zamora, Rubén. "¿Seguro de Vida o Despojo? Análisis Político de la Transformación Agraria." *ECA* 31, 335/336 (Sept.–Oct. 1976): 511–34.

Other Works

Anderson, Charles W. *Politics and Economic Change in Latin America*. Princeton : Van Nostrand, 1967.

Baloyra, Enrique A. "The Deterioration of Reactionary Despotism in Central America." Paper submitted to the Department of State in partial fulfillment of DOS Contract 1722-020083. Second draft. August 1981.

———. "Theoretical Aspects of the Transition from Authoritarianism to Democracy." Presented at the roundtable "The Transition from Authoritarianism to Democracy in Southern Europe and Latin America," Madrid, 19–22 Dec. 1979.

Cardoso, Fernando Henrique. "La Cuestión del Estado en Brasil." *Revista Mexicana de Sociología* 37, no. 3 (July–Sept. 1975): 603–30.

———. "On the Characterization of Authoritarian Regimes in Latin America." In *The New Authoritarianism in Latin America*, edited by David Collier. Pp. 33–57. Princeton : Princeton University Press, 1979.

Drew, Elizabeth. "A Reporter at Large, Jesse Helms." *New Yorker*, 20 July 1981, 78–95.

Garretón, Manuel A. "De la Seguridad Nacional a la Nueva Institucionalidad." *Revista Mexicana de Sociología* 40, no. 4 (Oct.–Dec. 1978): 1259–82.

Gil, Federico G., Enrique A. Baloyra, and Lars Schoultz. "The Peaceful Transition to Democracy." Paper submitted to the Department of State in partial fulfillment of DOS contract 1722-020083. Second draft. August 1981.

Giner, Salvador. "Political Economy and Cultural Legitimation in the Origins of Parliamentary Democracy: The Southern European Case." Presented at the roundtable "The Transition from Authoritarianism to Democracy in Southern Europe and Latin America," Madrid, 19–22 Dec. 1979.

Leal, Juan Felipe. "The Mexican State, 1915–1973." *Latin American Perspectives* 2, no. 2 (summer 1975): 48–63.

Lowi, Theodore. *The End of Liberalism.* New York: Norton, 1969.

Monteforte Toledo, Mario. *Centroamérica.* 2 vols. Mexico: Universidad Nacional Autónoma de México, 1972.

Purcell, Susan Kauffman, and John F. H. Purcell. "The Nature of the Mexican State." Woodrow Wilson International Center for Scholars Colloquium, Washington, D.C., June 1977.

Riz, Liliana de. "Formas de Estado y Desarrollo del Capitalismo en América Latina." *Revista Mexicana de Sociología* 34, no. 2 (Apr.–June 1977): 427–41.

Torres Rivas, Edelberto. *Interpretación del Desarrollo Social Centroamericano.* San José: Editorial Universitaria Centroamericana, 1971.

Wiarda, Howard. "The Latin American Development Process and the New Developmental Alternatives." *Western Political Quarterly* 25 (Sept. 1972): 464–90.

Wickizer, V. D. *Coffee, Tea, and Cocoa.* Stanford: Stanford University Press, 1951.

Wilkie, James W. *The Mexican Revolution.* Berkeley: University of California Press, 1967.

Wynia, Gary W. *Politics and Planners.* Madison: University of Wisconsin Press, 1972.

Zermeño, Sergio. "Estado y Sociedad en el Capitalismo Tardío." *Revista Mexicana de Sociología* 39, no. 1 (Jan.–Mar. 1977): 61–117.

Index of Names

Index of Subjects

Acción Comunitaria, 44

Agrarian front: and traditional oligarchy, 56; and ISTA project, 58–60, 62; and phantom organizations, 59; and violence, 91, 103. *See also* FARO; Oligarchy

Agrarian reform, 2; measures of, 1969–70, 45; ISTA project of 1975–76, 55–60, 103, 145, 179; initiative of 1973–74, 56; and military proclamation of 15 Oct. 1979, 88; and decrees No. 43, 153, 154, and 158, 91, 101; shortcomings under the PRG, 102, 139, 189; and rightist violence, 103, 138, 139; Phase 2 of, 145, 147, 149; and election of 1982, 176

Agraristas, 18

Agricultural products: indigo, 5; cotton, 25, 145, 147; sugar, 25, 145. *See also* Coffee; Export agriculture

Agricultural workers, 2; and unionization, 19, 31, 46, 47, 67, 98; salaries of, 30, 55, 91; political activation of, 59. *See also* Labor unions

AIFLD: officials assassinated, 117; investigation and trial, 127, 132, 205 (n. 36); and UCS, 138, 207 (n. 58)

Alliance for Progress, 42, 43

ANEP: opposed to ISTA project, 55, 57–59; as link between oligarchy and bourgeoisie, 57; heterogeneity, 60; and Public Order Law of 1977, 84; opposed to PDC in government, 98, 144, 146, 149, 152

ANSESAL, 92, 106

AP: origins, 113; and Reagan transition, 113, 144; composition, 114; criticizes junta economic policies, 145, 148, 149, 152; and disloyal Right, 146; and efforts to change Duarte junta, 148, 150, 151

Aperturistas, 16, 40, 91, 93, 96, 180

ARENA: formed by D'Abuisson, 150; in election of 1982, 168, 169, 212 (n. 2); dominates constituent assembly, 175; support for, 176, 177; and PCN, 179, 214 (n. 36); and

Reagan administration, 181

Argentina, 54, 108, 120, 184

Armed Force. *See* Military

Arrendatarios, 6

Authoritarianism, 1, 14; "new," 53–54; traditional, 63. *See also* Authoritarian regimes; Reactionary despotism

Authoritarian regimes: defined, 53; bureaucratic authoritarian, 53–54, 63, 199 (n. 3); *caciquismo conservador*, 54; PRG as, 160. *See also* Military rule

Banks: refuse to lend, 9; defy Araujo, 11; reorganized by Martínez, 11–13

Bar Association, 84

Beneficiadores, beneficios. See Coffee, processing

Bourgeoisie: as industrial faction of oligarchy, 18, 29–30, 32; and export promotion, 30; and political alliances, 30–31; and economic expansion of 1953–62, 43; and ISTA project, 55, 58, 59; and PRG, 90

Bourgeoisie-oligarchy relations: and diversification, 23, 26; as dispute for hegemony, 26, 28, 43, 62, 63; and joint political action, 58, 143, 146, 152

Bourgeois revolution of 1870, 5, 8

Brazil, 54, 120

Business organizations: Asociación de Ganaderos, 13; Salvadoran Chamber of Commerce, 55, 84, 144, 148; American Chamber of Commerce of El Salvador, 55, 149, 151; ABECAFE, 72, 103, 201 (n. 16); Asociación Cafetalera, 7, 13; ASI, 84, 98, 144, 145, 146; opposed to PRG, 98, 104, 144–48, 150, 151, 167; and disloyal Right, 109, 144; unity of action, 143, 146, 152; FENAPES, 144, 148, 152; CCEA, 144, 146. *See also* ANEP, AP, FARO

Caciquismo conservador. See Authoritarian regimes